"*Get Your Ass* ... ground-breaking ... in both the collection and anal... American oral culture. Indispensab... popular culture."

–**Henry Louis Gates, Jr., Harvard University**

"A stone cold classic! All you Hip Hop heads need to know this book if you want to know your roots."

--**Robin D.G. Kelley,** author of
Freedom Dreams: The Black Radical Imagination

"Bruce Jackson's *Get Your Ass in the Water and Swim Like Me* is a pioneering work that is as fresh today as when it was first published. As this collection, and Jackson's astute analyses make clear, black oral poetry and folklore are great literature. Funny as all get out, full of biting wit and dazzling wordplay, this book drops more science than Einstein while proving the genius of black folk who created meaning and defended their lives through signifying words. I hope the hip-hop generation takes a look at this book that documents where it all got started!"

–**Michael Eric Dyson,** author of
Mercy, Mercy Me: The Art, Loves & Demons of Marvin Gaye

Get Your Ass in the Water and Swim Like Me

African American Narrative Poetry from Oral Tradition

Bruce Jackson

ROUTLEDGE
New York and London

Published in 2004 by
Routledge
29 West 35th Street
New York, NY 10001
www.routledge-ny.com

Published in Great Britain by
Routledge
11 New Fetter Lane
London EC4P 4EE
www.routledge.co.uk

First published in 1974 by Harvard University Press

Cover image from the collections of the Library of Congress.

Routledge is an imprint of the Taylor & Francis Group.

Printed in the United States of America on acid-free paper.

10 9 8 7 6 5 4 3 2 1

ISBN 0-415-96997-2 (pbk)

Cataloging-in-Publication Data is available from the Library of Congress.

For Roger D. Abrahams and for Ira and Nina Cohen

and, most of all, for Diane

"But along with their scars, black people have a secret. Their genius is that they have survived. In their adaptations, they have developed a vigorous style of life. It has touched religion, music, and the broad canvas of creativity. The psyche of black men has been distorted, but out of that deformity has risen a majesty. It began in the chants of the first work song. It continues in the timelessness of the blues. For white America to understand the life of the black man, it must recognize that so much time has passed and so little has changed."

William H. Grier and Price M. Cobbs,
Black Rage, 1968

Preface

This is a book of *toasts* — narrative poems from black American oral tradition. Along with black folk sermons and lyrics of work-songs, spirituals, and blues, the toasts comprise an extraordinary body of folk poetry matched hardly anywhere in the world.

I've never met anyone who knows why these poems are called toasts. The best guess I've heard is, "They're poems and most drinking toasts are poems," which is not true at all. Though these may be recited while drinking, there is no connection between the recitation and the lifting of glasses, there is none of the toasting ritual involving cooperation of others. Recitation of these toasts is a performer-audience event, not a communal ritual. A drinking toast is directed toward a third party or idea, but these toasts are directed to nothing, at least not overtly; they are there to be acted, heard, and experienced.

Toast-telling situations are fun; the good performers recite in grand theatrical style. The audience often participates; a listener sometimes replies with a version he likes better, and other members of the audience comment on the differences in performance. They are dynamic events, full of sound and movement. Texts on a printed page are pale shadows, lacking for fine movements of the real events.

The first time I ever heard toasts was at the Indiana State Penitentiary in 1961. I had no idea what they were, but I knew here was a kind of poetry no one had ever told me about and which was worth telling other people about. I played some of the tapes for John Gagnon, senior research sociologist at the Institute for Sex Research (now professor of Sociology at SUNY/Stony Brook), and he told me about a recent University of Pennsylvania Ph.D. thesis by Roger D. Abrahams in which there were a number of similar texts. Abrahams' thesis was published the following year. It was an event of true scholarly importance, for not only did he include a number of obscene and erotic prose and poetry texts such as had rarely been published previously, but he drew attention to the fact and function of the rich body of black folk narrative that had survived and developed in the urban situation.

His book—*Deep Down in the Jungle ... Negro Narrative Folklore from the Streets of Philadelphia*—deals with black folklore from one small neighborhood. He was interested in the range and function of narrative forms in that community, and one portion of his book had to do with toasts. Since it was first published in 1963, there has been some mention of toasts in articles, but no large group of them has been published, nor has anything appeared which gives any indication of the scope of the genre. That is what I attempt here.

The variants published in this book are not all I collected but those that show the kinds of variation found in the toasts. Some have significant differences in plot and development, others vary in minor stylistic ways. At all times my interest was in showing the range of styles and the kinds of variation that do occur.

None of the texts in this book come from women performers. According to the men I've interviewed, there are very few women who do know toasts, and though toasts were sometimes performed while women were present, they were most often recited in all-male groups. My field work focused on the lore of lower-class black men; though I accept their claim that the toast is male property, I hope some scholar investigates what narrative traditions are extant among black women in this country. The toasts are often extremely misogynic, so it seems unlikely women would learn or recite them; it would be interesting to know if women have narratives that are equally misandric.

There are reasons why there may be more narrative lore among the men. Their society—as described by Hannerz (1969), Liebow (1967), Abrahams (1970), Reynolds (1974), and others—exists outside: on the streetcorner, in the bar, poolhall, place of transient employment. Women may visit those areas, but their domain is elsewhere. Their turf is the household, which doesn't offer as much opportunity for performance as those transient locations, nor are there as many passing outsiders with new poems to recite, new tales to tell, new versions to offer.

By saying the toasts are poems from oral tradition, I mean they may have had a number of authors rather than just one, or, to put it another way, various audiences have had an opportunity to modify the points or parts they didn't much like. The process of modification may have occurred over a considerable number of years, by different hands at different times. That is one of the major differences between written poetry and folk poetry; with written poetry, the audience makes its judgment after the fact; with folk poetry, the audience's judgment is part of the fact.

Folk audiences are no different from literary audiences, but they sometimes seem less pretentious about what they do. They do not pretend their decisions are based on high and immutable aesthetic values; they do not pretend they have no gut reactions to things; they do not pretend to like things which make no sense to them. In a way they are the harshest of audiences, for they are intolerant of what bores them and tend to discard boring things quickly and to reject boring performers immediately. The process of oral narrative is such that any active participant can change parts he doesn't like or understand or redesign parts not meaningful to his immediate audience.

Folk poetry is intolerant of private meanings, private constructions, for to survive it must be as available to the audience as the stories in a tabloid newspaper. The vocabulary of folk poetry is the public vocabulary, and when a folk poem moves geographically its vocabulary usually changes to keep it consonant with the local vocabulary. Often its characters are public characters whose roles are known well to the listeners. Such roles have no surprises, only articulations.

Folk poetry depends on fulfilled expectations: the characters will be who they are supposed to be, the words will mean what they are supposed to mean. It is an open literature; all primary meaning is on the surface. Eric Auerbach's comments on the surface reality of the Homeric poems (1957:1-20) hold true for much folk narrative. The sort of complex meaning found beneath the surface of a written poem is meaning that is latent, present within it, but the kind of complex meaning evoked from a folk poem is meaning *about* the way the poem relates to the tellers or the culture—little within the thing itself. Art poetry forges language into new frames to hold something that did not exist before the language was so shaped. Folk poetry must use prefabricated language, and the knowledge it contains must be preknown.

Written literature can outlive its maker and its original audience, so students tend to see written literature as existing on its own, independent of the maker and the user, and there are even pejorative terms used by literary critics for estimates of what the maker intended or the responder responded—the Intentional Fallacy and the Affective Fallacy. But the student of folk literature is denied such luxury. He knows that an item of folk literature has an ephemeral existence; it is transitory and idiosyncratic; the artist's perception of the audience's response and interest influences length and decoration and design. The telling situation of an item of folk narrative, the context, is as important as the text itself. A folktale told by a TV wit and the same tale told the same way by an Ozark farmer are not the same thing, however much the words may sound alike.

Students of written literature must concern themselves with meaning, but students of folk literature must also consider function. The joke, for example, is a powerful genre. It puts listeners in a dependent condition; that is why interruption by a listener with the punch line so infuriates the teller and why the failure of a punch line to elicit laughter deflates him and why well-told shaggy-dog stories elicit such frustration. In any joke-telling situation—and the recitation of toasts are like joke-telling situations—a number of dynamics occur simultaneously: the individual listeners are responding in terms of their aesthetic to the manner of performance by the teller, but they are also responding in terms of their own concerns (their fears or anxieties are being exercised or exorcised), and they must also respond to the social situation the telling engenders between them and the teller and between them and the other listeners.

Certain notions or roles within the narrative may have particular significance for the group using the narrative, but those things are by no means constants. When we consider the bravery of a folk hero, we do well to consider what the culture at that time thought of bravery, whether or not the perception of heroics changed over the time the folk narrative was in active repertory, and how that change influenced performance of the tale or how different perceptions were permitted by the same narrative structure.

Although the literary critic may focus on the act of creation, he is far more interested in the fact of it—the thing created, the object as forever fixed, the artist's final issue. Most critics consider focus on the creative act ancillary to their main task—analyzing the product—and the reason for that is the product is the only thing that makes the process meaningful in the first place, and it is only the product they can ever possess entirely. The various drafts and their meanings, the psychic states of the artist along the way are never fully open to the critic. Only the finished work is fully available, and only the finished work justifies the attention paid. But for the folklorists, the creative act is part of the product; each redaction of the text, each re-creation of the event is to some extent controlled or influenced by the situation. And the situation—involving all participants, their physical and psychological relationships to one another and to the material—can be very complex indeed.

This book does not intend to accomplish the range of folklorists' goals outlined above. Although I try to assay the function of toasts for the performers, there isn't enough data yet to fully understand how they function now and how they have functioned in the past. There are still many questions to be answered. How are toasts created?

If the toast tradition is as weakened as I think, has anything other than transistorized radios and television sets replaced it? If I'm wrong about that weakening, is there any change in repertory that has kept pace with changing times and moods? How has the psychosocial function of toasts changed in the past thirty years? How do travelling verse units work in the creation process? Why do some communities select certain segments of the available canon for frequent performance? How much of apparent community repertory is a function of community interest and how much a function of performer repertory? How do performers choose what toasts will go into their working repertories? Why are blacks the only American ethnic group with such a spectacular poetic tradition? There is much to be learned.

A number of friends and colleagues contributed help, advice, or encouragement at various stages of fieldwork and manuscript preparation, especially Roger D. Abrahams, Howard S. Becker, George Beto, James F. Beyers, Diane Christian, Ira Cohen, Susan Fawcett, John Gagnon, Edward Hall, Lesley Johnson, Judy Kolbas, Stephen Munn, Pol Ndu, Howard Nelson, Anthony M. Reynolds, Murray Schwartz, Gerald Sturman, Celes Tisdale, Phyllis Wallace, Alf Walle, and D.K. Wilgus. Students in the black folklore seminars I taught at Harvard and SUNY at Buffalo made many interesting comments about portions of this material, some of which I incorporated into this book. Ann Louise McLaughlin, my editor at Harvard University Press, taught me once again the pleasure of working with someone who cares.

Ten years ago, when erotic and obscene materials were not as generally available as they are now, the staff of the Institute for Sex Research at Indiana University gave me free access to their invaluable book and manuscript collections. The staff of the Texas Archives at the University of Texas permitted me to examine the unpublished manuscript in their enormous John A. Lomax collection. Much of the fieldwork for this study was done while I was a member of the Society of Fellows at Harvard, and I am ever grateful for the Society's financial and professional assistance from 1963 to 1967. Some later fieldwork was supported by grants from the Research Foundation of the State University of New York and the Graduate School of SUNY at Buffalo. The final work on the manuscript was done during part of my year as a Guggenheim Fellow, 1971–1972.

Portions of this book appeared, in different form, in the following: "What Happened to Jody," *Journal of American Folklore* 80:318 (1967), 388-396; "Circus and Street: Psychosocial Aspects of the Black Toast," *Journal of American Folklore* 85:336 (1972), 123-139;

"The *'Titanic'* Toast," in Harry Levin, ed., *Veins of Humor,* Harvard English Studies 3 (Cambridge, Mass., Harvard University Press, 1972), 205-223. Part of the material about "Jody" appeared in *Wake Up Dead Man: Afro-American Worksongs from Texas Prisons* (Cambridge, Mass., Harvard University Press, 1972). Some of the material quoted from Slim appeared in *In the Life: Versions of the Criminal Experience* (New York, Holt, Rinehart and Winston, 1972).

July 1974 / B.J.

Contents

The Toasts

The Toast World

TELLING AND LEARNING TOASTS

Toasts can be told anywhere—at parties, lounging around bars and streetcorners, on a troopship crossing the boring ocean—but they seem to be told in county jails more than anywhere else. There is so much time to kill in county jails and so little to do with that time, and so great a portion of the population in county jails is lower-class black (they are the people without money to pay a bondsman for freedom before trial or who must serve jail time because they lack money to pay a fine).

Some of the texts in this book were collected in a migrant camp in upstate New York, others come from a few large Eastern cities, but most were collected in prisons. I did not go to prisons to collect toasts, but toasts figured prominently in a large body of folklore and sociological material I collected during several years of studying prison communities. The location partially loads the nature of the collection: a greater number of toasts probably deal with crime and jail than one might find among the participants' repertoires in the free world, and a few toasts such as #46, "The Voodoo Queen," are specific to prison.

None of which disqualifies this as a representative collection of toasts; it simply qualifies it as a collection most of which came from prisons. As much evidence as there is for viewing toasts as the poetic literature of the street or partying black man, there is evidence to consider it, along with the worksong of the black convict in the South, as his jailhouse testament. It is in jail that these poems are recited as much as ever and more than elsewhere, and it is just those street roles of badman, pimp, hustler, and junkie described in so many of the poems that get those jailhouse tellers and auditors in jail in the first place.

A black informant in Texas replied, when asked if toasts were still told very often, "Oh, in jailhouses and city halls, county jail, when you're laying around with nothing to do and you've read all the books and can't get no more, you've run out of regular conversation and you start to crackin' jokes, telling toasts to pass the time away." Michael H. Agar (1971:176), reporting on a group of addicts in a treatment program in Lexington Clinical Research Center, said his informants said "toasts usually originate and are recited in prison settings or in treatment centers such as Lexington." Almost a third of Agar's informants "recited or heard them in the streets," but "almost all, 92 percent, indicated that toasts were primarily recited during periods of confinement." A white ex-dope addict, who had spent a great deal of time in New York City jails (the Tombs, the Bronx House of Detention for Men and Riker's Island) and also did several longer sentences in Dannemora and other upstate felony prisons, told me he'd heard toasts recited rarely in prison but often in the jails. "That was a real pleasurable part of the day in the Tombs," he recalled. "In state prison you don't holler out in the cell because if you do you get hit in the head the next morning. Guys are reading, studying, sleeping, you know. But in the Tombs, I'd hear guys hollering them out every afternoon. It didn't seem to be the guys with big bits, though, it was the floaters, the guys with thirty and sixty days." I wondered if the reason he heard so few toasts in state prison wasn't really because in New York the prisons are more racially segregated than the jails, but some black ex-convicts told me the same thing.

Although the toasts are told in jail more than anywhere else, they are an aspect of black culture, not prison culture; there just happens to be more occasion to perform them in prison and jail than outside. We have a tendency to define people in terms of immediate role: a man who has never performed a criminal or violent act in his life but who kills his wife in a fit of rage is forever afterward known primarily as "murderer," surely an excessive application of title. We think of men in prisons as "convicts" often forgetting that the cultural baggage they bear is mostly from the outside world, the world in which they grew up and — with a few exceptions — in which they spend most of their lives. A black convict has in his cultural bag some things from prison culture, but he has far more from free world black culture.

Toasts are learned from other people, from the performance of other people. One may have to hear a poem on several occasions in order to get it all down, and one may hear a poem told by several different people and incorporate portions from those different performances into one's own version, so any performance reflects not only the talent of the immediate teller but also something of the tellers he heard and liked and learned from. The process is not unlike the learning process undergone by the Serbian singers of heroic narratives described by Albert Lord in *The Singer of Tales* (1960).

Susan Fawcett, who teaches at Bronx Community College, asked one of her students how people learned toasts. "Sometimes a person might start one and might not know the whole thing," Joe said, "and another person might come in and finish it, it might not be one specific person. Like sometimes, if two or three persons know the same one, one person might say part and then another person might say, 'Well, let me do the other part, I like this part.' And they do it, and another person might do it. And then another person might come up and do a new one that nobody ever heard. That's how they learn and find more, you know, by starting saying them around different people they don't know."

In *Die Nigger Die!* H. Rap Brown wrote: "Signifying at its best can be heard when brothers are exchanging tales. I used to hang out in bars just to hear the old men 'talking shit.' By the time I was nine, I could talk Shine and Titanic; Signifying Monkey, three different ways, and Piss-Pot-Peet, for two hours without stopping" (1973:356).

Learning toasts is not just a matter of learning a lot of words that happen to be metered and rhymed, but also of developing and learning a performance style. It is not easy to deliver—without being boring—a poem of perhaps one hundred lines. No one listens much to a toast-teller who cannot *act*. Imagine a joke told in a monotone, a song sung without inflections, and you can imagine a toast told without the dramatic.

Toasts are not recited, they are acted; the teller does not just say a toast, he performs it. His voice changes for the various personae of the poem, and sometimes there is another voice for the narrator. There are differences in stress, in accent, in clarity of articulation for various characters. The toast is a kind of street theater, a theater involving only one performer at a time. People who can say the lines but cannot act them get little opportunity to perform, because they are boring.

A great deal of time is spent listening to others recite. One learns not only lines and groups of lines and entire poems but also what audiences like, what performance options are available. Things survive because audiences like them, not just because performers like them. A symphony concertmaster may include in the repertoire works the audience does not know or understand, but he can do that only because most of any concert consists of works the audience does know and accept, and they permit him to teach them what they do not already know. The toast-teller, like any folk performer, has far less of that didactic luxury. What his audience dislikes he may not perform; if he insists they simply go away or tune him out.

The learner listens to performers recite poems on several occasions. He hears different performers recite varying texts of the same poem and gradually assembles a version of his own, different from the others in style of performance and complexity of events, different in flourishes, such as the variety of ending formulas in some of the toasts, different in speed and stress. The toast narratives vary less, I think, than the much longer Serbian epics Lord describes, but the process of learning and the forces encouraging variation are the same.

What is most often found in the repertoire of a performer is what he has heard most often in the repertories of others. And what those others have performed most are the poems their audiences have responded to most favorably. In my experience, the most popular poems are "Signifying Monkey," "*Titanic,*" and "Stackolee." Dramatically, each does something different; each portrays a role that has significant parallels in the reciters' street world.

Many poems previously reported in the oral tradition of hoboes are in the repertoires of older toast-tellers. One such poem is #57 "Hoboes' Convention." I have not included many because samples of them are available in books such as George Milburn's *The Hobo's Hornbook.* Milburn expurgated all his material, but the poems I have in mind in most versions have nothing obscene or scatological to expurgate in the first place, either because they are mild and innocent or because they derive from popular literary sources. Among the poems Milburn reports having been heard in hobo camps and that I've heard black informants recite are "The Hobo Convention at Portland" (1930:28-30), "The Hobo's Last Ride" (131 133), "The Face on the Barroom Floor" (153-157), "The Girl in the Blue Velvet Band" (162-163), "The Tropic's Curse" (198-202; I collected this with the title, "Lure of the

Tropics" in Jefferson City, Indiana).

Similar poems are available in a variety of paperback anthologies, and several informants said they had in fact read some of them. Charles O'Brien Kennedy's *American Ballads* (1962 in the paperback edition though it was published a decade earlier) includes the following poems I collected as toasts: "The Girl with the Blue Velvet Band" (by John F. Leonard, 22-25), "Willie the Weeper" (82-83), "The Face on the Barroom Floor" (by H. Antoine D'Arcy, 102-106), "The Shooting of Dan McGraw" (by Robert W. Service, 160-163), "The Cremation of Sam McGhee" (by Robert W. Service, 178-182), "The Lure of the Tropics" (245-248), and "The End of the Trail" (233-234), which is similar to #78B, "The Wanderer's Trail," in this book.

The hobo tradition contributed not only specific texts to the toast repertory but also an important narrative technique: the catalog of names often found in hobo "monika [name] poems" (discussed by Milburn). "Hoboes' Convention" is almost entirely such a catalog, one that passed directly from hobo to black tradition, but note also the way similar catalogs are used in #46 "The Voodoo Queen," and #58 "Junkies' Ball"—both obviously black in origin.

A few, but not many, toasts are parodies of well-known poems; among them are #69, "Convicts' Prayer" (an adaptation or parody of "The Lord's Prayer"), and #59, "Junkies' Heaven," which is a parody of "The Night Before Christmas." Parodies, poems from popular verse books, and survivals of hobo tradition comprise only a small portion of the toast repertory. Most toasts come from the life experience of the people who tell and listen to them, and most have never been in print anywhere.

Some sense of how toasts are created and circulated can be gained by considering the background to #46, "The Voodoo Queen." I had heard about the poem long before I heard it performed. One day in 1963, when I visited the Ramsey Unit of the Texas Department of Corrections, someone told me about Voodoo, the best-known homosexual on the farm.

You ever read the story about Voodoo? Voodoo was out in the free world, wearing women's dresses, high-heeled shoes, lipstick, and all that. He had natural hair that he had processed and grown out. He looked like a woman. He lived with a man nine or ten months. And the man was giving Voodoo his paycheck, thought he was a woman. Voodoo told me all about it. I had already heard about it, read about it. I asked Voodoo,

"Well, how did you come by moving this deal [what did you do with your penis and scrotum]?" She said she had something to take it and make it run back up, something she put there to make it squishy, make it go back up in the stomach. And I said, "He didn't know what he was getting?"

And she said, "No. Fools aren't born, they's made every day."

That's what Voodoo is in here for. Had to kill that guy after he found it out. He went in the service and stayed for about five months or something and she was getting the check. The way he found it out was she got drunk or something and went to sleep and it wasn't pushed back up. He come by looking at it and he got ready to kill him. She woke up and had to kill him. She's doing time for murder. Stealing, well she never did anything like that. She was pretty well off. I think she got $3000 or $4000 in the Walls up there in the inmate account. Point was, she just wanted to be a woman, that's all. She never did like girls, you know. Liked to play with them, have fun with them, but as far as sex, she wanted boys. Down there right now, they say, "Voodoo, he . . ." Somebody say, "What do you mean *he?*"

The man told me a poem had been written about Voodoo, and she was so upset by it she tried to purchase it from the author; but it was too late: copies had been made and they had disappeared in the secret channels of the prison. I later met Voodoo and asked about the poem, and she said, "That wasn't a nice poem. I tried to buy it back, but they wouldn't sell it to me."

A year later, Big Ten, an inmate on another Texas prison farm, recited the toast for me. He had learned it orally; he knew there had been a manuscript around, but he had never seen it. The toast is metrically rough in many spots, far more so than any other toast in this collection, and it is clear it hadn't been in oral tradition long enough for those rough spots to have been smoothed over. I asked Big Ten why he liked the poem and he said, "It's just a good poem, that's all."

I think it is obvious that "The Voodoo Queen" is more than "just a good poem." It expresses some of the anxieties most threatening to an inmate in prison, the range of problems having to do with sexuality in an all-male culture, the conflicts arising over prison homosexual behavior. Big Ten couldn't talk about that—if he could, I don't think he would have needed the poem—but it was there. People tell toasts about what interests them, about what is important to them, about what frightens them. Toasts deal with heroes and problems; often the problems are real ones for the informants, and the heroes are the men they would like to be to deal with those problems.

Susan Fawcett asked her student friend Joe, "What were the subjects of most of the toasts you heard?"

> People who are in the fast life or underground, you know. Or it be somebody that's superstrength, you know. Somebody that's supposed to have real good capabilities of doing something that nobody else can do. Or he have all the material values that other people don't have. You know, doing something as far as pimping or hustling or shooting up some people, being a gangster or something. Or it's about some other kind of dealing, all dealing in a illegal thing. Usually if he's not a pimp he's a hustler, if he's not a hustler, it might be a jive bartender, or it just might be a guy that thinks he's bad, that throw his weight around . . . Usually at the time I heard them, when I was young, that was like a insight on being big for me personally. Say, "Yeah, I like that. Wow, he was bad!" . . . Seemed like everybody would like to be whoever that guy was.

One of the best narrators I met was a man I'll call Slim Wilson (for an interview with him, in which some of the material quoted below appears, see Jackson, 1973:145-159). He had done a little of everything: gambler, pimp, hobo, soldier, roustabout. He wasn't so much criminal—though he was that, too, and in fact was doing time for armed robbery when I met him and had previously done time for murder—as hustler. What seemed to get him into trouble was the kind of life he led in a world of chasing the dice and running whores, a world where there is no moral center but making it, no tomorrow, no absolutes other than that somewhere each night he will get some sleep. When he was gambling he would "follow the dice." He would be in a game, win some money, hear there was a big game somewhere else, go to the other place, and keep with it as long as his luck or cheating ability held up. The pace was sometimes gruelling. "It's harder to stand up at a dice table all night than to get a decent job and work a week," he told me. I asked why he did it, then.

> Well, I don't like for nobody to tell me what time to get up or what time to lay down, or blow a bell or ring a bell for me to eat, make my check out . . . I just don't go for it. So I find some other way.

It's not that I'm lazy. Hell, I have worked, I've worked hard.

I've skinned mules, goddamit, I've pulled logs, worked in saw-mills for a timber company, I've unloaded whole cars of coal by myself. I don't give a damn about working, but I just don't want no sonofabitch standing over me telling me, "Well, you've got to this and you've go to do that."

He talked of switching dice in gambling houses, hustling suckers in cooncan. "Cooncan," he said, "is a serious game. It's just about as serious as chess. And chess is sure enough serious. Because it's really wits, a game of wits, battle of nerves. Sonofabitch play cooncan all night, next day he can't hold a cup of coffee. 'Cause he's shot to hell. But really, Bruce, I'm no gambler. I'm a cheat."

"Cheat?"

"A cheat, yeah, I'm no gambler because if I tried to gamble, fuck, I'd lose my goddamned drawers. Everything I go at I look at it from being a way of making money, I'm looking to cheat . . . In work I do an honest day's work. But in cooncan, in gambling, I cheat. Just remind me not to gamble with you. I have did some honest work . . . I don't mind working. I just can't stand that no one standing up over me."

Slim is originally from Arkansas, but he travelled around the world, then settled in St. Louis. Many of his toasts were learned from his father.

My old man was a scoundrel and a old roustabout and what-haveyou, a gandy dancer, a poet, a soldier, and so forth . . . I'm just a chip off the old block I guess. He taught me quite a few intellectual poems. Well, they're not what you would call classics, but they're classics as far as a man of my father's standards would be calling them because usually his stems around a bunch of "motherfuckers," you know. And when he would run down a clean one I would marvel at it. Like that "Life's a Funny old Proposition" — that's a beautiful piece of poetry. Like "Sam Mc-Ghee," that's one of them. I think he got that out of a hand-book. And "The Lure of the Tropics," he got that and all those out of a handbook I believe. But they were nice and clean. Usually his were something like "The Blue Velvet Band," or "Lady Liberty." That's one he taught me,:

Gather round me fellas, I have a story to tell,
I want you to listen carefully so you can learn this lesson well.
You see I fell in love with a brown skin girl that carried my
    heart for a whirl,

but the bitch was like a timberwolf all year 'round.
She was on my side when I was on my feet and on my ass when
    I got down.
So you see, fellas, I've traveled this wide world over now, and
    I know there's only one bitch for me,
she has her face on a silver dollar and her name is Liberty.
She feeds me when I'm hungry, keeps my clothes out a soak
    [hock],
and as long as I got this fabulous old broad I can't be broke.

He taught me that, he ran that one down to me. What led up to that, I was in high school and I got strung out behind some old cottontail, you know. I come home and run the spiel down to the old man and he run that down to me. He said, "Boy, you just can't make it like that."

From his father he learned #19, "Hobo Ben," #32, "The Pimp," and many other toasts. "We used to sit around, we used to have parties at the house with the company there and they used to go just backwards and forwards with them."

"They make with those the way some people do with songs," I said.

Songs and conversation. You tell one and then I'll try to top it and so on down the line . . . It was not on just one occasion that I'd heard these things. I'd hear it from him, probably I'd get some of it then, and later on I'd visit another party and get some more of it. You find it quite common in my sect—not my race in particular, but in my sect, the group of people I hang around with. I'm a roustabout, I do everything, little bit of everything. You may see me today in a factory and tomorrow I may be hoboing, day after tomorrow I may be driving a Cadillac, you know. What the fuck, it's life. I'm not gonna say I'll be the sonofabitch that'll be paying for it, but I'll be driving it.

Slim's body was a palimpsest of his career. It was decorated with knife scars, gunshot wounds, and the thin razor line around his throat where a whore had cut it one afternoon in a bar when she saw him chatting with another woman. He was a fine raconteur, so all the stories were fun, but obviously there was a lot of anguish behind the fun. "There's a lot of comical things that happen to you," he said one time. "They're not comical, they're not worth a fuck *then*, but later on you sit back and look at 'em and crack up.

There's a lot of things that happened to me that at the time they happened I said, 'Oh man, Jesus Christ, if I live through this . . .'" He told about getting caught on a boxcar with a flat wheel, one he couldn't get off because he got a bad grip when he jumped it and could only hang on, while the stack was blowing hot cinders down his neck. Another time, when he was on the side of a car near Hutchinson, Kansas: "I caught the car wrong . . . Now when I come up there's this damned old bridge abutment and there ain't nowhere for me to go but just stick there in the side of that car and pray and feel them slats brushing my ass. 'Lord, if I get off a this one I ain't coming back this way no more,' I said."

But he was ready for more—after all those scars and nights in jail cells and everything else, he was ready for more. "Because every day to me, the life that I lead, every day is a book, it's a brand-new book, every day. When I wake up in the morning I'm not like most guys—they wake up with a plan: 'Today I'll do so and so.' The only plan I have is, 'Well, tonight I'll lay down sometime.' Other than that, take her as she go. Every day is a book. But it's beautiful. Because someday I'm gonna be too old to do these things. I'm gonna sit back: well, it wasn't no fun when it happened, but I'm glad now."

FUNCTIONS AND THEMES: VIOLENCE, SEX, AND THE FAILURE OF ROMANCE

The first function of any narrative, from the auditor's viewpoint, is entertainment. If it fails at that there is no further need for discussion of function because no one is there; the audience goes away. The entertainment may elicit a variety of external responses—tears, laughter, smiles, shouts—and moral evaluations ranging from approval to disapproval. These reactions are far from simple: the funny story often (some would say always) hovers just above a sharp point which would bring blood if touched directly.

The toast is different in its work from the joke. Jokes have one point, one discharge, but the toast often has several. It may use wit, it may employ the comic; the comic may be verbal or situational. As with jokes, the humor in toasts can be examined from several points of view. One may consider not only the social situation of the telling but also the broader social framework in which the teller and his audience function, and the relationships among the various narratives in active repertory. The telling of a humorous narrative is a very complex business, and only rarely do we manage to see much of what is really going on. But we should at least try to keep in mind that all those things are operative.

Toast-telling sessions are similar to joke-telling sessions (and sometimes mixed with them) in that a man might recite "Stackolee," and someone else might respond with another version, saying, "The way *I* heard it was . . ." or with another toast, such as "Signifying Monkey," "Dance of the Freaks," or *"Titanic."* The toast is a social genre. Ask *why* toasts are told and you will be looked at as if you were some sort of fool: everyone knows they are told to pass the time, they are told because they are funny, they are told so the teller can display his skill at assembling bits and pieces from here and there, so he can perform. But there are many ways men might pass the time, many things found laughable, many ways of displaying verbal skill; the choice among those options is as meaningful as the form of the particular option itself.

Toasts, like much folk literature, deal with problems of human relations, but they do it in a special, highly filtered and exaggerated, way. They contain much violence, some of it sexual. There are homiletics about good men and trustworthy women, about the wages of sin; there are short narratives, often highly obscene, close in form and content to the drinking toast; and there are longer narratives about badmen, tricksters, pimps, fools, prostitutes, hustlers, and squares. They often confront the same threats and problems as the listeners. But the toast protagonists deal with these difficulties with style and grace, and, when they fail, their failures are spectacular. The trouble with most difficulties in the real world is one cannot talk or fight them away, and one's failures are often silly or embarassing, hardly ever spectacular.

The three toasts most frequently heard are "Stackolee," "Signifying Monkey," and *"Titanic."*

"Stackolee" is about an irrational badman who engages in gratuitous violence and joyless sexuality, a man who fires his gun a lot but is almost totally nonverbal. He is the archetypal bully blindly striking out, articulating or discharging his rage on any passing object or person. His sheer strength and big pistol bring him fame, but there are for him no solutions, only occasional valve-openings.

"Signifying Monkey" is about a jungle trickster who by clever word-play — signifying — manages to send his archfoe, Lion, off to be stomped and mangled by the stately Elephant. The Monkey uses wile and cleverness to accomplish what he cannot accomplish with brawn: his mode is a verbal judo, for he uses his enemy's own excessive ego against him, and he does it all with words. In many of the poems he falls out of his tree while gloating and jumping up and down, giving Lion a chance to trap him. He usually tricks Lion into stepping back so he can "fight like a natural man," whereupon he leaps back into his tree and resumes his insults. He usually "wins," but his gains are not unmixed, for although he gets someone else to trample his enemy he still must stay off the ground if he wants to stay alive.

"Titanic" is about a laborer named Shine, who combines the ability of the physical hero with the verbal skill of the trickster or pimp hero. Shine cracks jokes as he swims away from the sinking ship and drowning whites; he ends up safely on dry land in orgies of sex and booze. Shine and the various Pimp heroes succeed through both verbal and physical skill, and their successes are the greatest. The Pimp wins his whore's affections not only by super-sexual abilities but by his great skill at braggadocio and insult. He finishes best of all, for he has not only women but everything money can buy.

All of these characters, who will be discussed in detail later, are exaggerations of roles known on the street. The streetcorner world (see Liebow, 1967, and Milner, 1972) includes those who make it with brawn and those who make it with brains, and a very few who make it with both. One takes what is there and sees if he can use it; another knows what he wants and cleverly figures a way to acquire it.

Ulf Hannerz disagrees with Roger D. Abrahams' division of toast heroes into "trickster" and "badman" types. This dichotomy, Hannerz says, "may be misleading, for smartness and toughness are only facets of a single if somewhat amorphous conception of ghetto specific masculinity which both Stackolee and the monkey serve. That is, most streetcorner men would be able to recognize both of them as cultural models for their own role, although they may personally emphasize one or the other" (1969:115). But most social models are extremes, for only in extremity is there little enough ambiguity for what is being modeled to be obvious. Badman and trickster certainly are extremes, and because steady extremism is usually socially intolerable, behavior suited to survival needs modulating devices. It may very well be that in both types of hero the men of the streetcorner society can see aspects with which they identify, but they too—in their folklore at any rate—make a clear distinction between them. We must respect that distinction if we are able to deal with the folklore at all.

It is easy to see the street roles portrayed in the toasts as models for street youths, but they are also terribly threatening to them: the badman will beat you up; the pimp will hustle your sister or your mother or your woman; the pusher will sell a product other people rob you to buy; the hustler will take your money. I suspect the toasts hold those roles up as models for behavior or success but simultaneously display some of them as figures to be distanced and laughed at. Stackolee not only makes a fool of almost everyone he deals with, he is something of a fool himself; remember, the poem always begins with a woman kicking him out of the house, and his violence never hurts her. Signifying Monkey makes a fool of Lion, but he must stay in his tree if he wants to survive. I think of Konrad Lorenz's observation on humor:

> Humor is the best of lie-detectors and it discovers, with an uncanny flair, the speciousness of contrived ideals and the insincerity of stimulated enthusiasm. There are few things in the world so irresistibly comical as the sudden unmasking of this sort of pretense. When pompousness is abruptly debunked, when the balloon of puffed-up arrogance is pricked by humor and bursts with a loud report, we can indulge in uninhibited, refreshing laughter which is liberated by this special kind of sudden relief of tension. It is one of the few absolutely uncontrolled discharges of an instinctive motor pattern in man of which responsible morality wholly approves (1971:285-286).

Except for the discursive homiletics—and there aren't very many of these: #8, "My Reflection"; #9, "Feeble Old Man"; #55, "Once I Lived the Life of a Millionaire"; #56, "Life's a Funny Old Proposition"; and a few others—the toast world is generally one of clearly defined and limned agons, a world with sequences of specific challenges or one massive response to one massive challenge. In each, the protagonists or antagonists fail the test or make the grade. Shine swims the sea, outspeeds the sharks, out-thinks the whites; Stackolee outshoots Billy and overcomes the whore; the Signifying Monkey uses wile to accomplish what he cannot accomplish with brawn; in the numerous misogynistic toasts the woman presents herself in a dominant or domineering role, and the man either successfully rejects her role assumption (as in the Pimp toasts) or submits to it (as in #30, "L. A. Street"), in which case the toast changes from a frame for a formulaic brag about masculinity to a vehicle for a homily about the loss of it; in the homiletics false goals are illuminated and their sorry wages detailed, or the inherent absurdity of this world is treated directly with resignation or cynicism.

Romance is always discouraged; in several of the narrative homiletics the failure of romance is used as an informing element in a relationship. In the others, especially the Pimp and Freak toasts, we have the obverse: an absurd reduction to the purely physical and its verbal equivalent. There is a terrific cynicism or resignation to loss in many of the poems that makes me think of Elliot Liebow's comments on futurity in the lives of the streetcorner men he studied:

It is a future in which everything is uncertain except the ultimate destruction of his hopes and the eventual realization of his fears. The most he can reasonably look forward to is that these things do not come too soon. Thus, when Richard squanders a week's pay in two days it is not because, like an animal or a child, he is "present-time oriented," unaware of or unconcerned with his future. He does so precisely because he is aware of the future and the hopelessness of it all (1967:66).

And:

Thus, the constant awareness of a future loaded with "trouble" results in a constant readiness to leave, to "make it," to "get out of town," and discourages the man from sinking roots into the world he lives in. Just as it discourages him from putting money in the bank, so it discourages him from committing himself to a job, especially one whose payoff lies in the promise of future rewards rather than in the present. In the same way it discourages him from deep and lasting commitments to family and friends or to any other persons, places or things, since such commitments could hold him hostage, limiting his freedom of movement and thereby compromising his security which lies in that freedom (1967:70-71).

Competition in the toasts is resolved immediately; no relationship survives its own exercise. It is a transient and fleeting world of ephemeral successes and quick triumphs. In "Stackolee," levels of meaning of interaction are all discarded and we have simply the nondialectical agon: the bartender is killed, the whore swived, another whore shot through her knees, and so on. As the recitation continues the auditors laugh and nod approval for his "badness," for in a well-done recitation there is always a double action going on: the action within the poem and the action of the performance. The audience responds to both, forming a third dynamic.

In the Pimp toasts, status or role is assumed through competition. "Stackolee" and the Freak toasts have no terminal goal; they are episodic and the internal movements are paratactic, as in dreams. This lack of manifest sequential necessity, I think, reflects some of the tellers' reality. The future, as Talley indicates, does not bear thought; things go nowhere. The only alternative to competition as a means of acquiring status or role is acquiring them by birthright, but this is a folk literature of the lower-class black male, and the rights of birth are pitifully skimpy. Moreover, the grounds on which successful competition may occur with real gain are terribly few. But since "Stackolee" and the Freak toasts do not admit functional competition, the rule they admit is of chaos only, the brutalizing clown or the clowning brute.

Sexual relations in the toasts are invariably affectionless and usually affectless; the female exists as a device for exercise and articulation of male options, not an integral member of a bilateral relationship. In the toasts where the woman is presented as a decent human being, sex is almost always absent. There is an apparent inconsistency too important to ignore: sexual conquest of the female is usually presented as being important (in "Stackolee" toasts it is, dramatically, an event equivalent to the perforation of the bartender), yet the object of the conquest is consistently denigrated. The object of the conquest has significance only insofar as it is there to be conquered, not for any sequelae to the conquest itself. One does not conquer the female to have sex; it is *with* sex (or, as in many of the Pimp toasts, with the verbal equivalent) one negotiates, executes, and terminates the conquest.

There is an important balance between physical and verbal skill. It would be difficult to underestimate the power of verbal skill, not only in the toasts but in the culture using them. That verbal skill is appreciated is obvious to anyone listening to Dozens or Sounding sessions: the audience is trained to recognize a well-turned insult. (See Abrahams, 1970:39-42, for a discussion of this form of ritualized insult.) In the toasts, verbal agility is often the basis of contest between the pimp and whore: he first bests her in an insult or bragging session, and then superfucks her into adulating respect for "that too." His words are his plumage.

For the middle-class male the acting-out of aggression—striking, screaming, smashing, any of the things that naturally occur to one at such moments—is bad behavior; it will get one excluded from the best clubs, it will cut off one's party invitations. But among lower-class males words are sometimes perceived as displacement—which they often are—and a man who *always* talks his way out of anxiety situations is considered clever but not really very manly.

Words open a variety of options mere physical actions cannot afford. The scenario of a situation with limited verbal play and fixed physical options can be boring and violent. I recall John Gagnon telling me that when he worked on the Institute for Sex Research study, *Sex Offenders* (Gebhard et al., 1965), he and his colleagues found that many rapes occurred when the woman said "no" in situations in which the man had not really expected rejection or in which he thought "no" was code for "Yes, but coax me more," or "Be manly: take me." By the time the actor realized it really meant "no," no gracious form for disengagement remained, so he either had to leave (in humiliation and with some sense of foolishness for having misperceived things so or being inadequate) or fuck her. If he fucked her, there was the chance he would fulfill the curious folklore notion that a woman well-swived immediately feels great affection for her violator, whatever her previous attitude to the act or about him. In the folk notion, the worst that should happen is the woman will write it off as a bad experience. Gagnon and his colleagues found that many of the men arrested after situations like this were surprised that they should be considered rapists or that the woman would have called the police.

The middle class is not so prey to that form of rape, primarily because it has verbalization techniques which permit disengagement and a status system which requires gradual approach, one that takes rejection so seriously it carefully avoids the fail-safe point unless the results are clear; it often takes a lot of fencing to achieve that clarity. The middle-class male is trained never simply to reach out and stroke, however much he might want to, which is perhaps why he writes and talks so much.

Even in the Pimp toasts, the pragmatic aspect of pimping—getting a women to turn tricks and give the man her money, money he will use for clothes, cars, and entertainment—is often forgotten by the end of the poems. He is usually, in the toasts and often in the real world too, far more interested in her submission than her income.

But the problem in winning the woman with fucking is that there is nothing left to do in that affectionless world. What remains is only an object as inferior as the protagonist insisted it was at the beginning, for all function is then denied it. Whenever the toast Pimp proves his point he loses, for his proof is only of his own superiority, which occurs by denigrating or violating the woman. Setting up an object for conquest while simultaneously nullifying its value has a deathly consequence: the battle is never won, for there is no prize, and each competition restates the argument. Sexual gratification cannot result, so the most one might hope for sexually is exhaustion.

Sexual activity in the toast world is conventional, and basically conservative. Variation, when it does occur, has a specific dramatic purpose. Cunnilingus is loathed; when the male does it, the act signifies his sexual submission, which in turn is emblematic of his functional emasculation. The Milners, in their study of black pimps and prostitutes in San Francisco, wrote that one of their informants "went on to say that Black women are turning on to White men because White men will indulge them with oral sex (cunnilingus), while a Black man 'won't do that,' because it's too submissive a role. Much teasing occurs on the subject of oral sex as a sign of being a trick" (1972:218). They describe a dialogue among some pimps on the subject, during which "Eldorado Eddie" says: "Well, once a bitch wanted me to eat out her pussy and she was going to pay me two hundred dollars. But I didn't do it, 'cause I got the idea she didn't just want to pay for pussy-eatin', she wanted to buy her a little *manhood*, dig?" (219). And Elliot Liebow noted:

> The sexual exploitation of women does not refer to sex practices. The streetcorner man's heterosexual sex practices are wholly compatible with the observation that "(lower-class) taboos are more often turned against . . . any substitution for simple and direct coitus . . . (substitutes for intercourse) are considered a perversion . . ." Kinsey, Pomeroy, and Martin, "Social Level and Sexual Outlet," p. 305. Anal and oral intercourse, for example, are thought of as belonging exclusively to the homosexual world. Even the labels or terms designating or describing cunnilinguism—used so commonly by servicemen and working-class males generally as contemptuous terms of address or in comradely jest—are very seldom used (1967: 143n).

In the toasts involving cunnilingus, the man is often at first in a down-and-out role, broke and hungry in an alien town. The woman picks him up and he at first rejects her request for cunnilingus. The narratives then develop in one or two ways: either he fucks her into uncomplex submission, or he submits to her. Without affect or place for affection, we have room for gesture and symbol only, and the man who submits to the woman's desires in these narratives, even though he is supported financially by her, adopts the role of symbolic inferior: he is Samson shorn.

Fellation is just the obverse: the male requires it to signalize his domination over the female, not for any particular erotic value. In #37, "Corner of 47th and South Park," the man refuses the woman's request for cunnilingus and instead:

> So I fucked this whore from the living room to the dinin' room
>   stairs,
> she fell down on her knees, I thought she was gonna say her
>   prayers—
> but she done kissed me on the dick.
> She said, "Daddy, you done fucked me till I farted, you done
>   fucked me till I pissed,"
> said, "now, if there ever was a heaven, it must be this."

Note that the critical line about her submission is unrhymed and uncoupled, as always a signal to the listener of high significance.

Buggery serves approximately the same narrative function, that is, the man is *using* the female sexually rather than participating with her, as in these lines from #29, "Cocaine Nell":

> Then I'm gonna make you gaze in a lookin' glass
> and throw some vaseline right in the crack a your ass,
> then I'm gonna shove my rod in your open hole
> and try to pacify your ornery soul.

Often in the toasts the pimp threatens the women not with a beating, but with a promise that he will put his shoe "up your ass," an image designed and perceived as far more humiliating than a simple kick.

Except for these situations, and the Freak toasts (which are sexually bizarre but involve actors previously defined as freaks of one kind or another), sexual activity is straight and uncomplex, more or less unvaried, characterized only by some exaggeration and exhibitionism.

PIMPS AND THEIR LADIES: INSULT AND REPUTATION

The dope-dealer, rumor has it, has lost his street prestige. Though he still runs around in a big shiny car and sports $150 alligator shoes, he is more and more perceived as a man who rips off his own; he's making it, but he's as evil as the white predators from outside. He's neither the folk hero nor the role model he was in years past.

But the black pimp seems as big as ever. He makes his money by trickery: he tricks his whores; his whores "turn tricks" and call their customers "tricks." Most of the customers and some of the whores are white. And all the money comes rolling into his pocket. At once he fills a sparkling range of roles or options: he turns away women Whitey comes uptown to buy; he slaps senseless any of his women who hold out money; he is paid absolute respect by those women and has to do little in return except be himself; and in *his* family it is the women who have to feel guilty and inadequate if they don't bring home what he considers enough money. Whether or not all of this is true doesn't matter: that's the image and he works very hard at maintaining it.

Christina and Richard Milner wrote of the pimp's image to the neighborhood kid:

> They see their older brother or cousin or neighbor with a big flashy Cadillac "talkin' that jive" and "high-sidin" about his roll of hundred dollar bills with its diamond money clip and they are impressed.
>
> The idea that sex can buy all this and a brighter future than the society seems to offer is heady wine for ghetto teenagers who are fed up with school, fed up with religion, exposed to heavy dope, and (perhaps) experiencing their first ego-testing love affairs. Here is tangible proof, measured precisely in dollars and cents, of a teenage girl's feminine lure of which she is yet uncertain. Here is tangible evidence that a boy is really a man who not only can get money, but get it from a girl who is all "hung up" on him and will do anything to keep his attention. That's manhood: money and power over women. If he or she gets arrested, their "education" continues in reform school or jail, and when they get out they are ready for their advanced courses at the "College of the Street" (1972:141).

In toasts, a woman is frequently perceived as viciously aggressive, and the pimp's task and triumph is redirecting that aggression so she's after someone else's money, and instead of taking him for a ride she's buying him a car. The cynicism is described by Elliot Liebow:

> Men and women talk of themselves and others as cynical self-serving marauders, ceaselessly exploiting one another as use objects or objects of income. Sometimes, such motives are ascribed only to women: "Them girls [whom the men on the corner hang out with], they want *fi*nance, not *ro*mance." But more often, the men prefer to see themselves as the exploiters, the women as the exploited, as in assessing a woman's desirability in terms of her wealth or earning power or in equating being "nice" with having a job. At a party, Talley waits for Jessie to arrive and grins with anticipation. "She's not pretty," he said, "but she's got a beautiful job" (1967:137-138).

In a footnote, Liebow points out that such exploitation is by no means limited to black lower class: "This kind of exploitation was also found in a lower-class district of London where 'there is also an important exploitative component in the 'love-relationship,' at least on the man's side . . . The boy may be overly exploitative, not only of the sexual intercourse which the girl permits, but also of what he can get out of her financially'" (137n.).

But Liebow found the talk and actions of his streetcorner men were not consonant: "In action, however, the impulse to use women as objects of economic or sexual exploitation is deflected by countervailing impulses and goals, especially the desire to build personal, intimate relationships based on mutual liking or love. It is the interplay of these opposing impulses which accounts, at least in part, for the discrepancy between the way men talk about women and the way they act with them" (145).

There are various reasons for such discrepancy. Part of the attitude toward women is determined by the machismo of the situation: a group of rootless men standing around a streetcorner talking are going to express different attitudes about women than any one of the same group in a relationship with a specific woman. And, in fact, this inability to build the relationships Liebow sees as desired contributes to the negative verbalizations.

In any event, the figure of the Pimp, for younger ghetto males especially, focuses these various concerns, and therefore is of major significance in toast repertory.

Though sexual contact occurs in only some toasts, many, especially, focuses these various concerns, and therefore is of intensity. In these, the woman challenges the man and he either devastates her with an excoriating verbal reply or performs a superfuck and *then* responds verbally (as, for example, #22A, "Pimping Sam"). The dramatic and psychological identity of the invective and insertion is obvious.

In many of the toasts, especially those about badmen and pimps, names and reputations attached to names are treated with extraordinary seriousness. This is not surprising in the street culture world where reputation is one's primary coin: if known as a certain kind of person, one is invited to take part in hustles, one is quickly entitled to hustle women. Lee Rainwater writes:

> Boys and young men participating in the street system of peer-group activity are much caught up in games of furthering and enhancing their status as significant persons. These games are played out in small and large gatherings through various kinds of verbal contests that go under the names of "sounding," "signifying," and "working game." Very much a part of a boy's or man's status in this group is his ability to win women. The man who has several women "up tight," who is successful in "pimping off" women for sexual favors and material benefits, is much admired. In sharp contrast to white lower-class groups, there is little tendency for males to separate girls into "good" and "bad" categories. Observations of groups of Negro youths suggest that girls and women are much more readily referred to as "that bitch" or "that whore" than they are by their names, and this seems to be a universal tendency carrying no connotation that "that bitch" is morally inferior to or different from other women. Thus all women are essentially the same, all women are legitimate targets, and no girl or woman is expected to be virginal except for reason of lack of opportunity or immaturity. From their participation in the peer group and according to standards legitimated by the total Negro slum culture, Negro boys and young men are propelled in the direction of girls to test their "strength" as seducers. They are mercilessly rated by both their peers and the opposite sex in their ability to "talk" to girls; a young man will go to great lengths to avoid the reputation of having a "weak line" (1966:184).

The Milners make a similar statement:

> To be a man means having the *respect* of others. Black soul singer Aretha Franklin's record of the song "Respect" was enormously successful with Black audiences. In the White society, respect is to a large degree institutionalized. You must respect a man because he is a judge or a professor or a corporate executive. In the ghetto, without the institutionalization of respect, a man must earn respect by his own personal qualities, including the ability to defend himself physically. In informal gatherings in a bar or on the street corner the man will constantly be testing each member of the group. A man will be bluffed to see if he is a coward, teased to see if he has a sense of humor and stability, jousted with to see if he has wit and humor, trapped to see if he is a policeman or informer. In addition to *boy* (which is so terrible it is almost never used), the worst verbal insults to manhood are *punk, fruit,* and *trick,* in approximately that order (1972:45-46).

Reputation on the streets is important, but in the toast the demand for recognition of what one's name means seems at times to go far beyond the merely important; the question becomes critical and ontological. The first time Stackolee is violent is when the bartender disregards his name. In the Pimp toasts, the same sort of challenge—couched in terms of reputation—produces the incredible invective.

Stackolee's response to the bartender's rejection of his name and the insult exchange in "Pimping Sam" may seem extraordinarily excessive, but excess is not rare in folk literature. Knowing how to name things and when to use the name is important in many cultures. Vainamoinen in *Kalevala* defeats Joukahainen not with the swords Joukahainen wants, but with recitations of magic sounds, recitations of *names.* Huizinga notes that contest—the source of justice and law—was not originally concerned with ethics, but rather with winning and losing (1955:85). Eskimos, he points out, settled quarrels with ridicule contests, the resolutions of which had nothing to do with the truth of the matter, but only with the verbal skill of the contestants—quite similar to Pimping Sam and Wicked Nell.

Reputations are important because they say who you are; names are important because they identify what reputation you own; words are important because they are a kind of battle; violence is important because it does what words fail to do.

Every time I have heard the Pimp toasts told, the audience responded with most energy to the insult sections. The response is typically parapractic: when an act or event occurs the reaction seems far out of proportion to the stimulating conditions. A minor insult is followed by a massive attack, a slight accident produces enormous anxiety; such responses are really concerned with matters nowhere near the surface of the immediate discourse. (In prison, for example, homosexual jokes produce excessive laughter, an excess that makes sense only when one understands the sexual insecurity felt by many men in prison when challenged by the range of roles open to them: queen, punk, stud, abstainer.)

We might suspect a similar process operative in the toasts when an extremely violent or vindictive response follows a relatively minor action or statement by another protagonist. That process is obvious in the narratives themselves, but the psychoanalytic insight about the parapraxis is just as relevant to the listeners' responses.

I am not anxious to get into the arguments about the kinds of threat the black woman poses to the black ghetto male. (I'm not convinced those threats are unique among blacks; the "battle of the sexes" was not invented in the ghetto.) It is clear, however, that for those for whom the toasts *are* an active device, there is or was some sort of threat, some clear differences in social and economic roles such that the woman often had more security, more place, more status than the man. The apartment and children that bound her, that restricted her mobility, also meant she got the welfare payments, meant she had a *place* in the world, while the man often only had places he could go.

Part of the problem is well described by two black psychiatrists, William H. Grier and Price M. Cobbs: 'Because of the institutionalization of barriers, the black mother knows even more surely what society requires of *her* children. What at first seemed a random pattern of mothering has gradually assumed a definite and deliberate, if unconscious, method of preparing a black boy for his subordinate place in the world. As a result, black men develop considerable hostility toward black women as the inhibiting instruments of an oppressive system. The woman has more power, more accessibility into the system, and therefore she is more feared, while at the same time envied. And it is her lot in life to suppress masculine assertiveness in her sons" (1968:63).

The Milners comment on that statement: "The pimping subculture can be seen in this light as both a rebellion of the son against the mother's suppression of his masculine assertiveness and as his utilization of the female's power and accessibility into the system for his sustenance. He is sometimes sadistic, sometimes loving toward the Black woman in her dual role as protector and emasculator. His role as the super-masculine pimp is an ingenious compromise between manhood and infantilism. He is both 'baby' and 'Daddy' and his lady is both 'baby' and 'Momma'" (1972:225-226).

This may explain the parapractic response when the men verbally attack women in the toasts. Her threat can never really be named, perhaps because she is so formidable, both literally and symbolically. If the male is worried by her ability to castrate him, how does he retaliate in kind? Medusa symbolized the problem visually: one might cut off her appurtenances all day long without permanent damage, yet one casual eye-to-eye glance could freeze the man forever. Freud wrote:

> The hair upon Medusa's head is frequently represented in works of art in the form of snakes, and these once again are derived from the castration complex. It is a remarkable fact that, however frightening they may be in themselves, they nevertheless serve actually as a mitigation of the horror, for they replace the penis, the absence of which is the cause of horror. This is a confirmation of the technical rule according to which a multiplication of penis symbols signifies castration.
>
> The sight of Medusa's head makes the spectator stiff with terror, turns him to stone. Observe that we have here once again the same origin from the castration complex and the same transformation of affect! (1959B:105)

The final solution to the Medusa problem required artifice — her weaponry was directed against herself, while Perseus stood on the other side of the mirror. Perseus never really conquered; what he did was control her power and trick her into killing herself with it.

Freud's further comment suggests the function of the exhibitionism in the Pimp and Badmen toasts:

> If Medusa's head takes the place of a representation of the female genitals, or rather if it isolates their horrifying effects from their pleasure-giving ones, it may be recalled that displaying the genitals is familiar in other connections as an apotropaic act. What arouses horror in oneself will produce the same effect upon the enemy against whom one is seeking to defend oneself. We read in Rabelais of how the Devil took to flight when the woman showed him her vulva.

The erect male organ also had an apotropaic effect, but thanks to another mechanism. To display the penis (or any of its surrogates) is to say, "I'm not afraid of you. I defy you. I have a penis." Here, then, is another way of intimidating the Evil Spirit (106).

If the woman's threat were corporeal, the male might respond in kind: but hitting her doesn't do it, and few normal men can ever really outfuck normal women. How is her threat emasculating? Why does it challenge masculinity? No weapon in the ghetto man's armamentarium can counter the woman's sexual power of withholding, no weapon will touch that social and economic security (however minimal it is in fact) she seems to enjoy.

Many commentators have discussed the difficulties between men and women in lower-class black communities, some pointing out that many of those difficulties are a function of lower-class, rather than lower-class black, culture. But what matters here is only that some such problems *do* exist and they find expression in the folklore. Ulf Hannerz commented about

the experience of unstable personal relationships, in particular between the sexes. It is a well-known fact that among lower-class urban Negroes there are many "broken families" (households without a husband and father), many temporary commonlaw unions, and in general relatively little consensus on sex roles. Thus, it is not much an exaggeration to speak of a constant "battle of the sexes," and the achievement of success with the opposite sex is a focal concern in lower-class Negro life. From this area come most of the lyrics of contemporary rock-and-roll music. It may be objected that this is true of white rock-and-roll as well; to this it may be answered that this is very much to the point. For white rock-and-roll is predominantly adolescent music, thus reaching people with similar problems of unstable personal relationships. In the case of lower-class urban Negroes, such relationships are characteristic of a much wider age-range, and music on this theme also reaches this wider range (1968:457-458).

But music must represent male *and* female, since both listen and dance to it, both are potential customers for records and concert tickets. Toasts are for men only, and the rage can be far more explicit and unambiguous. Or it can seem that way, for in the toasts misogyny is rarely directed at real problems but at surface aspect of womanhood, and the result is the great concern among toast protagonists that women capitulate to maleness. Pimp's verbal invective produces total capitulation: I am yours; do what you will with me. The failures by the male produce total submission by him; the pussywhipped man is the closest thing to the faggot, and the ending of #30, "L. A. Street"—"but I'll be a cocksucker [cunnilinguist here, but more generally a fellator] tomorrow"—does not suffer a gratuitous ambiguity.

Oedipal conflict is handled rather neatly, or summarily, in the toast world: the father is flatly rejected. It takes no great Freudian commitment to see Shine's leaving the ship and its captain as a rejection of more than simple white authority.

Signifying Monkey, perhaps, manages the same end with his words. Lion is still the more powerful and always will be; in many versions his very noise renders Monkey impotent sexually. Yet Monkey arranges to have Lion mangled and usually manages to avoid Lion's angry revenge for that manipulation. He knows he can never accomplish those ends physically, just as the child who grows up may never overcome his father physically: the youth's physical advantage destroys his victory, for the elderly father is protected by a code, the younger father by his power.

The Oedipal question never occurs in the Pimp toasts; the specific nature of the prostitute/pimp relationship precludes it. The prostitute is sex without future function, she is never the mother. Between prostitute and pimp there is a peculiar inversion of normal sexual roles. The woman beds other men without passion, without love, without joy, without guilt, all solely to supply the pimp his wants. The prostitute can sleep around without ever betraying; the more she does, the greater the evidence for her dependence on the pimp. He need not even be sexually superior in reality, he need only be agile verbally. That the pimp is himself dependent, that the relationship is symbiotic, rarely is allowed to become overt.

I think it rather simpleminded to say, as many have, that the black woman poses a threat to the black male, hence all sorts of folk forms automatically and totally flow forth to cope. That is one of those gross cultural oversimplifications that work only if one ignores all the rest of human behavior. "The black woman poses a threat" tells us nothing but that black women and black men are like the rest of us, for the opposite of that statement is that the woman would pose no threat at all, and that surely is not the condition of middle-class white America or lower-class white America. The woman who strokes can crush by varying the intensity of her grip, just as the man can. "The black woman poses a threat" notion supposes sexual relations among human beings are normally events of no danger, psychic or otherwise, which is nonsense.

There is danger in all significant human relationships, and it is danger either or all parties may and can generate and ratify: the danger of withdrawal. Most of us know of situations in which one partner has refused to engage in depth because of fear that the relationship subsequently will terminate. A refusal to commit oneself to interpersonal relations often speaks of a desperate *need* of such relations, a need so great that the fear of having and losing is worse than not having at all. Most of us have heard children scream to parents or spouses to one another: "I don't need you!" and known clearly that the reverse was not only the case but what was meant.

I think it important here to keep in mind that folk literature is *literature*. It is a part of expressive culture, but it is not all of culture, it is not all of action. It is one way of handling some things, but only one way, appropriate only to certain circumstances at certain times. One does not recite the Pimp toasts to one's mother, or, for that matter, to one's woman; these are for the men only and they serve needs men have in situations where they are asserting their independence, solidarity, and verbal skill.

At the end of their long and detailed description of the working lives of West Coast black pimps and whores, the Milners again raise the question of why the Pimp should be a culture hero. "Beyond the surface flash, the fine cars and colorful clothes, what accounts for the player's charisma? First, the pimp hero is a trickster. By the use of wit and guile he earns a rich living and maintains aristocratic tastes without having to resort either to violence or to physical labor." They believe he faces life as it is and is pragmatic and functional in a devious and complex world (1972:271). But more important, they say, is that the pimp "controls women. Few other American heroes, secret or otherwise, can claim that ability" (1972:273).

If the trickster or early nineteenth-century American black folklore, the Rabbit, was doing his trickeration against larger animals who wanted to kill or control him, and if the trickster of late nineteenth- and early twentieth-century American black folklore, John, was doing his trickeration against the cruel master or boss who wanted to get more out of him than was reasonable to require, the Pimp trickster of the mid-twentieth-century period is working his trickeration against everybody: outsiders and insiders, his own kind and others, men and women, whites and blacks. In the vicious world of the streets, he seems a brutal, but not unreasonable, revision of the American Dream, the Horatio Alger story.

BADMAN AND TRICKSTER: FUNCTIONAL OUTSIDERS

Folk literature often sets forth models for behavior, either positive (those you emulate) or negative (those you eschew). Stack is neither, at least not on any literal level. His style is not viable, for the population in the land of irrational badmen is constantly decreasing, and that in any society is intolerable. As I noted earlier, the regard for the badman is ambiguous, for though he does have power he is also dangerous.

But analogically he may seem reasonable: confronted by a situation known to all auditors of the poem, his first response is to ignore it, then in gross caricature work it out—but elsewhere. That the working-out is caricature is not surprising. Social reality admits no easy solution, perhaps it admits none at all, and the analogic truth of humor is more appropriate than the literal truth of biography.

In current street argot, the word "bad" often means its exact opposite: "That's a *bad* car" is a compliment. The word is not without some ambiguity, especially among older blacks, for whom the expression "bad nigger" brings forth a constellation of meanings. Grier and Cobbs write:

One of the constant themes in black folklore is the "bad nigger." It seems that every community has had one or was afraid of having one. They were feared as much by blacks as by whites. In the slave legends there are tales of docile field hands suddenly going berserk. It was a common enough phenomenon to appear in writings of the times and to stimulate the erection of defenses against this violent kind of man.

Today black boys are admonished not to be a "bad nigger." No description need be offered; every black child knows what is meant. They are angry and hostile. They strike fear into everyone with their uncompromising rejection of restraint or inhibition. They may seem at one moment meek and compromised— and in the next a terrifying killer. Because of his experience in this country, every black man harbors a potential bad nigger inside him. He must ignore this inner man. The bad nigger is bad because he has been required to renounce his manhood to have his life. The more one approaches the American ideal of respectability, the more this hostility must be repressed. The bad nigger is a defiant nigger, a reminder of what manhood could be (1968:65-66).

No wonder that in these convulsive days the word should shift in meaning, for "badness" in the old days and "badness" now in one sense are exactly the same thing: violent rebellion against the system of controls. The rise in black militancy has loudly proclaimed that suppressing everything in order to make it on the white man's terms isn't worth it, the pay isn't high enough.

The we may consider such characters as Stackolee pathological, but that reading does not diminish their legitimacy; it merely provides another adjective with which to try to come to terms with them. We are used to assuming that "normal" behavior and "normal" thought processes are adequate for a community's functions, but it is by no means clear that such is in fact the case. Reality and literature offer too many examples to the contrary. Durkheim wrote: "Crime is, then, necessary; it is bound up with the fundamental conditions of all social life, and by that very fact it is useful, because these conditions of which it is a part are themselves indispensable to the normal evolution of morality and law" (1964: 66n).

The ultimate Badman, the one who fears or respects nothing, is dangerous to his own community, but he still has a certain value and that value is not minor. While doing research in some prisons a few years ago, I realized that the madmen (not mad enough to be committed to another type of institution, but mad enough to respect none of the powerful convict organizations) were sometimes the only factor preventing the development of an absolute totalitarian system among the inmates. The nut does whatever he wants, and if someone says, "Do that and we'll kill you," he says, "Kill me," or he says nothing at all but keeps on doing what he wants to. In the country of machismo, to kill a madman is like killing a child; it is taboo, he must be let free. In being free he is a continual challenge to hegemony, and the hegemony of totalitarianism is such that any successful challenge always keeps it from being total.

I think the Badman, as role, has some of the same functions. Stackolee "doesn't mind dying"; he cannot be threatened by the system because he is forever outside it. By being himself outside and occasionally functioning within, he keeps the system from being total, and that supplies a measure of freedom which never lets anything take total control. Even though he is dangerous to everyone, his gratuitous freedom bestows some measure of freedom on everyone else.

Two of the more important characters of Afro-American traditional narrative are Badman and Trickster; both figure prominently in the toasts. Although Trickster is traditionally the more childlike, Badman is the more childish. He often acts gratuitously, seems more anxious to display his badness or his "coolness" than attain any particular goal or end. Trickster is practical. He is goal-oriented (in this regard the Trickster of black tradition often differs from his American Indian counterpart, who is often self-destructive). Badman focuses on process only, on style; his is a surface world of pose and counterpose, a world of perceived challenge and synaptic response. He rarely considers consequences, while Trickster is always conscious of them. (Trickster sometimes makes mistakes and gets into trouble because his tricks don't work, but that does not mean he wasn't thinking of consequences, only that he miscalculated when doing the predictions.) This is why Trickster is so adroit at role-playing and Badman so well known for "playing the role." In the folk world there is an immense difference in the two: role-playing means one can assume a variety of faces for a variety of situations; playing the role means one offers one face only, often in spite of the realities of the situation.

Roger D. Abrahams says: "Where the trickster is a perpetual child, the badman is a perpetual adolescent. His is a world of overt rebellion. He commits acts against taboos and mores in full knowledge of what he is doing. In fact, he glories in this knowledge of revolt. He is consciously and sincerely immoral. As a social entity he is rebelling against white man's laws. As a male he is revolting against the woman's attempt to emasculate him. As a poor man he is reacting against his perpetual poverty" (1970A:69-70). I think Abrahams' suggestion of Jungian reduction of Trickster-child misses something vital. For the real-life child it is the *game* that matters; the game ends when one may no longer play one's assumed role, there is no goal to the game external to itself (see Huizinga, 1955). This is the way Badman works, not Trickster.

Adults operate in situations that may often be described by game theory (Stock Markets, War, Cops and Robbers, Seductions, Cowboys and Indians, Professors and Students, and so on), but the players are not necessarily more committed to the games than the goals. Those who are goal-oriented can alter role, shift immediate desires to future situations in which the gratification is more felicitous or satisfactory or feasible. This is the mode of the Trickster without his flourishes. Trickster is the adult. He is not amoral out of childishness so much as out of pragmatism.

The tough guy, the general offender who "doesn't mind dying," engages in an undirected rebellion against an unspecified opponent. He finds specific objects at which to hurl his rockets from time to time, but they are selected randomly or appear coincidentally. He does not, in his folkloristic avatar, delay gratification; his exercises in immediate gratification, however, never satisfy. His mode is that of the sociopath and the dream.

Abrahams sees the Trickster/Badman dichotomy in quite different terms. "The trickster provides a full escape for those Negroes who have been offered no opportunity to feel a control over their own lives, no method for developing their egos through a specific action. As such, the trickster may reflect the real childlike state of a severely stunted ego, or a veiled revolt against authority in the only terms available. At the same time, the performer and audience are enabled to express some of their aggressive impulses in this acceptable form." And, "Where guile and banter are the weapons of the trickster, arrogance and disdain serve the badman. He does not aim to be a god, but rather to be the eternal man in revolt, the devil. He is the epitome of virility, of manliness on display" (1970A:69,70).

I wonder. Though Stackolee may be rebelling, one would be hard put to find a focus for him, from his point of view or the tellers' perceptions of his point of view, in the "white man's laws." The verb "rebel" usually takes, assumes, or implies the preposition "against" and a noun; Stackolee simply strikes out at everyone he meets at the Bucket of Blood. To have the behavior of the rebel without the focus suggests the sociopathic. He may be "the epitome of virility," but what do we then do with our suspicion that satyriasis reflects not manliness but, on the contrary, the profoundest insecurity, that it is a false synedoche? Something else: however much we may wish to romanticize the folk hero, we play a better game if we limit our romanticism to that entertained by the folk, and for the folk, *mesure* and self-control — coolness — are as manly as an erection, and these the Badman neither has nor understands. Stackolee never gets what he wants, for he constitutionally loathes what he gets. If anyone is a model of success in the toasts, it is the Pimp, for he combines the cleverness of the Trickster with the power over others demanded by the

Badman — and he is loved and paid for it.

No conscious decisions are made in the violent and Freak toasts. A decision is a conscious and deliberate *act* requiring awareness of alternatives (otherwise there is no deciding to do) and prediction of alternate consequences (otherwise deciding is meaningless). Stackolee and his analogs do not make decisions; they react to stimuli.

The violent toasts do not seem to form a significant part of the repertory of older Southern or Southern-born blacks, but they are very much in the repertory of the group between sixteen and thirty years old. For members of this group, some of these toasts may represent a vicarious reinforcement of their own defense mechanisms (for example, verbal skill and sexual prowess in "Pimping Sam," toughness in "Stackolee," hipness in "Signifying Monkey"). Toasts, especially violent ones, may act as safety-valve devices, which, according to Lewis A. Coser (1964:209), "lead to a displacement of goal in the actor: he need no longer aim at reaching a solution of the unsatisfactory situation, but merely at releasing the tension which arose from it. Where safety-valve institutions provide substitute objects of the displacement of hostility, the conflict itself is channeled away from the original unsatisfactory relationship into one in which the actor's goal is no longer the attainment of specific results, but the release of tension." Except for the Freak and violent toasts, most of the narratives and homiletics tend toward stabilizing the social system; they are usually reinforcing. The Freak and violent toasts have no goals; they are self-contained. These toasts perhaps consolidate the minor deviant proclivities and acts of the auditor community in a semblance of entertained but antagonistic normality.

George Herbert Mead has written that "the attitude of hostility toward the lawbreaker has the unique advantage of uniting all members of the community in the emotional solidarity of aggression. . . . Seemingly without the criminal the cohesiveness of society would disappear and the universal goods of the community would crumble into mutual repellent individual particles. The criminal does not seriously endanger the structure of society by his destructive activities, and on the other hand he is responsible for a sense of solidarity, among those whose attention would be otherwise centered upon interests quite divergent from those of each other" (1964:209). That statement should be modified slightly, for society's reaction to the stylized criminal (the one articulated in art, such as "Stackolee," or *Bonnie and Clyde,* or *Butch Cassidy* and the Sundance Kid) is not necessarily hostile; it can also find safety in pretending detached amusement. Since such figures are paradigms for social disorganization, they may serve as an extreme boundary for minor deviance, making all else seem at least tolerable, perhaps even reasonable. And characteristics that make them notable as criminals may at times, or all the time, be perceived as positive values, even within the society with which they are supposedly at odds.

We should note that the Badman, Stackolee, is all style; Pimp is a role. A role always implies recognition of other actors, of an order, possibly a hierarchy. Role and style are not the same: Lyndon Baines Johnson and John Fitzgerald Kennedy had the same role—Democratic Presidents of the United States—but their styles were quite another matter. Stack's responses are not in terms of a role, as are the Pimp's, but his personal style. Role implies a social structure (actions suitable to social position, norms and pre-rogative of social position) and is dependent on a sense of coherent structure. To this, Stack does not and cannot relate. The Pimp's anxieties relate to level, Stack's to identity. Stack's problem is far more basic, it is ontological, although he does not perceive it as such.

SHINE AND THE *TITANIC:* GOODBYE TO CHARLIE

The sinking of the *Titanic* on April 14, 1912, produced several million words of prose, several motion pictures, a few songs—and one poem. This toast has been heard by a very small number of white Americans and by several million blacks. That is both curious and ironic, for not only were there no blacks on the *Titanic*'s passenger list, but neither were there any in the crew. The ship seems to have been all white, and the one item in American folklore that widely documents its sinking is the toast, a genre performed almost exclusively by blacks.

Shine is the lowliest worker in the giant ship; his station is in the bowels of the *Titanic,* down among the coal piles and boilers. He doesn't so much beat the white man as show practical intelligence while the white is stupidly proclaiming faith in his machine, a machine which, like many others, the black could not have.

In white folklore, the black man is supposed to be oversexed and financially incontinent (there is even a pejorative term for a person who spends money too freely: "nigger rich"). Shine says he understands that those things have their place: money is good only on shore, which is where *he* is going; as for sex, he is obviously able to get enough of that on dry land, where it is safer to do that sort of thing anyway.

Shine expresses little hostility toward the whites (though the audience delights in their physical incompetence and probable fate). He laughs at their offers, and refuses to risk his neck to save theirs, but he never expresses glee at their situation. He simply offers practical advice: "Get your ass in the water and swim like me."

He is the one hero of the toasts who perfectly mediates between the street extremes of Trickster and Badman. He is smart enough to jump ship when the rich whites aboard still trust its purported infallibility, strong enough to swim past several natural obstacles, and sexual enough to finish with a grand encounter with a mob of women. And he is the one toast hero who uses whites as foils for his adventures and displays.

Roger Abrahams, after describing the style of heroism Shine embodies, says, "Here is a Negro story that overtly pictures the enemy as white. The white man has been one of the authority figures against whom he has been rebelling. But here he achieves that greater act of rebellion, the turning of his back. This is then something of a declaration of independence" (1970A:81).

For some time I thought Abrahams' statement wrong, but now I find it suffering only from slight excess (see Jackson, 1972B). The white man may be presented as Shine's foil in this poem, but hardly as his enemy. That the white man is *not* presented as an enemy, but only as someone rather opaque and clumsy, is what is perhaps most startling.

Among the three hundred toast texts I have collected in the field, the various papers and collections done by students in my folklore classes at Buffalo and Harvard, and the few papers and books that have published toast texts, I have found only *two* that explicitly deal with whites and blacks: #52, "Ups on the Farm," a poem I collected only once in Texas (about a black who refuses to work for a white farmer because he knows he will have difficulty in collecting his wages), and *"Titanic."* In *"Titanic"* there is articulated a black rejection of bribes and status symbols, and in the toast canon that is a rare rejection indeed. Some commentators, such as Labov and his colleagues, say in Shine we find "total rejection of white middle-class society" (1973:335), but that is clearly nonsense: Shine is offered wealth and sex, and if those are valued only by whites then the rest of the world's population seems to operate under a sore delusion.

Although *"Titanic"* is one of the three best-known toasts and has compelling and clear themes, it has spawned no thematic analogues. One doesn't wonder that the theme of black and white turns up in *"Titanic,"* but rather that it turns up nowhere else in the toasts. (The theme does sometimes turn up in folksong, as in Leadbelly's blues-ballad about the sinking of the *Titanic,* which includes a verse about the Captain's rejecting heavyweight champion Jack Johnson and saying, "I ain't haulin' no coal." See Lomax, 1936:182.)

It can hardly be accidental that the protagonist is named Shine, a white man's term that is unambiguously derogatory. "Shine" never had the casual currency among blacks that "nigger" did. One still hears in parts of the South phrases like "all us niggers..." and, in the North and South, "he's a *bad* nigger," an expression approving someone's toughness. A character named Shine appeared in some early nineteenth-century minstrel routines, but he never became a character in black prose narratives. Even so, only two of the performers of the ten texts collected here felt any need to identify him: Slim, who contributed the C- and D- texts, says he is "a fella called Shine/he was so dark he changed the world's mind," and "he was jet black and he change anybody's mind"; and Rudy Ray Moore, a nightclub performer who was the source of the H-text, says, "Up stepped a black man from the deck below that they called Shine." Remember that "Black is beautiful" is a recent perception. Many older blues praise "high yellow" women and complain about very black women, and in much folklore the "coal-black nigger" was portrayed as dumber, meaner, and tougher than the mulattoes. Blacks were not free of white stereotypes.

At an obvious level, this toast is a response to racial indignities, but it would be a mistake to view it in those terms only. The paucity of overt racial themes in other toasts suggests that if we want to know what *"Titanic"* is about we should consider other interpretations as well.

Shine's leaving the ship and its captain is a denial of more than mere white authority. The captain is the agent of all power at sea; he is the repository of all authority, the ship is his extension, the sea his medium. Shine rejects the first two and masters the dangers of the third. Not even the sexual temptations offered by members of the captain's entourage are sufficient to draw Shine back to that drowning fold. He cuts loose and strikes out on his own, his own man now. His silly reversion at the end—he is either drunk or trying to recover from an orgy—is no reversion in a temporal sense; he is childish, perhaps, but he is not childlike, and that is what is humorous about his role. He has earned the right to be childish if he wishes, for he was practical when practicality mattered. He has refused serious offers of sex in trade and now he may casually trade in sex. The authority figures are gone. Shine is solidly on dry land and may now play the childish game without fearing revocation of his status. One thing no one can take away from him is the fact that he is grown up.

Many observers have written about the problem of powerlessness among the poor and the various social and psychological costs of that situation. Much of the focus of the toasts has to do with the nominal opposite: power is of central concern in most of them. In the toast world, power comes from two sources: physical force or verbal skill. Badmen rely primarily on extraordinary physical ability or psychotic disregard for personal safety; the pimps and Signifying Monkey use words to establish their power; but Shine combines both physical and verbal hero qualities. He is the only one who has enough sense and perhaps competence to swim away from the sinking supership, but while he is doing that he constantly chatters away. Unlike the pimp, talking and acting physically are discrete events for Shine. His power is total—body and mind—and so he alone gets home free, perfectly safe to fuck and signify as he wishes. That all this happens while a shipload of rich whites drown is a gorgeous bonus.

BEYOND POETRY

Although there is little overt concern with racial matters in the toasts, that does not mean such concern isn't very much present. It is. Denying its relevance would be like saying water is not a significant element in the life of a fish because he takes no appreciable notice of it.

American racism is there, always there. It lurks somewhere beyond the sound of the toast-tellers' voices, and rarely is it forgotten, even among kids living in the heart of a large ghetto who never encounter directly and almost never see whites anywhere but on a television screen. It is at the employment line where the black will be hired last, paid least, fired first. It is in street encounters between whites and blacks, when both look at one another with fear and hate which neither can quite fully account for but which each knows full well is there.

We have been considering fictions here, fantasies, but they are attempts to deal with a difficult and problematic reality. Reality testing is hardly a defect among lower-class black youth; they suffer not from too little reality testing but too much of it. Their daily functioning is a sequence of tests, challenges, combats. Unlike the middle-class white, their world is unstable in most directions; the promises made are so seldom kept that, in order to survive, they must continually evaluate, estimate, consider, manipulate, and plan. The game of Dozens, for example, suspends for a time one's need to respond to challenge totally. The satisfaction of the game comes not only from giving insult, but taking it, from moving the plane of action to a purely verbal level. In the process of this action certain anxieties are excited and eased: one may explore one's own, and the cathartic effect applies both to audience and speaker. By replying, one may attack one's own internal exchange of Dozens, one's own ambivalence, because one can defend the hated/loved person, the situation (see Dollard, 1973). When the stage is reached at which the response in control loss is too dangerous, when the youths are too large to afford casual fistfights anymore, for example, because they can hurt each other too badly, Dozens are rarely played. From a participant situation there is a shift to audience/performer situation: instead of gladiators battling it out in a verbal arena it is an artist performing in a theater; the arena and theater may be the streetcorner or house or bar. One listens to others make music (to which one may dance — with a woman in a cooperative rather than competitive situation), and one listens to others narrate toasts and jokes.

In the toasts a performer-audience situation always exists. One does not play them for oneself, the way a guitarist might spend hours playing for himself. The satisfaction for the teller requires an audience, the structure and focus of performance. The content of the toasts — both latent and manifest — often reenacts the same danger situations the Dozens were concerned with, the same danger situations the songs are concerned with, the same loss of object and loss of love and absence of power and control.

Stackolee, for example, accepts his woman's rejection; he offers her no protest even though she offers no real new reason for it. He assumes he deserves it, he really believes something is wrong with him; the fact of his belief is enough to make it true and he then becomes a berserk, a person for whom there is no language but violence, no truth but the act just ended. For many years the American black man was perhaps in exactly the same position: he was told he must, and was often convinced he should, accept outrageous handling because of some defect that had nothing to do with his individual self, a defect with him from parturition to death, a black Calvinism of a perfect and unredeemable sort.

But recent developments in the black community have modified the status of the toasts' protagonists, thereby limiting their further utility. The role of hustler is no longer generally accepted as a legitimate way of coming to terms with an intolerable situation; other options are open now, options that do not require parasitical exploitation of everyone else.

It is impossible to prove that toasts are performed less than in the past. There isn't enough data. Except for Abrahams' research in Philadelphia, I know of no intensive collection project in a small area which tried to document the working repertory of young black men, and one cannot go back to Abrahams' neighborhood for its composition has changed significantly in the fifteen years since he worked there.

But there is some data which, though not conclusive, supports my contention about the failing health of the tradition. The first is, everyone I've asked about the matter—informants quoted in this book, black friends and colleagues, street workers—has the same impression. The change is attributed to a difference in racial attitudes, to an increasing middle-class orientation, to the general shift in American culture away from narrative performance. Inexpensive and lightweight transistor radios, tape recorders and record players, and the omnipresent TV set have had an extraordinarily stultifying effect on almost all aspects of folk performance. The second bit of evidence is how many of the toasts seem to be over twenty-five years old. Except for #45, "The Voodoo Queen," the poems composed by Peter (#62-66), and perhaps a few others, it would be hard to date many items in this collection after the early fifties. Most can be dated—by diction or thematic content or relation to earlier published sources—to the 1930s. If the amount of composing is reduced, I think it can be assumed that the amount of performance also is reduced.

Toasts long served to quieten the need for other kinds of action, they dulled other kinds of perception. That service and dulling no longer work very well, and for that reason performance of toasts outside places like jails is attenuating. The old tools do not work any longer, so they atrophy and eventually perish. What is left is an almost detached kind of recitation, spectacle rather than adventure. Spectacle is not good enough when one cannot hide the real world, nor when the real world offers more attractive options.

The Toasts

ABOUT THE HEADNOTES

It is standard practice in folklore annotation to give the name of the informant and the date and place of collection. Folklorists find the informant's name useful in case someone later collects in the same area and wants to compare versions of an item through a neighborhood or family or even with the same informant over a period of time. Because of the nature of the material presented here and because of the present institutional affiliations of some of the informants, I decided not to use real names. I have, however, used pseudonyms consistently throughout, so all toasts identified as having been told by "Slim," for example, were in fact told by the same man. Any scholar who has a legitimate need for the real names of any of the informants can obtain such data from the Center for Study of American Culture, State University of New York at Buffalo. The original tapes for all the toast sessions are housed in the Center's Archive of Folklore, Traditional Music and Oral History.

Each headnote tells where the toast was collected (Ramsey, Ellis, and Wynne are prison units of the Texas Department of Corrections; Jefferson City is the site of the Missouri Penitentiary), the date of recording, and whatever bibliographical or glossing data seem necessary. Such data are meant to be suggestive, not exhaustive.

Badmen, Crime, and Jail

1. STACKOLEE

A. Henry, Ramsey, 17 November 1965
B. Joe, Ellis, 24 March 1966
C. Frank, Ramsey, 17 November 1965
D. Bobby, Jefferson City, 22 June 1964
E. Gene, Wynne, 19 March 1966
F. Manuscript fragment sent by Phyllis Wallace, of the Delinquency Study Project, Southern Illinois University, as heard from a Chicago informant in 1967
G. Bob, Connelley Migrant Camp, Barker, New York, 17 August 1970

The character Stagolee or Stackolee figures in ballad and prose narrative tradition as well as toast tradition. He is found throughout the South and much of the industrialized North. B. A. Botkin, in his entry on "Stackalee, Stackerlee, or Staglee," in Leach (1950:1080-1081), writes:

> Negro bad man who, according to the ballad, shot and killed Billy Lyon (Lion, Galion) in a barroom brawl (some say in Memphis and some say in St. Louis) for stealing his "Magic Stetson." Legend says . . . that this magic hat for which Stackalee sold his soul to the Devil, enabled him to assume various shapes, from mountains to varmints, to walk barefooted on hot slag, and to eat fire. When he got too ornery for even the Devil to stand, the latter caused him to lose his hat and his magic, via Billy Lyon, and ultimately to burn in hell.

Stacker Lee, for whom many Negro children along the Ohio and the Mississippi were named, was one of the four sons of Captain James Lee, founder of the Lee Line, and was celebrated for his prowess with the ladies as well as steamboats. The packet *Stacker Lee* (nicknamed "The Stack," "The Big Smoke," "Stack o' Colluhs," and "Bull of the Woods" and noted for its size and speed) plied between Memphis and Cincinnati, St. Louis, and Vicksburg. The original Stagolee is said to have been a stoker or rousabout on this boat, also the son of a woman who was chambermaid or cook on this or another of the Lee boats; and the ballad is said to have been composed on the levees, where it was sung.

Mississippi John Hurt narrated several tales about Stackolee in which the badman was presented as white; Hurt's song version follows the traditional lines about Stack killing Billy in a fight over the Stetson hat (see Jackson, 1965). For an excellent discussion of Stackolee as song and toast character, see Abrahams (1970A:76-80, 129-142), which includes good discographical and bibliographical notes. D. K. Wilgus sent me a bawdy version of the song from his Western Kentucky Archive, along with two Kentucky versions of the toast. There are many recordings of the song, one of the best of which is Mississippi John Hurt's "Stack O'Lee Blues," Okeh 8654 (original number 401481-B, recorded 28 December 1928). Labov et al. (1973:336,343-344) print a text and offer some commentary on the toast. Also see Abrahams (1970B:45-47) for a Texas variant.

Cunnilingus is universally loathed in the black toasts because it seems to symbolize female domination and has the male in a servicing position; in the few exceptions the actor is meant to be perceived as a fool. There is one other exception: the D-text of "Stackolee." But this version was told by a white informant, a Missouri penitentiary inmate who had learned it from blacks while a child. Stack's line, "Looked at her pussy, said it was good enough to eat," is never found in any black toast I've heard; the woman's reply, "You better do it, daddy, or you'll never see the streets," would in the black toasts produce terrific invective. In the white version it produces nothing; the next line finds the hero in an alley sometime later, and no more mention is made of the whore. Note the teller's frequent use of the word "bastard," a word which never appears in the black texts, for it never developed among blacks the insult function it has among whites.

One other text of "Stackolee" was contributed by a white

informant, the E-text. The weakest poetically of the taped versions, it exhibits several rough attempts to keep the rhyme scheme going by introducing inconsistencies in the names of one of the characters: Ben Lee becomes Ben Lion and Ben Lair.

The A-text is a good version of the usual black redaction of the narrative. There are six agons: (1) the opening scene, both low-key and negative, gets him to the Bucket of Blood; (2) encounter with bartender; (3) encounter with bartender's mother; (4) encounter with whore; (5) encounter with Billy; and (6) encounter with court.

He begins with dissatisfaction, frustration, and rejection: his cards are bad and his woman through with him. In almost all versions of "Stackolee" the opening scene is the most realistic part of the toast: usually he is without money and owner of bad cards or unlucky dice; sometimes he also has a "fucked-up Ford"; and he is almost always rejected by a woman.

His reaction to the woman's rejection — "so I said, 'Fuck it,' you know" — is strangely neutral: it is not directed at the woman but is instead rhetorical. The inside quotation marks are almost superfluous, for one could read the line as equivalent of a shoulder shrugged in resignation. The line is recited without stress; it is metrically short and does not rhyme, so it is not structurally mated with any other line. (The only other unmated line in the poem is the one in which he gives his name: "I said, 'My name is Stackolee.'" The only unrhymed couplet, "So I walked around the room and I seen this trick, / and we went upstairs and we started real soon," results, probably from a misremembering: "soon" should be "quick.") Usually such a line would be dropped, since in metered and rhymed verse in oral tradition dangling lines tend to be easily forgotten. The line's importance, the reason it survives without the usual mnemonic coupling, is contextual. Stack *never* says very much; he never articulates affect verbally: when moved, he strikes or acts out. He does not use the usual range of mental mechanisms to cope with anxiety, he discharges — in each of the six agons except this one.

Considering the subsequent action, his passivity here is at first surprising. For the crime of not knowing Stack's name the bartender is killed, then the dead man's mother is insulted, the whore is not just fucked but is publicly penetrated in the grand style, several people are shot or maimed, Billy is killed, and the judicial process is a farce.

I suggest that the sequence is a kind of physical alternative to the *verbal* handling of a similar threat in the Pimp toasts. In those the woman demands that the man define himself, and he invariably responds with highly structured invective and braggadocio. Stack's masculinity has been challenged or frustrated or rejected (or all those things) in the first agon, and in the rest of the narration he affirms his masculinity in a set of grossly exaggerated and stylized actions against a stranger, a mother, a whore, another Badman, and society. Among the few roles he doesn't manage to attack are those of father and friend, the latter because the sociopath can entertain no friendship, the former for reasons I noted in the section on Pimps.

He cannot use words to cope with conflict. After having handled the bartender, mother, and whore, Stack is named by someone else before the confrontation scene. Billy must be identified as a worthy competitor, so Billy gets to shoot someone; Stack does the same, to put them even. Their duel is not even described. The sequence of events is not causal; it is coincidental. The order could be shifted, for the protagonist lacks a positive articulable goal, a manifest motivational grammar, a motive.

In some versions Billy does not appear at all; in these, Stack kills only the bartender and his sister. The endings are often flippant: Stack responds to a life sentence with, "Judge, that ain't so cold," and the judge says, "No, but your black ass will never get on parole. Now laugh at this: case dismissed."

1A   STACKOLEE

It was back in the time of nineteen hundred and two,
I had a fucked-up deck a cards and I didn't know what to do.
My woman was leavin', she was puttin' me out in the cold.
I said, "Why you leavin' me, baby?" She said, "Our love has grown cold."
So she kept packin' the bags, so I said, "Fuck it," you know.
So I waded through water and I waded through mud
and I came to this town called the Bucket of Blood.
And I asked the bartender for something to eat,
he give me a dirty glass a water and a tough-assed piece a meat.
I said, "Bartender, bartender, don't you know who I am?"
He said, "Frankly, my man, I don't give a goddam."
I said, "My name is Stackolee." He said, "Oh, yes, I heard about you up this
      way,
but I feed you hungry motherfuckers each and every day."

'Bout this time the poor bartender had gone to rest —
I pumped six a my rockets [bullets] in his motherfucken chest.
A woman run out the back screamin' real loud, said, "I know my son ain't
        dead!"
I said, "You just check that hole in the ugly motherfucker's head."
She say, "You may be bad, your name may be Stack,
but you better not be here when Billy Lions get back."
So I walked around the room and I seen this trick,
and we went upstairs and we started real soon.
Now me and this broad we started to tussle
and I drove twelve inches a dick through her ass before she could move a
        muscle.
We went downstairs where we were before,
we fucked on the table and all over the floor.
'Bout that time you could hear the drop of a pin —
that bad motherfucker Billy Lions had just walked in.
He walked behind the counter, he seen the bartender dead,
he say, "Who put this hole in this ugly motherfucker's head."
Say, "Who can this man's murderer be?"
One motherfucker say, "You better speak soft, his name is Stackolee."
He say, "Stack, I'm gonna give you a chance to run before I draw my gun."
Bitch jumped up and said, "Billy, please."
He shot that whore through both her knees.
A pimp eased up and turned out the lights
and I had him dead in both my sights.
When the lights came back on poor Billy had gone to rest,
I had pumped nine a my rockets in his motherfucken chest.
The next day about half-past ten
I was standin' before the judge and twelve other good men.
They say, "What can this man's charges be?"
One sonofabitch say, "Murder in the first degree."
Another say, "What can this man's penalty be?"
One say, "Hang him," another say, "Give him gas."
A snaggle-tooth bitch jumped up and say, "Run that twister through his jivin'
        ass!"
My woman jumped up and said, "Let him go free,
'cause there ain't nobody in the world can fuck like Stackolee."

It was back in the year of forty-one when the times was hard,
I had a sawed-off shotgun and a marked deck of cards.
I had a faded blue suit and a slouch down hat,
I had a T-model Ford and no payments on that.
I waded through water and I sloshed through mud
till I came to the place they call the Bucket of Blood.
I said, "Say, Mr. Bartender, please, will you give me something to eat?"
He gave me some bitter-assed water and tough-assed meat.
I say, "Say, man, you must not know who I am."
He say, "Frankly, sonofabitch, I don't give a goddamn."
I said, "Say, man, my name is Stack, and I'm from down the way,"
He said, "I don't care about your name bein' Stack and from down the way,"
say, "I meet a hungry person like you each and every day."
About that time the poor boy was dead
with three of my thirty-eight rockets in his head.
A little later on a lady walks in, she say, "Where can the bartender be, please?"
I said, "He's layin' over in the corner with his mind at ease."
She said, "Oh, no, my son," say, "he can't be dead!"
I said, "You better look at them three wide-assed holes in his head."
Little later, about you would hear the drop of a pin,
that's when Billy Lane walks in.
He said, "Who can the murderer of this poor man be?"
I said, "Me, Stackolee."
He said, "I'm gonna give you just one chance to run
before I draw my old Gatling gun."
Now just about the time I got him in my thirty-eight sight
a waitress slipped over and cut out the light.
But now when the light come on old Billy was dead,
he had two more rockets in his head.
Early the next morning at quarter to ten,
they carried me before the judge and twelve other men.
He said, "What can the charges of this poor man be?"
They said, "Murder, your honor, in the first degree."
Judge said, "Well, son, I'm gonna give you a little old sixty-year sentence."

I said, "Judge, sixty years ain't no sentence, sixty years ain't no time,"
I says, "I got a old buddy over on Ellis doin' ninety-nine."

1C   STACKOLEE

Back in forty-nine when times was hard
I carried a sawed-off shotgun and a marked deck of cards.
I stumbled through rain and crawled through mud
on this bad town called "Bucket of Blood."
I asked the bartender for something to eat,
he give me a muddy glass a water and a fucked-up piece a meat.
I said, "Mister," I say, "you must not know who I am."
He say, "Frankly, son, I don't give a damn."
Before I realized what I had did,
I had shot him six times through his motherfucken head.
His wife's run out and said, "That's my husband, he can't be dead!"
I said, "Well count them six slugs in his chickenshit head."
The sister ran out and said, "Call the law!"
And I bust two caps [fired two shots] right dead in her jaw.
Well when I went to court it was rainin' a downpour
the court was in a uproar
and this is what happened to me:
one woman say, "Hang him," one say, "Kick his ass till his face turn pale,"
one say, "Give his jivin' ass the electric chair."
Well, the judge looked at me and say, "Son, I feel sorry for you
and I tell you what I'm gonna do."
He say, "You won't hang and you won't burn,"
he say, "but your jivin' ass will serve two life terms."
I laughed, I said, "Judge," I say, "that ain't so cold."
He said, "No, but your black ass will never get on parole."
He said, "Now laugh at this: case dismissed."

1D   STACKOLEE

"This is supposed to be about two colored studs. It's truth. In New Orleans.
That's a true one. I mean, it's *true,* though. Did you know that?"

Was back in thirty-two when times were hard,
I had a sawed-off shotgun and a cold deck a cards.
Wore a brown Squire suit and a big beaver hat,
and if you motherfuckers ever saw me I was dressed like that.
Wore brown suede shoes and a diamond-studded cane,
had a twelve-inch peg with a be-bop chain.
Now times turned hard and the weather grew cold,
my old lady kicked my ass out, said her love had grown old.
So I took me a walk down to Rampart Street
where all the bad motherfuckers are supposed to meet.
I walked through six inches a shit and ten inches a mud
to a place they call the Bucket of Blood.
Called to the bartender to give me a bite to eat,
he give me a muddy glass a water and a tough piece of meat.
I say, "Say, sonofabitch, don't you know who I am?"
He said, "Frankly, mister, I don't give a damn."
He said, "I've heard of you down the way,
I meet you raggedy-ass bastards damn near every day."
Well, the motherfucker never said much more,
for one of my bullets laid the bastard dead on the floor.
A lady walked in, said, "Oh, God, please."
I said, "Speak softly, mam, his mind is at ease."
She said, "Please don't tell me my son is dead."
I said, "If you don't believe it, cunt, look at the hole in his head."
She said, "I've heard of you, you bastard, your name is Stack,
but you better not be here when Billy Lion gets back."
"I'll be here when the time comes and pass,
and fuck your Billy Lion right dead in his ass."
So there sat a broad all sexy and sweet,
so I walked right over and I pulled up a seat.
I said, "Say, bitch, don't think me silly,
but who is this stud that they call Billy?"
She said, "He's tall, dark, and handsome like he's supposed to be."
She reached in her purse and pulled out a square [cigarette].
She said, "Don't worry, daddy, he's no where."
Well I could see right away the bitch went for this clown,
I said, "Move along, cunt, I'm puttin' you down."
Over the next table the whore give me a smile,
said it looked like I hadn't had any in quite a while.
I said, "My wife kicked my ass out and locked the door

and I been lookin' around for a good-lookin' whore."
She looked at her watch, it was half-past eight.
She said, "Come on up my place, daddy, we'll get things straight."
So I went right up and I locked the door,
I just had to get a look at that frantic whore.
Looked at her pussy, said it was good enough to eat,
she said, "You better do it, daddy, or you'll never see the streets."
Woke up in an alley and went back to the bar,
and there at the end stood Billy Lions,
a bad motherfucker, there's no denyin'.
He said, "Who can the murderer of this good man be?"
I said, "Me, motherfucker, my name's Stackolee."
He said, "Yeah, I heard of you down at the shitty ditch,
but you tore your ass when you fucked my bitch."
Lady jumped up and hollered, "Oh, Billy, please!"
And he shot that bitch clean to her knees.
A man jumped up and hollered, "Someone call the law!"
And he shot that bastard clear through the jaw.
He landed on the floor with his hands on his face
and pieces of his jaw scattered all over the place.
I fucked all the whores and drank the place dry
and fell on the floor with blood in my eyes.
A cop walked in and said, "Who can this drunken bastard be?"
Lady said, "Speak softly, officer, his name is Stackolee."
Woke up next mornin' it was a half-past ten,
in front of a judge and twelve good men.
The judge said, "Well, now, what can the charges against this good man be?"
It was drunk and rape and murder in the first degree.
Said, "Well now, Stackolee, you've led a simple life,
fucked your sister and killed your wife.
There's only one thing left for me to do, that's give you twenty years' time."
I said, "Well, fuck, judge, that's nothin': my mother's doin' twenty-nine."

1E   STACKOLEE

I staggered in a place called the Bucket a Blood.
I said, "Barkeep, barkeep, give me something to eat."
He give me a glass a blood and a piece of fucked-up meat.

I said, "Barkeeper, don't you know who I am?"
He says, "Frankly mister motherfucker, don't give a goddamn."
I reached in my pocket and pulled out my forty-four,
I shot him twice and he hit the floor.
A bitch jumped up and said, "Barkeep, barkeep, where's the barkeep?"
I said he's in the corner with a peace at mind.
Another bitch jumped up, said, "Stack, you better come with me,
but watch out for my boyfriend, Ben Lee."
I went with her and everything was fine.
We fucked on the chair, we fucked in the bed,
and up the stairs come Ben Lion.
A clatter of smoke and a roar of fire,
and there lay Ben Lair with his ass in the air.
The judge said, "Son," say, "I give you life."
A bitch jumped up and said, "Give him gas."
Another bitch jumped up and said, "Shoot 'lectricity through his mother-
    fucken ass."
Judge said, "Son, I'm gonna change my mind,
I'm only gonna give you ten years' hard time."
Said, "Gee, judge, that's no time,
I got a brother on Levenworth jackin' ninety-nine."

1F   STACKOLEE

When I was young in my prime
I had all the bitches on my mind
I had money every single day
I even had green bags stashed away
I doned on reefers and grubbed on dope
I inhaled gas like it was smoke
I walked in water I walked through mud until I came to a town
    called Bucket O' Blood
I went into a bar—asked the bartender for somethin to eat
He gave me a dirty glass of water and a fucked up piece of meat
I said "Bartender Bartender, do you know who I am?"
The bartender said, "Frankly, I don't give a damn!"
That was all was said. I put two of my rockets in the mother fucker's head.
Lou came in rappin strong said Billy Billy you can't be dead.

I said count my rockets in his head, She say Billy Billy please.
I say look at that mother fucker down on his knees. Then the lights grow tight.
Two mother fuckin sisters tried to break for the door.
They won't try that silly shit no more.
Then I started again until I came to a town called sin.
Cops started fallin in.
One jumped up and blew gas.
I jumped up for the deck and caught a rocket in my mother fuckin neck.

(*From Manuscript*)

1G   NINETEEN THIRTY-TWO

In nineteen thirty-two when the times was hard
I had a crooked pair of dice and a marked deck of cards.
I went to Cliff's and what did I see?
I seen a hundred motherfuckers were a havin' beans.
I said, "Look, motherfucker, gimme something to eat."
She gave me a clean glass a water, a dirty piece a meat.
I said, "Look, bitch, don't you know who I am?"
She said, "Frankly speaking, motherfucker, I don't give a good goddamn."
Before that bitch realized what she had just said,
she had a thirty-two bullet right between her motherfucken head.

2. STACKOLEE IN HELL

Bobby, Jefferson City, 22 June 1964

This was recited by the same white man who recited the long
D-text of "Stackolee" above. The opening is similar to the popular
song version of the battle between Bill and Stack. The rest of the
poem takes a direction quite different from the usual poem about
Stackolee: here, he is gunned down by the mother of a man he
killed, and in the rest of the poem performs as a superstud rather
than homicidal badass. See the second stanza of #42, "Casey
Jones," for another version of the bad stud in Hell, fucking
anything that gets in his path.

STACKOLEE IN HELL

The other night I thought I heard a dog bark,
but that was Stackolee and Billy Lion gamblin' in the dark.
Stackolee says, "Now, Billy Lion, you stay here in this shack,
and I don't want to see you move your motherfucken ass till I get back."
Stackolee went home and got two smokin' forty-fives,
he came back and placed 'em between Billy Lion's eyes.
Billy Lion said, "Oh, Stackolee, don't take my life.
I got four cross-eyed kids and a cripple-assed wife."
He said, "I don't want your four cross-eyed kids or your cripple-assed wife,"
said, "All I want's your cocksucken life."
Shot him five times right through the head,
left him on the floor quivering till he's dead.
Then he went and told Sister Lou just what he'd done,
said, "Say, Sister Lou, I just killed your no-'count cocksucken son."
She said, "Well, Stackolee, you know that's not true.
Hell, you and Billy been friends for a year or two."
He said, "Look, bitch, if you don't think he's dead,
go down and count those five fucken holes I just put in his head."
Stackolee went walkin' down the track
and Sister Lou snuck up behind him and shot him in the back.
He shit, farted, stumbled, fell on his face
right down in front of Joe's place.
Stackolee's wife come runnin' out the door hollerin'
"Stackolee, Stackolee! Somebody killed my Stackolee."
He rolled over and said, "Look, bitch, when I die don't dress me in black,
'cause if hell don't suit me I'm comin' back."
There was a rumble in the earth and a roar in the ground,
that was Stackolee changin' hell around.
He said, "I want tables over here and the chairs over there,
and don't a motherfucker move while I comb my hair."
The devil said, "Look, Stackolee, I heard you's a pretty bad man in that upper
    land,
but you know you're down here and met another bad man."
Said, "Okay, Devil, you get your pitchfork and let me get two smokin' forty-
    ones,

and us two bad motherfuckers'll have us some fun."
The Devil got his pitchfork and Stackolee got two smokin' forty-ones,
and those two bad sonofabitches did have some fun.
Stackolee shot the devil right through the heart
and he lit up like a human torch.
Caught the old lady bent over shovelin' coal,
put twelve inches up her hole.
Four little devils runnin' around,
hollerin', "Mother, mother, stop him 'fore he fucks us all."
Well he fucked St. Peter and he fucked St. Paul,
he'll be a fuckin' motherfucker time the roll is called.

3. BROCK HANKTON

Seymour, Wynne, 18 March 1966

According to the informant, Hankton "was a badman in Austin, Texas. A real man. He was in Austin in '34, '35. He got killed in '35. He got killed by a fella named John Henry. Everything in that toast is true. All those names is facts." Seymour learned the toast in a Texas prison in 1937. Lt. Harvey Gann of the Austin Police Department wrote me that some oldtimers in the Department remember a badman named Hankton who was in fact killed in a fight sometime in the 1930s, but he couldn't supply any other information about the event.

Unlike Stagolee, the badman here is done in specifically because of his rudeness. A "little bum" makes a pitiful plea for some booze; Brock insults him and is killed by John Henry, whose "whole-hearted desire was to kill him a man," but who, unlike Stack, waited for a proper opportunity to fulfill that desire. Stack gets no satisfactions, only occasional valve openings. This poem's characters are rational, "Stackolee" is reactive. Note the hobo recitation type of monika listing for the participants in the funeral, suggesting the poet knew something of that other tradition.

3   BROCK HANKTON

On October the sixth it was a terrible night,
that was the last time that bad Brock Hankton remember seeing the light.

Brock left off a Sixth Street about a quarter till eight,
and he drove on Eleventh in his Ford V-8.
He stopped into Lewis' place where all the boys was having fun,
Brock got kind of hankty [suspicious] and he felt for his gun.
He walks up to the bar, says, "Bartender, got any whiskey for sale?
If so, give me a pint, and make it snappier than hell."
There stood a little bum in the corner, he said, "Mr. Brock, can I have a
    glass?"
He said, "You better stand back, motherfucker, before I kick your goddam
    ass."
There stood the bum's friend, John Henry, with his knife in his hand,
his whole-hearted desire was to kill him a man.
He said, "Kickin' asses, Brock, have came to the past,
and if you kick that kid tonight you'll kick your goddam last."
Well, Brock was already hankty, so he jumps under the light,
and before he knew it he was hit with a knife.
He pulled out his pistol and he begin to cuss,
you ought to seen the Negroes kickin' up dust.
Because they knew that Brock was bad
and it just wouldn't do to make him mad.
He made three shots inside of the place,
and he made ten steps forward and fell dead on his face.
Then an ambulance begin to run, sireens begin to whine,
the driver said, "Let's go, Doc, somebody must be dyin'."
Then he drove up to the curb, all of a sudden he stopped,
driver jumped out, said, "I'm a motherfucker if that ain't old Brock."
Said, "What hospital must we take him to?"
Say, "Carry him to the undertaker, the only place will do."
Now he was carried to the undertaker by the name of Fella, but he couldn't be
    seen,
so they carried his body to an undertaker by the name of Cain.
So the day of the funeral everyone was sad,
'cept old Ice-house Jim, that motherfucker was glad.
Now there was Pants-Pickin' Lead, Big Ed Ned,
Butt-Cut and Shorty, and Wirehead Ed,
there was Fast-Fuckin' Fanny, Razor-Cuttin' Annie
and Mary Lou, dressed in her high-powdered blue.
She told Mary Mack, said, "What can I do?
Brock was your man but he was my man too."

So after the gamblers came from around so far,
up drove Buttercup Marshall in Cub Greasey's car.
He gets to the door and he makes a little bow
and he speaks to the people ahead.
He said, "What I got to say, I must say it softly, for I know that Brock is dead."
He said, "Of course at the time I'm a little bit late,
I had to help Buttercup Marshall in his Ford V-8.
So before the preacher close his Bible and all kneel to pray,"
he say, "any more a you friends a Brock have any thing to say?"
They all got together, said, "Goodbye, Brock, you know we hate to see you go,
but the good book say you got to reap just what you sow."
So after Brock Hankton's funeral, Ice-House go down to Mary Mack,
and he begged and he pleaded for her to take him back.
She said, "Ice-House, Brock Hankton was the only man that I ever loved,
and I wouldn't take you back if you was the last ice-sellin' motherfucker that
they had in the world."

4. DOLOMITE

A. Recorded by James F. Beyers from the performance of Rudy
Ray Moore, Governor's Inn, Buffalo, New York, June 1970.
B. Manuscript sent by Professor G. M. Sturman, M.I.T., as sent
to him by a friend from Harlem in 1967

Dolomite is the ultimate badass: he drinks, fights, and fucks,
and in between seems to brag about what he has just done or will
do next. He suffers none of Stackolee's inarticulateness or the
Pimp's limited perspective.

4A   DOLOMITE

Some folks say that Willie Green
was the baddest motherfucker the world ever seen.
But I want you to light you up a joint and take a real good shit and screw your
wig on tight,
and let me tell you about the little bad motherfucker called Dolomite.

Now Dolomite was from San Antone,
a rambling skipfucker from the day he was born.
Why, the day he was dropped from his mammy's ass,
he slapped his pappy's face
and said, "From now on, cocksucker, I'm running this place."
At the age of one he was drinkin' whiskey and gin,
at the age of two he was eatin' the bottles it came in.
Now Dolomite had an uncle called Sudden Death,
killed a dozen bad men from the smell of his breath.
When his uncle heard how Dolomite was treatin' his ma and his pa,
he said, "Let me go and check on this bad rascal before he go too far."
Now one cold dark December night,
his uncle broke in on Dolomite.
Now Dolomite wasn't no more'n three or four,
when his uncle come breakin' through the door.
His uncle said, "Dolomite,
I want you to straighten up and treat your brother right,
'cause if you keep on with your dirty mistreatin',
I'm gonna whup your ass till your heart stop beatin'."
Dolomite's sittin' in the middle of the floor playin'.
He said, "I see your lips quiver, Unc, but I don't hear a cocksucken word you
     sayin'."
This made his uncle mad.
He led off with a right that made lightnin' flash,
but Dolomite tore his leg off, he was that damned fast.
Now the men of San Antone gathered around that night
to see if they could do something about the little bad rascal called Dolomite.
They took a hundred of the baddest, the boldest, the ugliest men in town,
finally drove Dolomite's ass down.
Put him in jail, ["Really got him!" someone in the audience yells].
they held him without bail.
If you think his mammy was happy,
you should have seen his pappy.
Now it's been eight long years since Dolomite's been faded,
the average motherfucker would a long long been dated.
Now the warden called Dolomite, said, "Dolomite,
I'm gonna tell you what we're gonna do.
We gonna give you a dollar and a half and a damned good meal,
if you promise to leave us alone

and get your bad ass out of San Antone."
Dolomite took the dollar and a half and the damned good meal,
and said, "I'm gonna tell you old, jive, ancient, moldied, decrepit mother-
     fuckers how I feel.
'Cause you can all suck my dick, nuts, and ass down to the motherfucken bone,
because I ain't *never* comin' back to San Antone."
Now Dolomite wasn't no more than thirteen when they let him out the gate,
he got a job in Africa kickin' lions in their ass to stay in shape.
He got kicked out of South America for fuckin' steers,
he fucked a she-elephant till she broke down in tears.
Now Dolomite worked five years and a day, got his pay,
Said, "Well, I believe I'll go back to that jiveass U.S.A."
Well, the news of the heavyweight fight was being broadcasted that night,
and a special bulletin said, "Look out for storms, atomic bombs, and
     Dolomite."
Well the first thing Dolomite encountered
was two big rocky mountains.
He said, "Mountain, what y'all gonna do?"
He said, "We gonna part, Mr. Dolomite, and let your bad ass through."
Now Dolomite went on down to Kansas City,
kickin' asses till both shoes was shitty.
Hoboed into Chi.
Who did he run into but that badass Two-Gun Pete.
He said, "Move over and let me pass
'fore they have to pull these triple-A's out your motherfucken ass."
Went on down to forty-second Street,
not for no shit, but for someplace he would sleep and eat.
Run into that Chi Mabel, of all the whores she was the boss.
She'd suck you, fuck you, and jack you off.
She said, "Come on down to my pad, Dolomite,
we gonna fuck and fight till broad daylight."
Dolomite said, "Bitch, I had a job in Africa
kickin' lions in they ass to stay in shape."
Said, "I got run out of South America for fuckin' steers,"
said, "I fucked a she-elephant till she broke down in tears."
Mabel said, "I don't care where you goin' and where you've been,"
said, "I'm layin' to wrap this good hot juicy pussy all around your badass chin."
     [Some people in audience laugh and clap, one says, "All *right*, all *right*!"]
Dolomite said, "Bitch, it's best you not fuck with me,
I better run you down some of my pedigree."

Said, "I swimmed across muddy rivers and never got wet,
mountains has fell on me and I ain't dead yet.
I fucked an elephant and fucked her mother,
I can look up a bull's ass and tell you the price of butter.
I fucked a mother elephant down to a coon,
even fucked the same damned cow that jumped over the motherfucken moon."
Said, "I rode across the ocean on the head of my dick,
and ate nine tons a catshit and ain't never got sick.
And you talk about wrappin' your good hot pussy all around my badass chin,
bitch: you ought to be blowin' up my ass trying to be my motherfucken friend."
Oh, but Mabel farted,
that's when the fuckin' started.
She let her pussy do the mojo, the pop-grow, the turkey, and the grind,
left Dolomite's ass nine strokes behind.
She threw pussy up Dolomite's back, come out his ears, down his sides, run out
    of his pocket,
damn near pulled his asshole out of socket.
But Dolomite suddenly made a mojo turn,
had the crabs around that bitch's asshole hollerin', "Burn, baby, burn!"
But the next mornin' they found Mabel dead,
with her drawers wrapped around her nappy-assed head,
and the crabs was madder than a motherfucker
to see Dolomite eat 'em out of their goddamned supper.
But Dolomite kept on kickin' asses and fuckin' up the hall,
'till finally his roll was called.
They had his funeral, carried him down to the graveyard.
Dolomite was dead, but his dick was still hard.
The preacher said, "Ashes to ashes and dust to dust,"
said, "I'm glad this here bad motherfucker called Dolomite is no longer here
    with us."

4B   DOLOMITE

Dolomite first originated in San Antone
Baddest mother-fucker the world has ever known
When Dolomite was born he jumped on his mother's stomach
Smacked his father in the face
Said "listen mother-fucker

I'm taken over this place"
At the age of one
Dolomite was drinkin' whisky wine and gin
At the age of two
He was eatin' the bottles the damn stuff come in.
Now Dolomite had a cousin named Sudden Death
At the age of four
First walked 'cross the floor
And said to Dolomite
Said "Dolomite if you don't stop this mistreatin'
I'll kick your ass till your heart stops beatin'"
Dolomite laid there as if he was dead
Finally he turned to Sudden Death and looked at him
And this is what he said
"I saw your lips movin' but I aint heard a damn word you said"
Quicker than the human eye could see
Sudden Death pulled his razor and sliced Dolomite
Nine times 'cross the knee
Got over confident and took one more stroke
And that's when the mother-fuckin' razor broke
He turned with a flash and started to move
As if he was doin' the hundred yard dash
While he was runnin' he thought to himself
"I know I can fight him so I'll go back and kick his ass
'Til he loses his mother-fuckin' eyesight"
He turned with a grin and something hit him on his chin
He slid for six miles and when he awoke
He no more could smile 'cause his mother-fuckin' chin was broke
Dolomite grabbed Sudden Death by his cabbage lookin' head
And squose him 'til his mother-fuckin' ass-hole bled
Sudden Death went stone blind 'cause he knew he was dyin'
The sheriff got his ten best men to bring Dolomite in
Dolomite was sentenced to ninety-nine years in jail
And the other mother-fucker would have been dead
But Dolomite just stood there scratchin' his mother-fuckin' head
Sheriff tole Dolomite "I'll give you a dollar and a half and a good
Square meal if you'd get out of San Antone
And leave us decent people alone.
Dolomite took the dollar and a half and said
"I'll tell you mother-fuckers just how I feel

You can kiss my ass right down to the bone
If you catch me back in this place called Ole San Antone."

(*From Manuscript*)

5. JESSE JAMES

Phil, Wynne, 9 July 1964

Phil says he's known this toast over thirty years. Abrahams has a very different version (1970A:163-164), one similar to his Stagolee texts in its major movements. Probably the most interesting aspect of this text is the final couplet: Jesse's wife, rather than the betrayer Bob Ford, is blamed for the murder. The toast becomes a curious homiletic rather than a badman narrative.

There are a number of ballads in general circulation about Jesse James. A bibliographical note on the version closest to this text is found in Laws (1962:176-177).

5   JESSE JAMES

Come all you people whilst you present at hand,
say, I want to tell you a story about a bold bad man.
From St. Louis, Missouri, down the Mississippi stream,
from Louisville, Kentucky, down to New Orleans,
say, now, we've had some good men, we've had some bad men,
but the most a you all done forgot their names,
but all the little children nowadays can tell you 'bout Jesse James.
There was a man sittin' down readin' a history of Jesse James' life
and the wind blew his door open and he died from fright.

Jesse told Frank to saddle up his horse—
for that outlaw gang he was strictly boss.
Jesse sittin' down greasin' his forty-fo',
Frank told his cousin Bob, said, "My brother's figurin' on dough."
Jesse told Frank, "Say, now, what do you think,
say early next mornin' we rob the Pitchfield bank?"
Early next morning 'bout nine o'clock
the Pitchfield banker got an awful shock
Jesse kept him covered with his forty-fo'

whilst the gang sacked up a half a million or mo'.
They cut the money equal, Jesse said, "Now I'm through,
boys, if you want to continue robbin', say, that's up to you.
'Cause I decided to make a change in life,
I'm goin' out West, gonna get me a wife."
So one day while Jesse's wife had business in town,
Jesse stayed at home just to straighten things around.
'Bout an hour's time the doorbell begin to ring,
up steps Bob Ford, a member of the outlaw gang.
"Hello, Jesse." "Hello, Bob.
Well I haven't seen you since the Pitchfield rob."
Bob comes up with a awful tale,
says Frank and all the boys is bound in jail.
"And I want to get you to help me rob the Western Mail."
Jesse jumps up on a rawhide chair
to hang his wife's picture up who he loved so dear.
Bob taken dead aim at Jesse James' head;
the news spread all over town: Jesse James is dead.
Now, boys, if you ever decide to be a outlaw you don't need no wife,
'cause a pretty woman's picture cost a bad man's life.

(*From Manuscript*)

6. BOOTHILL McCOY

Henry, Ramsey, 3 July 1964

Like Jesse James in the previous toast, Boothill McCoy is proba-
bly a hero out of white narrative tradition. The poem is so similar
in structure to the Robert Service sort of poem that I would be
surprised if it hadn't seen print at some time, although I haven't
yet discovered any such source.

6   BOOTHILL McCOY

It was just about sundown in a border town
that was called the Gatesways to Hell,
where women and men indulged in sin
that's damn near too frightenin' to tell,
where dogs fought cats and cats fought rats

just for a drink of polecat rye,
where men was cold and women was bold
and much too ornery to die.
Say in this town of sinless souls
there lived one Boothill McCoy,
who played with his guns in the morning sun
like a kid playing with a toy.
Say, Boothill's draw was lightnin', in fact it was frightnin',
too fast for the naked eye to see.
Boothill was so fast he could take a lookin' glass
and beat his own self to the draw.
Say, in this town where sixgun was law
and the code was to shoot,
Boothill's lightnin' draw settled a many a dispute.
And though the undertaker was the moneymaker
for every day he sold a pine box suit.
Now hated around and not wanted in town
Boothill kept much to his self
until he craved a fight and a little red-eye
just like anyone else.
And in town to get his supplies one day
who should he chance to meet?
Big Bob Clint and Rawhide Flint
who had sided with Sadie McCrea.
They called him down in the heart of town,
And said, "Boothill, make your play."
With a piercing yell, Boothill fell,
while blasting between his thighs.
He shot Bob Clint, Rawhide Flint
with two slugs apiece between the motherfucken eyes.
And while dodgin' a slug that suddenly tugged
at his rawhide-fastened vest,
he shot McCrea to save the day
with the remaining slugs in his motherfucken chest.
He picked up his hat and pulled to his feet —
a job well done, you sonofagun —
and then he went sashaying down the street.
Then he came to a saloon where a lonely tune
played throughout the night.
He walked to the bar and ordered rye

while his eyes took in the sights.
And at the end of the bar who should he chance to meet?
Half-breed Joe from Mexico
who was rappin' with Commanche Pete.
"What're you doin' here?" Commanche sneered,
displayin' a gunman's crouch.
Now this wasn't no talk to a deadly gunhawk,
but Commanche himself wasn't no slouch.
And no one knew when Boothill drew
till they saw Joe hit the floor,
almost torn apart with a slug in his heart.
While still on his feet, he blasted Pete
even before his gun cleared the slot.
Now things went well until that fateful day Boothill made his play
on a stranger who just hit town.
Light as a feather they both slapped leather,
but only one of them bad motherfuckers hit the ground.
Yes, Boothill fell, through the gates of hell,
just as all bad gunmen did,
but he never knew that he had drew
on that fabulous young Billy the Kid.

7. HERMAN FROM THE SHARK-TOOTH SHORE

Henry, Ramsey, 3 July 1964

  This is a poem about a super con-man, one who can sell anyone anything anytime, but it is cast in the frame of a tutorial experience, which means the narrator can use that device to involve himself in the action in a manner that lets him get the most out of the first-person involvement. I suspect the poem may have been in print—lines like "make him think he was a Buddha and could grow hair under a wooden head" are not usual in the toast canon—but it has been adapted to the teller's situation. Note the Texas segments, which even involve a former Texas governor, Allen Shivers.

  The toast includes one of the earliest examples of the word "player" to mean "pimp" I know of (see Milner, 1972, for a fine long description of the modern player's perception of his operations). The term "short-coin" turns up in many of the toasts.

It should really be "short-con," that is, small con games.

The Kid Weil mentioned in the toast is Joseph "Yellow Kid" Weil, one of America's most famous big con-men. He was born about 1875 and worked well into the second quarter of this century. According to Scott (1961:336): "Weil operated all over the Middle West, but especially in Chicago. He would pose as a mining engineer or respectable banker and always took immense pains to substantiate the story he told. He would rent or borrow imposing business premises; forge letters of credit or testimonials from eminent financiers; even, on occasion, reproduce nation-wide magazine articles with his own photograph substituted for the celebrity he wished to impersonate."

7 HERMAN FROM THE SHARK-TOOTH SHORE

All you cool cats, bop daddies, and pennyweight pimps who think you know
    the score,
listen while I tell you of your superior: Herman from the Shark-Tooth Shore.
It was early one mornin', the temperature read about twenty below,
I was on my way to the Union Station to beat some sucker for his dough.
And upon arrivin', stashin' myself in the restroom to make my daily score,
that's when in walked this cool cat, Herman from the Shark-Tooth Shore.
He was a well-dressed cat about six feet or more,
I thought he was a mark, so I tried to beat him for his dough.
But my approach was intercepted, he smiled and shook his head,
say, "Why, son, you're far too clumsy, you couldn't even beat [con] the dead."
Say, "Pickin' pockets, why that's a hustle for a lame,
why don't you try short-coinin', that's a far more prosperous game."
Say, "Come along with me and let's have a heart-to-heart chat,
let me tell you some of my experiences when I was broke and down and out
    flat."
He took me to his mansion on the Shark-Tooth Shore.
It was so tough I never saw one like it before.
There was a gold gate hung on a wall of brick,
a windin' sidewalk of silver ten inches thick.
His mansion looked like a huge castle standin' there,
why the French cathedral in Paris couldn't touch it anywhere.
He says, "Sit down, son, let's have a heart-to-heart chat."
He say, "Dig some of my experiences when I was broke and down and out flat.

I used to rob people, cold-cock 'em in alleys with baseball bats,
I'd eat ten-cent meals and hoghead jowls
and half the time I didn't know what a decent meal was."
Say, "I slept in boxcars with my friends and my cubs,
then I wore shoes with holes in 'em that showed my very toes."
Say, "But I left all that behind me, made my way to fame
when Yellow Kid Weil taught me the game.
He taught me how a fool should be led,
to make him think he was Buddha and could grow hair under a wooden head.
He told me, "You take a fool and set him high upon a ridge,
and make him believe how much money he can make by buyin' the Brooklyn
    Bridge."
Say, "Now you get a fast-steppin' whore
and before you know it your pockets will be lined with suckers' gold."
Say, "You take San Francisco, that's a real prosperous land,"
say, "come along with me, son, and watch how I play my hand."
And on the way to San Francisco, to a rich man named Twain,
for a cool ten thousand he sold this mark the train.
And standin' in San Francisco the very next day,
to the mayor of San Francisco he sold the San Francisco Bay.
And to a rich man named Ortez who had lived in California all his life,
he sold the mark the island of Alcatraz.
Say, now, I stayed with the Herman for two long years, until I learned the
    game,
and I made my way home to start my road to fame.
I remembered everything the Herman had taught me in the very same way,
and I used the very same methods to beat a sucker each and every day.
And in San Antone to a rich man named Joe who had lived there all his life,
I sold the fool the Alamo.
And standin' in Houston on Main and Grey,
to ex-governor Allen Shivers I sold the Gulf Freeway.
It was the end of summer, just about the beginning of fall,
I decided to take a trip to the Windy City, pay my friend the Herman a call.
It had been five years since I had been to the Shark-Tooth Shore.
I pulled a long golden chain and a sweet young maiden opened the door.
She was youth itself standin' there in the sun,
a sweet young maiden not a day over twenty-one.
And I looked at her and said with a silly grin,
"My name is Mister Henry, is my friend the Herman in?"
She said, "Come in, have a seat.

Take his luggage, Gentry, while I prepare him something to eat."
And upon arrivin' with my food, and then she softly said,
"I'm sorry, Mr. Henry, but your friend the Herman is dead."
She say, "Now eat and I'll show you to your room,
and tomorrow I'll take you out and show you the famous Herman's tomb."
Next day she mousefully cried all the way
to the gigantic tomb where the famous Herman lay.
There were a note of pride in the inscriptions, they seemed to ring a bell,
for whoever wrote them knew the Herman very well.
For this is what they read:
"Here lies Jed P. Whittaker, the greatest con-man of all time,
and I never saw the time, day or night, when he couldn't make hisself a dime."
And to Miss Whittaker I asked what had brought about the Herman's end.
She say, "Wine, cocaine, and heroin has beat him for his win."
Now all this talk about short-coinin', the Herman was a player too.
This I know, for I saw him talk the Queen of England out of her royal senses
    down to a chickenshit whore.
So all you cool cats, bop daddies, and pennyweight pimps who think you know
    the score,
just remember your superior: Herman from the Shark-Tooth Shore.

8. MY REFLECTION

A. Joe, Ellis, 24 March 1966
B. "The Wanderer's Trail," Seymour, Wynne, 18 March 1966
C. "All You Tough Guys that Thinks You're Wise," Sam, Indiana
   State Prison, Michigan City, Indiana, 30 March 1962

9. FEEBLE OLD MAN

A. Phil, Wynne, 8 August 1965
B. "Feeble Old Man and a Kid Named Dan," Joe, Ellis, 24 March
   1966

The performer of the 8C text is white; he had learned the toast
in Deer Lodge Penitentiary (Montana) some years before. There is
a similar poem in Milburn's book (1930:256-257), titled "The
Hobo's Warning." I collected versions similar to the 8A and 8B
texts from several other Texas informants; the general textual

consonance suggests some published versions of the poem. Reynolds (1974:9-10) has a Los Angeles Variant.

Both "My Reflection" and "Feeble Old Man" are homiletics of a kind found in both hobo and jailhouse repertories. The poems have some clear relationships, such as the catalogs of experiences used to establish authority, and since the narrative segment of "Feeble Old Man" comprises only a small portion of the whole, it is not surprising that some of the catalog sections move back and forth in performances of the two toasts.

8A   MY REFLECTION

Now peoples, as I gaze tonight at the pale moonlight
through the doorways of my prison cell,
I'm thinkin' of a past that hard as cast
and a record that's black as hell.
Now I've been around from town to town
did everything a man could do,
but the places I've went and the time I've spent
in the outside world have been few.
Now I committed every crime that you can find
in pictures and storybooks,
I've shot my cue with society pure
and I've dealt with the dirtiest of crooks.
I've spent spells in some of the best of hotels
and I've slept on the cots in the slums,
I've built fires beyond the Northern stars
and I've ate with the dirtiest of bums.
Now my life has been such a failure
along this thorny trail,
until my shoulders are drooped and crooked
from laying on bunks in jails.
Of course I only loved but one woman
and I loved her for only a while
She did like all the others —
she walked off and left me with a smile.
Now I never thought she'd let me down
in eleven thousand years,
and each time I think of what's become

it almost brings the tears.
But now I'm sittin' here in deep meditation
thinkin' of a home that's far away,
I know that someone's there waitin',
it's a mother that's old and gray.
Now I left my mother many years ago
and I promised her to return.
Oh, God! how I wish I'd a kept that promise
and went down that road to learn.
But my life has been such a failure,
I got crime wrote all over my face,
and I'd rather not see my dear mother
if it would bring her name to disgrace.
Now I had a whole lot of friends and partners
who helped me commit lots of crimes,
but they all turned to snitches, boys,
and they caused me to be servin' this time.
I was lied on, cheated, and double-crossed
from time and time again.
But if ever I can get out of this trouble,
only a dog can be my friend.

8B   THE WANDERER'S TRAIL

This is a tale of a wanderer's trail,
of a man with his back to the wall.
Some smart guys who think they're wise,
but they can't conquer their downfall.
But me, myself, I'm a wise old egg,
I can lie, steal, or beg.
I've been overheard over thousands of dead
and I've slept on the banks of the Rhine.
I've listened to y'all's toasts sincerely,
now I want you to listen to mine.
As I gaze at night at the pale moonlight,
through the doors of my prison cell,
thinkin' of a past which is hard as cast
and a record as dark as hell.

I've committed every crime that a man could find
in the laws or statute books,
I've shot my cue in society pew
and I've mingled with the worst of crooks.
I've juggled trays in New York cafes,
hopped bells in hotels in Chi,
I've toted a pack down a B and O track
hopped redball freights on the fly.
I've built jungle fires beneath northern stars,
ate mackerel with the dirtiest of bums,
and I've stayed a spell in some of the best hotels
and I've slept on cots in slums.
In this case a woman's always the reason,
but that was only for a while,
for she did me like all the rest,
she left me with a smile.
My shoulders are drag and droopy
from travelin' so thorny trail,
I now feel the aches and pains
where I've slept in jails.
My life have been such a failure,
from travelin' so thorny trail,
my shoulders are saggin' and droopin'
from sleepin' on bunks in jails.
As I sit in deep meditation,
thinkin' of a home which is far away,
I know that there someone is waiting,
a mother and father who is old and gray.
Many many years ago I promised them that I would return,
oh, how I wish that I could keep that promise
and down that old lane could turn.
But my life have been such failure
with criminal wrote upon my face,
I would rather not meet them now
and to bring their name to disgrace.
I've had lots of pals and partners,
who helped me commit a lot of crimes,
but they all turned snitches to the cops
and caused me to do a lot of time.

If I ever get lucky and should accident and go free again,
I'm gonna get me a dog for a partner,
And I know I'll have me a friend.

8C   **ALL YOU TOUGH GUYS THAT THINKS YOU'RE WISE**

All you tough guys that thinks you're wise,
take heed and avoid your downfall.
For I'm a wise egg, and I can lie, steal, and beg,
and I've traveled this whole world around.
I been east and I been west and I been with the best
when it comes to covering ground.
Why I juggled a tray in a New York cafe
and I hopped hotel bells in Chi,
and I've carried a pack down a B & O track
and I've popped redball freights on the fly.
Now, you know, all my life I've been a wanderer
up and down that old cinder trail,
and all the happy memories I've got left
are the few days I've spent out of jail.
Why I've laid in my cell and I've suffered like hell
for the want of a shot of dope,
I've prayed in despair to be sent to the chair
or bumped off at the end of a rope.
I have prayed without hope to the goddess of dope,
to whomever with whom I have served.
So just hark to the tale of the wanderer's trail,
just look what it's done to me.
You better stay out in the sticks with the rest of the hicks,
that's a convict's warning from me.

9A   FEEBLE OLD MAN

Say, there was a feeble old man and kid they call Dan,
whiles sittin' in the prison cell one day,
they spoke of life and their days of strife
just to while the time away.
Now the kid he spoke of jewels and gold to be had whiles playin' the game,
he worried not over the sentence he'd got,
for he knew in the future would bring him fame.
He'd turn a few tricks and baffle the dicks,

leavin' not a clue to find,
whiles makin' his retreat back to easy street,
with the thoughts of the stir behind.
Now the old man he listened, and his eyes they glistened,
and when the kid was through,
he said, "Now, lad, listen to dad,
at the funny story I will tell to you."
Said, "Now I have played them all, both big and small,
and I've struck them pretty rough,
but it's the Hoosey mob that's on the job
that's quick to call your bluff."
Said, "Now I had to shoot while heistin' the loot,
'cause my life was treasured then,
like a wolf at bay I fought my way
through a mob of bloodthirsty men."
Say, "Now I'm a number one rambler of request,
I'm known in every burg around Chicago,
from Paris to Key West."
Said, "I've preached in Kansas City,
I've sold jobs in St. Paul,"
said, "I've slid out on the cuts in Texas,
and I've went hungry at them all."
Said, "I've ballyhooed in a smalltown circus,
throughout the middle west,"
says, "I've played the county fairs in Georgia,
and I've been the city jailers' guest."
Say, "I've even did the heavy on a New Orleans levee,
and I've cooked in lumbercamps in Maine."
says, "I even gathered fruit in California,
in the sunshine and in the rain."
Say, "I've even been a cub reporter on many small town sheets,"
say, "I've run a all-night lunchstand in Denver,
and I've sold some crackers cheap."
Say, "I even served the Foreign Legion,
and in the shade I've did swell,
but as I think of these gray bars before me,
that reflection is flashes and spells."
Says, "I gaze tonight at the pale moonlight,
through the doorbars of my prison cell,"
says, "I'm thinking of the past that is hard as cast,

with a record as black as hell."
Say, "I've traveled around from town to town,
and the time I've went and the time I've spent
in the outside world is few."
Say, "I even built jungle fires beneath the northern stars
and eaten Mulligan with the dirtiest of bums,"
Says, "I've stopped in spells at the best hotels,
and I've slept in dirty cots in slums."
Says, "I've even committed most every crime that you can find
that's in the statute law book.
I've even shot my cue in the society pew,
and I've mingled with the best of the crooks.
So I was like you, Dan, I wasn't afraid to try it once more,
but a village clown got me hands down
while makin' a jewelry store."
Say, "I made a draw, so did the law,
and both our rods spit lead,
I only stood until the smoke was clear
and the village clown lay dead.
Now the Hoosier mob got on the job
boy, I didn't have a chance to run,
I stood on the brinks and tried to think,
but they outwitted me, son.
They throwed me in jail and held me without bail,
chalked up with first degree,
But I wasn't so game when trial day came
with the chair confrontin' me.
I tried to grin but I had to give in,
my soul was torn with strifes.
I held my breath for the verdict 'Death,'
but they sentenced me here for life.
So I'm here yet, son, with life almost done,
all ways of hopes have fled."
Say, "It won't be long before I will join the throng,
and be a number among the dead."
Say, "You are young now, Dan, you have just begun,
you had a dear old mother out there,
it's up to you to make her dream come true,
now, boy, why don't you play the old game on the square?"
Now the kid's head dropped and the old man stopped,

he said, "Dad, I believe you're right.
So the best plan is to make a man."
"Goodnight, lad." "Goodnight, dad." "Good night."

9B   FEEBLE OLD MAN AND A KID NAMED DAN

I was servin' time in a Southern town
and by some queer luck I overheard
a real strange story told by a lad and a old jailbird.
Now there was a feeble old man and a kid named Dan
sittin' in a cell one day,
they was talkin' about life and strife
just to pass the time away.
Now the kid he told of silver and gold
to be had while playin' the game,
and worried not for the sentence he got
for the future would bring him fame.
He told of the tricks he used to beat the dicks
how he left no clues to be found,
how he made his retreat back to easy street
and left all the studs behind.
Now the old man listened while his dim eyes glistened,
and when the lad was through,
he said, "Listen, lad, I want you to listen to dad,
and the story I'll tell to you."
He said, "Boy, I played them all, both big and small,
I found some to be mighty tough.
Once a hooligan mob was on the prod
and was quick to call my bluff."
Said, "Lad, I committed every crime that you can find,
in pictures and story books,
I've shot my cue with society pure
and I've dealt with the dirtiest of crooks.
I've juggled trays in New York cafes,
hopped bells in hotels in Chi,
I once carried a pack on my dim young back,
and I watched a million brave soldiers die.
Say, lad, I'm a gambling man,
I gambled by request,

I played 'em big from the Golden Gates of Frisco
all over the west.
But gamblers make sinners, lad,
that you are yet to learn,
it will lead you from the road to righteousness
down to the road to ruin.
And, lad, as each man live his life
it's always a woman involved,
and this one was my wife,
I held her close to my heart.
Now we was happily married
and our life was like a sweet song,
until I came home late one night
and caught my wife doin' wrong.
I didn't say what you have said,
not do what maybe you would have done,
I downed my sorrows drinkin',
and met the world havin' fun.
Now this was just twenty-five years ago,
if my memory serve me right,
I hit the trail to my downfall, lad,
and I'll never forget that night.
That's when this police clown caught me with my hands down
while robbin' a jewelry store.
I made a quick draw but so did the law
and both our guns spit lead.
I'm only here to swear that when the smoke was clear
the village cop he lay dead.
But, lad, I had to shoot or be caught in a loop,
and my life was treasured then.
So I was like a wolf at bay as I shot my way
through the mob of bloodthirsty men,
but this hooligan mob was then on the prod
and I had no place to run.
I stood by the bank and I tried to think,
but they all outwitted me one.
So I was thrown in jail, held without bail,
    charged with murder in the first degree.
Lad, I wasn't so gay when the trial day came,

for the chair confronted me.
Now I held my breath for the verdict of death,
but they sentenced me here for life,
and I'm here yet, lad, with life not done,
all hopes of my freedom have fled.
And it won't be long before I join the throng
and be numbered among the dead.
But you, young yet, lad, you have a mother and a father out there,
it's up to you to make their dreams come true,
so why not live it on the square?"
As the old man stopped, the lad's head dropped.
He said, "Dad, I guess you're right.
My future plan is to be a man.
Goodnight, dad." "Goodnight."

10. SUBJECT TO A FALL

A. John, Ramsey, 17 August 1965
B. Victor, Wynne, 18 August 1965

"The Walls" is one unit of the Texas Department of Correc-
tions, but the term's meaning here is more general: it means
prison, any prison. Although this is basically a homiletic about the
criminal life, it demonstrates the common toast misogyny: what
gets the crook back working is "some dame that'll give you a smile"
or "some old bigshot dame."

10A   SUBJECT TO A FALL

Boys, you're subject to a fall and trip to the Walls
if you live the life of a crook,
'cause you're dealin' hands with no good bands
and soon you'll wind up with the book.
You're stealin' in the nights in the brightest of lights,
you'll probably get by for a year or more.
The first hit you get will be a small bit
but that won't worry you so.
It's when you land back out there with only your fare

from the village you were sent up from,
you say to yourself, "I sleep on a shelf,
why live the life of a common bum?"
But your money runs low and you go for more dough
just for some old dame that'll give you a smile,
you pull another job, probably split with the mob
and hit the bright lights for a while.
You'll put your pistols up for good and have a chance to settle down if you
    would,
but you say, "One more haul and then that'll be all."
Then you hear the cop's whistle blow.
One more crook and you'll wind up with the book—
Jim, that's all she wrote.
I got ninety-nine.

10B   SUBJECT TO A FALL

Say, you subject to a fall and a trip to the Wall
when you livin' the life of a crook,
you be dealt in the hand of some no-good band
and you probably wind up with the book.
You can steal at nights in the brightest of lights
and get by for a year or more,
the first sentence you get will be a small bit
and that won't burn to the core.
You'll pull a job and split with the mob
and hit the bright lights for a while,
and your money run low and you go for more dough
when some old bigshot dame give you a smile.
You make one more haul and say that's all
and put up your pistol for good,
you may get away and say it's okay
and have a chance to settle down if you would.
Then you hear the cop's whistle blow and you know it's the end of the show,
'cause you've had your last pistol to tote,
and you're one more crook and wind up with the book
and man, that's all she wrote.

11. DERRINGER YOUNGBLOOD

Jack, Ramsey, 2 July 1964

The toast isn't particularly coherent; the parts are there, but linkages are left out, as are the identities of most of the characters. The poem probably once was quite a bit longer, but this narrator remembered only the gunfight sections and the opening and closing couplets.

11   DERRINGER YOUNGBLOOD

Derringer Youngblood, the jet-black nigger,
strong as a jackass and quick on the trigger.
One day Derringer said, "Boss, my heart is gettin' sore,
I guess I'll go back South and see my wife and kids once more."
That's when they started to hightail to take on lunch,
when Derringer got suspicious and gave Youngblood the hunch.
He said, "Hey there, Jelly, can't you see,
how all a these people's a watchin' poor me."
Say, "They're lookin' for us anyway on this route,"
say, "I'll take down the bulls and we'll both back out."
He said, "I got one gun, it's a forty-five
and when we leave I wants to leave alive."
He said, "We's in a hurry, we don't wanna be late.
Look on the left-hand corner and get the four of the eight."
They got the four of the eight and hit the Tom Pine trail.
When they stopped driving they was twelve miles past Tom Pine's house.
Then somethin' kept pressin' on Youngblood's mind,
there was thirty-two coppers on the road behind.
He said, "Hey there, Jelly, don't drive too fast,
I'm killin' every motherfucker that attempts to pass."
That's when he fell to his knees throwin' steel and lead,
they found thirty-two coppers on the roadside dead.
Sooner or later poor Robin got caught,
that's when they took everything he ever stole or bought.
He got a letter from his father sayin', "You tore my heart and you rode my
      trail,
now I don't give a damn if you die in jail."

Says, "When you was in jail I sprung you from that,
and I'll scatter your brains with a Stetson hat."
Said, "There's one more thing I'll swear I will do,
I will burn in hell just to be with you."
Say, "If I happen to go to heaven and I'll meet you there,
I'll shoot your name on the golden stair."

12. SATAN'S PLAYGROUND OF HELL

Frank, Ellis, 22 March 1966

The opening couplets of this toast seem literary — they are far more periodic and adjectival than most toasts — but the poem soon moves into standard toast imagery and rhythm. The shift comes at the place where the rhyme scheme breaks down: "Well they walks off two tens and a five-spot richer. / Well I got the whore pimpin' for me, you know." "Lay in" is a prison term that means having permission to stay in the barracks for medical reasons.

12   SATAN'S PLAYGROUND OF HELL

Evil-mannered, underfed, underbred, restless, godless rule of light,
cold by day and treacherous by night,
frolic for the weak, enjoyment for the brute,
manned by pimps and prostitutes.
Full of heroin, cocaine, and rum,
big city chick town, here I come.
They say a man is supposed to reap exactly what he sow,
fast sights, bright lights, and supersonic whores.
Now this is a life of ease and pleasure and often seems swell,
but all that it gets you is a quick tombstone and a one-way ticket to hell.
I was on Broadway and Main when a East Coast chick passed my way.
I said, "Hey, baby, would you like to have a drink with me?"
She say, "I'm waiting for someone, punk, can't you see?"
About that time along come two badges patrolling their beat,
arrested this whore for prostituting on the street.
Well I walks up and I makes a play,
I say, "Take these two tens and let this lady stay on the streets today."

Well they walks off two tens and a five-spot richer.
Well I got the whore pimpin' for me, you know.
We became very tight, in fact we got very close that very same night.
Well after eight months she had did pretty swell,
brought in money, fuckin', she was pure hell.
One day she came in,
she said, "I'm sick and I need to lay in."
Well the broad had been doin' pretty good
and I thought that I should let this broad lay in.
So she said we would need money while we laid up,
"Won't you mind pullin' a stick-up?"
Well I stepped out on Thirty-fourth and Moore,
about six blocks where I sticked up this store.
Well it wasn't too long before I was apprehended and put in jail,
and $65,000 worth was where they set my bail.
Well I knew my fate for armed robbery and murder,
but I wish this no-account bitch well
'cause I'm destined to meet her in Satan's playground of Hell.

13. EDDIE LEDOUX

A. Seymour, Wynne, 18 March 1966
B. Henry, Ramsey, 2 July 1964

The confused sections in the B-text all seem to be mishearings or misrememberings of lines that are perfectly clear in the A-text: the meaningless "a streak that hit him just right" should be something like "seemed to have hit him just right," and "He let out a yell like a potato pell" should be something like "He let out a yell like a scream from hell." These curious incoherences survive because of the mnemonics of the rhyme and meter schemes: Henry has to fill out the couplet and he has to fill out the line and decides that garble is better than nothing because dropping the first half of the line would introduce even more confusion or a greater gap in the narration. The same mnemonic imperative accounts for similar garbling in field-collected texts of many folk ballads.

13A   EDDIE LEDOUX

There's some strange and queer tales that come through all jails,
this one I happen to believe it true.
It's the strangest tale that a man ever heard,
it was told to me by Eddie LeDoux.
He say he was sittin' in a cell in a Southwest jail,
where he landed doin' three days for vag.
A drunk came in, his eyes lit up like a hungry pup
as I handed him a tailor-made fag.
Now, you see, he was broke and the three-inch smoke
seemed to have hit him just right.
As his mind ran back over the memory track,
this is the story that he told that night:

He say he was doin' ten in an Eastern pen
where his buddy was sentenced to die,
for he was one of the mob who was caught on a job
and the state said he must fry.
He said a rat had squealed like a pig to be killed
and asked for the mercy of the state,
so to even the score, they gave the rat four,
when he should have got the gate.
"He let out a yell like a scream from hell
that echoed through cell block three,
and this other guy who was sentenced to die
was placed in the cell with me.
I'll never will forget the night the date was set,
that's the night he was sentenced to die,
he wanted to chat with that lousy rat,
for he was just that sort of a guy.
He wanted to shake the hand of the lyin' man
who had lied his life away,
but the guard said, 'Nix,' that he was on to all the tricks
'The governor might grant you a stay.'
Now it was 12 o'clock sharp in the death cell block,
when the guards they strapped him in,

he let out a prayer as he sat in the chair,
' Oh, Lord, forgive me for my sins!'
Now this snitch with the four-year hitch,
again he yelled like a scream from hell
that echoed through cell block three:
'Cut it off, I lied!' the snitch he cried,
and, 'Oh, God, how it's killin' me!'
So I guess you can guess the rest: the snitch went west
and he died when the lights went on.
Me and Eddie LeDoux, we helped bury the two,
in the cold, cold breaks of dawn."

13B   EDDIE LEDOUX

Wise and queer tales float through all the jails,
but this is one that's supposed to be true.
For the queerest I've heard was told by a bird
who called himself Eddie LeDoux.
I was sharin' a cell in Northwest Hell,
ten days I was doin' for vag,
when this chap winds up like a harmless pup
and I slips him a tailor-made flag [cigarette].
Now this guy was broke with a three-inch stroke,
a streak that hit him just right,
and he looked back over his memory track
this is the tale that he told that night:

He say, "Boys, I was doin' it all [life sentence] at the Southeast Wall
where my partner was sentenced to die.
He was one of the mob that helped to pull the job
and the court said that he must fry.
Say, his partner squealed and then appealed
on the mercy of the state,
but to even the score, they gave him four
when he thought he would get the gate.
He let out a yell like a potato pell
that echoed through cell block three,
and this guy that was sentenced to die

was put in the cell with me.
Say, I never will forget, the date was set,
the day he said, 'Goodbye.'
He wanted to chat with that lousy rat,
say, look, he was just that sort of a guy.
He wanted to shake the hand of the low-down snake
that had swore his life away,
but the guard said, 'Nix, I'm onto all the tricks
and the governor may grant you a stay.'
And it was twelve o'clock in the death cell block
as the guards was strappin' him in.
He mumbled a prayer as he sat in the chair,
sayin', 'Oh, God, forgive me of my sins.'
A fearful jump of his repose —
death took control of his tiresome soul.
Now this snitch with the four-year hitch
went ravin' mad, you see.
He let out a yell like a scream from hell
that echoed through cell block three.
'Cut it off!' he cried, 'I lied, I lied,
oh my God, it's killin' me!'
Now you can guess the rest, the snitch went west
and died when the lights came on,
and Eddie LeDoux helped bury the two
at the cold, cold break of dawn.''

14. LIMPTY LEFTY McCREE

Phil, Wynne, 20 August 1965

   The slang here is anachronistic; in his own speech, the inform-
ant would never use terms like "cracked it by the shield" (talked to
police), "stickin' in the slammer" (while in jail), "shuckman"
(someone who hustles squares), "gun" (pickpocket), "clipped a
dance moll for a swab" (got some money out of a dancehall girl),
"paid a trey or a fin" (was worth $3 or $5, or $300 or $500),
"highballed the trick" (saw what was going on), "clucked" ("got
chicken," i.e., ran), "lit a shuck" (ran fast), and so forth. The
toast obviously dates from the early twenties. The first four lines

are introductory, then the toast shifts from third- to first-person narration. The narrator used so much argot that I suspect the charm of the toast rests in the opportunity to use the arcane terms, some of which are apparently misremembered or incoherent. Once the action shifts to first-person narration, we get a story of a hustler in **Cincinnati** who was spotted by a square and picked up by the police; he is released, goes out on the street again, and is once again arrested. He claims he is an ordinary citizen ("I tried to put the square on them"), but they recognize him and take him off to jail to stay a while. The homiletic message—the good woman Carline who tries but can't help the man who's gone afoul of the law, and the advice to avoid crime—is dated. One meets fewer and fewer good and true women in the later poems, and younger toast-tellers rarely have such homiletic messages in their repertories.

14   LIMPTY LEFTY McCREE

Say, I beg your pardon, ladies and gentlemen, will you give me your attention please?
And I'll tell you the story of a notorious pickpocket, who name was Limpty Lefty McCree.
He was a true disciple of the field, he never used a hammer,
or cracked it by the shield while stickin' in the slammer.
It was down big old Cincinnati, in the year of '21,
it was on one big Saturday evenin', that's when my troubles first begun.
It was on that Sixth Street to Market, between Central Avenue and Plum,
that's the worst old place in ragtown for a shuckman or gun.
I clipped a dance moll for a swab, it paid a trey or a fin,
but an old squarejohn seen the play come off and he run and told the men.
So I should have left that tip at once, no doubt you may say,
but howbeever I didn't know that old squarejohn highballed the trick and I continued on the play.
And whiles roamin' down the settlement and signin' down the gray,
my buddy clucked and I looked up in the face of a plainclothes man.
He nipped me by my coatsleeve and lamped me with a wicked eye,
but in those previous moments, boy, I framed my alibi.
Now they carried me through the usual tests, but that's the question of every law,

but by having years past of experience I stood it without a flaw.
So I lit a shuck back to my regular old pad and jumped into a different tog,
but the minute I hit that firin' line, boy, you can bet I was gainin' like a dog.
That's when a hand fell softly on my shoulder and I kinda looked around,
looked up in two of the faces of the toughest dicks in town.
I tried to put the square on them but they looked at me and laughed,
said, "Well, well, Limpty Lefty McCree, we got you right at last."
So they called up for the wagon, and the crowd all gathered around,
I sent a word over on Carline to tell my little girl that I was jailhouse bound.
Now they throwed me in the slammer, on a hard old bed of oak,
no doubt if any you boys ever been there, you know this ain't no joke.
Now my little girl she was blue, she was true-blue,
she went round about the town tryin' to save me, that's all one little girl can do.
Now brothers of this disciple's field, who livin' this most unrighteous life,
while travelin' through this big pigiron world
tryin' to make a hellofa rep everywhere you go, takin' other people's dough:
stop! and look and reason above all things,
for one little wrong poke you take nowadays will cause your ship to sink.

15. I WAS SITTIN' IN THE JAIL TO DO A STRETCH OF TIME

Slim, Jefferson City, 23 June 1964

Slim learned this toast from a white inmate in a cell in the solitary block. Its theme and structure are familiar enough. The poem opens with a framing device—the narrator describes something that happened in another place, another time—which sets the stage for a common court experience: the black hustler who gets a "quarter" (twenty-five-year sentence) from a white judge who won't even remember his name the next day.

15   I WAS SITTIN' IN THE JAIL TO DO A STRETCH OF TIME

I was sittin' in the jail to do a stretch of time
when through the door stepped two friends of mine.
I could tell by the look on their face they didn't have a cocksucken dime.
So I took 'em over to the corner and I sat 'em down
and pulled out my Country Gentleman [bourbon] and began to run it down:

"Fellas, when you cross the street be prepared for your doom,
'cause there's some lousy motherfuckers in that silver courtroom.
Now that judge looked at me like I was a roach on the floor,
and said he was gettin' tired a me dartin' in and out a his goddamned door.
He said, 'Wilson, I'm gettin' tired a you fellas runnin' around here doin' these
    nickel-assed crimes,
jumpin' up here before me and ain't got a cocksucken dime.'
I said, 'But, your honor, I can truthfully say,
when the crime was committed I was miles away.'
Say, 'My people bought a home out in California, you know,
that's where I always be when I ain't got no dough.'
'Bout this time the prosecutor walked in
and my heart felt like a thousand motherfucken pins.
He says, 'Your honor,' say, 'that's old stick-high jivin' Wilson playin' the part
    of a simp,'
say, 'if you let him out, on the corner this evenin' he'll be screamin' he's a
    motherfucken pimp.'
Say, If you let him out a here talkin' that bunk,'
say, 'before sundown he'll have his arm full a that no-good junk.'
Judge say, 'Yeah, I heard about you.' Said, 'You been playin' these high-class
    broads, these broads a the upper class.'
Say, 'I'm gonna see if you can't shake this quarter off your goddamn ass.'
I said, 'But, your honor, how 'bout my children, my sickly wife?'
He say, 'Contempt of court! Clerk, change that shit to life.'
Now they had me up, they had my ass and they had my feet off the floor,
they was draggin' me out the courtroom door.
Judge say, 'You know what, Willie, it's a damned shame,
but this time tomorrow, I won't know your cocksucken name.'"

16. THEY CAN'T DO THAT

John, Ramsey, 23 August 1965

    "I learned this in jail from old jailhouse rats like myself," John
said. A similar poem was sent from a federal prison in manuscript
to John A. Lomax in the middle 1930s; the typescript, with a

number of other items from prisons, is in the Lomax papers at the University of Texas Archives (no date or name is on the typescript). See Milburn (1930:233-234) for a similar poem from hobo tradition. This is one of the rare stanzaic toasts.

The cynicism about lawyers expressed in the second stanza is hardly rare among a population which sees justice as being directly proportional to income, a population whose experience with lawyers is obviously less than successful.

16   THEY CAN'T DO THAT

Boys, you know it's a damned shame when you have been fucked and also framed.
Now here you is with fifteen years or more
for some deeds that was done by some other sonofagun and you wasn't even in on the dough.
When you leave the courthouse you'll tell your friends how they framed you and left you flat.
You know, it make any man sore as hell to hear a guy set around and say, "Aw, man, they can't do that."

But I'll tell you when it's hell: when you're laying in your cell in some lousy old county jail,
and some lawyer's come and shook you down for every cent of your cocksucken kale.
and kicked your best girl out in the streets and sold all the fixtures in your flat,
and here comes a jailbird slidin' up to you and says, "Aw, man, they can't do that."

When I finish my roundup on earth and start my bit in hell,
I hope to see 'em fry each and every guy that's ever let that word yell.
When he be standin' up on them big red hot coals and his body meltin' down in fat,
I'm gonna slide up to Tom Devil and say, "Look out, man, you can't do that!"

17. LIFE OF A JUNKIE

Henry, Ramsey, 2 July 1964

This is a particularly long toast, whose length is caused by several long, repeated formulaic sections. It is a classic story of the learning of evil ways: the youth begins drinking wine ("blood"), then is introduced to marijuana. He tries to hustle a woman, but she tells him alcohol ruins his health and puts him down as a kid who spends Saturdays making noise in movie theaters. Not only that, but she claims if she did treat him well, if she fellated him ("gave you some head"), he would gossip about it. She tells him what she needs (rather, she says what the street male likes to think the street female wants when she realizes what she needs). Years later, when he is hip and on drugs, he meets her again. She compliments him on his clothing, then again puts him down by saying he must make it by honest work ("hamin"). He hits her and she fellates him. But he begins to shoot heroin and gets hooked. His connection is arrested and no one will have anything to do with him because the police ("the heat") are watching him and he is in withdrawal ("sick"). He goes to jail to lament his fate, the life of a junkie. Although the middle section of the poem suggests the general misogyny of the pimp toasts, the poem turns into a homily about the evils of dope. Note the use of the word "lame." I'm not sure when "square" replaced "lame" in slang usage (it seems to have occurred sometime in the late forties or early fifties), but the older word has a more forceful visual referent: a cripple, one who can't make it physically.

17   LIFE OF A JUNKIE

All this happened about fifteen.
I was strollin' in the park as I usually do, when I meets this stud.
Well, by me bein' hip, I could tell he was high, but I thought it was off a wine.
So I started shootin' the bull like I do all the time.
I told him like I did every stud
that it wasn't shit for me to drink two or three fifths a some real good blood.
He looked at me and laughed and said, "Well, well, say, ain't it a shame:
I found myself a lame."
So he pulled out a match and a brown cigarette
and lit it and said, "Chump, this is weed."

Now I was scared as hell but didn't want him to know it,
I was a lame, but didn't dare show it.
Well, of course, I been smokin' shit for about seven years now, and my
    knowledge is pretty fair.
So I meets this broad I once tried to make when I was a wine-drinkin' square.
I takes her out for a Saturday night whirl.
Later on that night I hits on her to be my girl.
She looked at me and laughed in my face, which was much to my disgrace,
she told me some shit I never will forget until my dying days.
She say, "Sonny, why don't you get hip with all that peach fur around your
    lip?"
Say, "Don't you know when you drink it make your breath stink; a fifth, a pint,
    or a sip?
You goin' around lushin', fuckin' up your youth,
when you should be usin' that health to try and gain yourself some wealth.
Say, now, another thing I have to tell:
I be goddamned if you ain't in the show every Saturday raising hell."
Say, "Now I bet you couldn't do me no good in bed,
and would run and tell everybody if I gave you some head."
Say, "I'm a no-good whore from the word say 'Go'," say, "Turning out is all I
    need.
And judging from your ways and actions," say, "Daddy, you just ain't my
    speed."
Say, "Do you think you could teach me to deal, rob, and steal, beat some poor
    lame for his bread,
turn a trick or suck a dick in case I could sell some head?"
Say, "Would you whup me when I'm right and cuss me when I'm wrong, drag
    my fine big ass across the floor?
When you learn all these things and teach them to me, then I might be your
    whore."
Say, well, Jack, that was seven years ago, when I was a wine-drinking square,
but now this bitch comes back into my life, and wo! my knowledge is fair.
I said, "Baby, don't you remember me?" And I stepped back and looked at the
    whore.
And she said, "Why sure I do, don't they call you Joe?"
We walked the street and chatted a bit, bitch told me I looked swell.
I couldn't say the same for her, 'cause I could tell she hadn't been doing so
    well.
I took her to my pad, my pad was mad, I always featured a pad as hard as this.
We smoked some shit and shot a bit and laid across the bed to nod.
Two or three hours later after we finish fuckin',
the bitch turn over in the bed and begin to suckin'.

She told me I had some wonderful eyes,
and she always admired a man my size.
she say, "Joe, you have a short [car], some fronts [suits], and a fine ticker [watch] too,"
Say, "Yeah, Joe," say, "you're well-to-do."
Say, "What time do you go to work in the mornings, is your job very hard?
Judging from the way you dress and the things you own you must work at Carrol's shipyard.
And knowin' you like I do, I know you got these things by hamin',
I'm willing to bet you got three, four jobs and spend your weekends lamin'."
Bam, Bam! The bitch was getting up off the floor.
Say, "Whore, when you talk about my short and my fronts,
why I change clothes four times a day in every month.
And work: the hardest work I ever did was teachin' a bitch to steal,
and the heaviest thing I lifted in seven long years was a stack of hundred-dollar bills.
I got twenty-four whores that knows I'm death on a bitch when she's ratty.
I could tell them to shit and they'd pull down their drawers and say, 'What color, daddy?' "
Well, the bitch could tell I was getting mad now by the cold look in my eyes,
so she turned over in the bed and gave me some head and sung "I apologize."
Well, all the studs I knew was on stuff [heroin] now, and their habits was a good mile long,
but I thought I could chip [shoot heroin occasionally] and never get hooked, for my will was strong.
But my old hustlin' partner, John, he really knew the score,
he told me if I kept chippin' I would soon be woe.
But I could still count my haircuts, John's head was bald.
Wasn't shit he could tell me, 'cause I thought I knew it all.
But through some rat I trusted, old John gets busted and left me in a terrible rut.
I told John I would get that rat if it's the last thing I do.
But the chump had left town because he knew his goose was cooked,
and the same day John got his time I found that I was hooked.
I was sick as hell and the monk was on me [he was in withdrawal],
all the junkies froze 'cause the heat was on me.
Say, I wished I could kill that motherfucker that got me hooked, but I couldn't find the time,
for this good dope kept me on the run for not listening to that good friend of mine.

Say, well, my habit was getting longer, my loot was getting shorter,
and my fix was five and five in twelve drops of water.
Then I meets this bitch that gave me some head,
and she tells me she have eyes for making' me some bread.
But to make a long story short, I gets busted,
and they whups me up something terrible and carries me to jail.
The judge don't want the public to know how they fucked up my head, so he
    ups and denies my bail.
I laid on my bunk, thought I'd go insane,
I hollers, I pleaded and I screamed, but the doctors wouldn't do a thing.
The same day I got my time they carried me to Huntsville, where I was still
    sick.
They put me in the hospital where I damn near kicked.
And after I'd been there about three months or more I met my old hustlin'
    partner John.
I could tell he was in power, so I asked him for a fix.
He say, "Well, well, if it ain't bright boy," Say, "Why the last time I saw you,
    you had wealth.
Now look at you, beggin' for a fix 'cause you can't help yourself.
And up in the county jail begging all the doctors who's real good friends a
    mine,
for one last fix so you can come on cut back this time.
And when they froze, you thought your head would split,
until one day you got a visitor and you composed yourself a bit.
But when you got downstairs and saw it was your bitch,
she started talkin' that Virgin Mary shit.
But when you saw the bitch was in fear of her life, that's when you really got
    rough.
You told her you would soon be loose and do her some abruse [sic] if she didn't
    find a way to get you some stuff.
You went on back upstairs and called all the cats around you,
told 'em what a cap you had made on the snap, but you didn't know the bitch
    was leavin' town.
Say, when you enrolled in the life a the streets,
didn't you know a junkie's life was anything but sweet?
But since you've been out you've learned new names for the game,
such as till-tapping, the carpet, the rope, and the drag, [all con games] which
    all leads up to one thing."
Say, "When you was in school

you was the kind that couldn't learn 'cause you was a hip damn fool.
With your connections fair and your hustlin' girls is square,
you was the dapperest stud on the scene.
But through some rat you trusted your connection gets busted and left you in
    a terrible rut.
And then dope hit the ceiling and that's when you really started feelin'.
You sold your short and pawned your fronts, which wasn't enough,
and when you was so sick you was damn near dead,
that's when you went out and sold your motherfucken head.
And then you meets this bitch that gave you some head,
and she tells you she have eyes for makin' you some bread,
but you knew the bitch didn't have no class
with all them bandages around her motherfucken ass.
But you took a chance on the bitch anyway and called her a trick,
but you didn't know the hotel manager was a snitch.
And up come the boys in blue, cuts your head something terrible, and carries
    you to jail.
The judge don't want the public to know how they fucked up your head,
so he ups and denies your bail.
So here you are with seven years to think it over,
and when you kick this monkey you'll live any type life —
except the life of a junkie."

Pimps, Whores, and Other Lovers and Friends

18. JOE THE GRINDER AND G.I. JOE

Phil, Wynne, 7 July 1964

When he finished reciting this toast, Phil said, "See, when G.I. Joe was overseas, Joe (or "Jody") the Grinder moved in with his wife. So when the war broke up he come back, got him a van and backed up there, got him all the fine furniture and all the best clothes and everything." There was an obvious delight among the listeners that the "no-good whore," Juanita, had her material goodies taken away by the returning hero. When he recited the toast on another occasion, Phil added this couplet: "He said, 'Oh yes, Jody, I want you to meet my Japanese queen — / and will you please hand me over that Longine?'" Someone listening said, "That's right. He took the goddamned watch too!"

This toast is related to a well-known army marching chant; from that chant developed a Texas convict worksong (see Jackson, 1967 and 1972C). Jody is named in the brief blues "Joe the Grinder," recorded in 1939 by John A. Lomax from the singing of Irvin Lowry in Gould, Arkansas (which appears on Library of Congress Archive of American Folk Song record AAFS-14). The marching chant was popular throughout World War II and is still sung by some American troops. Alan Lomax prints a marching song "Sound Off," about which he says, "In many variants this was sung by all Negro outfits in World War II" (Lomax, 1960:595). Roger D. Abrahams collected a shorter version of this toast in Philadelphia in the early 1960s (see Abrahams, 1970A:169-170). Woody Guthrie, in an undated note in *Born to Win,* cites the song as background for "the best of marching I saw in my eight months in the army" (1966:22).

It is not surprising that Jody should survive transfer to prison from the army, or that he should figure in the toast world. Army life during wartime and life in prison anytime have a number of aspects in common, and one item of particular importance is concern about who is doing what with and to the woman one left behind. In black folklore, this concern is personified in the songs and toasts about Jody Grinder—"Jody" a contraction of "Joe the," and "Grinder" a metaphor for coital movement. The toast is dated by its content and slang: "solid news" and "solid sender" were out of circulation by the early 1950s; Japanese war brides didn't start receiving much attention until some time after the American occupation of Japan was well under way, probably about 1947. The atom bomb and fall of Japan are so central they supply an early cutoff date, so one would be safe assuming the toast was written between 1947 and 1950.

18   JOE THE GRINDER AND G.I. JOE

Say, old Joe the Grinder was coppin' a snooze
when the world got hip to some solid news.
Say now, there was a no-good whore with a man overseas,
sayin', "Get up, Jody, wake up, please!"
Say, "I know you'd rather burn in hell,
but it's all over the headlines: Japan just fell."
Then old Jody he turned over with his eyes all red,
he said, "I beg your pardon, baby," says, "now what is that you said?"
She said, "I know you're high, motherfucker, and resting fine,
and I know you heard me the first damn time."
He said, "Baby, that can't be right,
because I know those damn Japs just begin to fight.
And anyway, I know those Japs,
they have to be invaded before they scrap."
She said, "No, no, Jody," say, "back in Pearl Harbor the Japs had their day,

but General Douglas MacArthur made a comeback play."
Say, "There may once have been a time when those Japs wouldn't quit,
but that atomic bomb has stopped all that shit."
Jody said, "Now I don't dig this play."
Say, "I'm goin' up on the cuts and see what the other cats say."
She said, "Jody darlin'," said, "Don't be mad,
but whilst you up on the cuts, try to dig you up another pad."
She say, "I'm sorry, darlin', but that's all she wrote,"
she say, "my old man may be here on that next damn boat."
Jody say, "Don't front me with that shit because it's not anywhere,
and this is Joe the Grinder and damn that square."
Said, "Now I'm not interested in your point of view,"
say, "Now turn on the radio and get me the news."
Now the news he got, Jack, was a solid sender,
old Tojo was just signing unconditional surrender.
He said, "Turn it off, baby," said, "I don't want to hear no more,
and see who's knockin' at that motherfucken door."
He said, "Wait a minute, baby, before you answer that knock."
say, "Will you get that bottle and pour me a shot?"
He said, "That's all right, Jody, I'm already in,"
Said, "Let's all sit down and have a drink a gin."
He said, "I can tell by the look in both a your eyes
that I took this joint completely by surprise."
He say, "Hush, whore, I know what you gonna say before you begin:
that you and Jody just damn good friends.
But I want to put you and Juanita wise,"
says, "There's a lots a firepower in this forty-five.
And before some dreadful mistake is made,"
he said, "Jody, will you kindly pocket that old rusty blade?"
He said, "I heard you say you didn't give a damn,
but will you hip him, baby, to who I am?"
She say, "Yes, daddy, if you want him to know:
Mr. Joe the Grinder, meet Mr. G. I. Joe."
He said, "Now you people pull up a seat
and I'll make my little story short and sweet."
He said, "Jody, ever since Pearl Harbor back in forty-one,"
say, "You've played the cuts and had your fun."
Say, "You even shuck my old lady, and that ain't all,
you even carried her to the Allotment Ball.
You carried her to the park and you carried her to the zoo,

then you finally decided you'd just move in, too."
Say, "Now you know you and Juanita didn't play fair,"
say, "Now you face to face with this same damn square."
He said, "Oh, yes, I picked up on your wardrobe as I came down the line,
and from what I hear about it, it's awful fine.
Now's that all right, baby, I'll get around to you,
I picked up on your wardrobe and it's foxy, too."
Say, "Now I have a little chick over across the way
and those togs may come in handy for her some day."
Say, "Now if you people will be cooperative and give me a helping hand,
we can soon have all this jive in my moving van."
Boy, he took the rug off the floor, he took the mattress off the bunk,
he took the divan, cookstove, and the wardrobe trunk.
He took her shoes and stockings and her highest priced dress,
he took a combination Victrola and a cedar chest.
He said, "Load up, Jody, and load up fast,"
say, "I'm 'bout ten seconds off your motherfucken ass."
Said, "Now when you load this van you don't have to be ashamed,
'cause lots of other Jodys is doing the same damn thing.
I know you people interested in what I'm going to do."
Say, "I'm gonna open up a hopjoint on Cedar Avenue.
And you can pick up on me 'most any old day
when me and my new old lady step out to play."
Now he made a military bow as he backed through the door,
he said goodbye to Jody and his dogassed whore.

19. HOBO BEN

Slim, Jefferson City, 23 June 1964

   Slim hoboed, as did his father, from whom he learned this
toast. The "Seymour shoes" about which Heavy-hipted Hattie rags
Ben are shoes with soles so thin and so full of holes one can see the
newspapers stuffed inside. The poem is both an obvious fantasy
("Someday my pockets will be stuffed with big bucks and I'll show
them") and a homiletic ("Don't judge a bum by his cover"). The
verbal terms of the misogyny are obviously close to the Pimp
toasts.

19   HOBO BEN

The party was going at the Shady Nook,
the bitches was braggin' about the fools they'd took,
when through the door stepped Hobo Ben,
he hadn't had a dollar since God knows when.
He was shakin' with the palsy, his eyes was red,
his lips was chapped but they heard what he said:
"Ladies of culture and beauty so refined,
is there one among you that would grant me wine?
I'm raggedy I know, but I have no stink,
and God bless the lady that'll buy me a drink."
Heavy-hipted Hattie turned to Nadine with a laugh,
and said, "What that funky motherfucker really need, child, is a bath."
Said, "When you lift them crazy Seymour shoes
I bet you my ass the bottoms are made of the *Daily News*."
Said, "Get moving, motherfucker, before I call the Man,
'cause if I had a dime it wouldn't reach your hand."
Said, "Lizzie Lou, of all the dames that hawked this game,
now there's a tramp just for you."
Lizzie Lou was four-foot-two and weighed five-fifty-five,
the fat funky motherfucker was an answer to a hippo's desire.
She sat there speakin' with a southern drawl,
she said, "I wouldn't let him suck the come from my drawers."
"Shut up, whores, and be polite, I only listened to your spiel because I was
        raised to be polite,
but I think you've said enough for one motherfucken night.
Nadine, you lowdown scroungy bitch,
you sittin' there like a dog with the seven-year itch.
And look at you, Hattie, I brought your mother from the house of God to the
        house of sin,
and if you tell the truth, bitch, I broke you in.
You whores layin' around here with the winos' shakes and the nymphos' itch,
you can't sell enough ass to make a bedbug rich.
But if you do happen to score for a pint of wine
you start braggin' you done made big time."

Say, "If you find a sucker to give you a quarter for that trim,
if syphilis don't kill him you'll marry him."
Say, "You whores layin' round here talkin' 'bout you'll call the Man,
you better try to keep your ass in this corner of shade
'cause if the Man come you make a sad motherfucken parade.
Accordin' to all the high-class bitches that I've ever seen,
compared to schoolgirls you whores are sure 'nuf green.
Now look at all these pretty green hundred dollar bills
and look at Hazel turning green around the gills.
I know you bitches thought when I walked in I was busted and down on my
    luck,
but the next time you see a gentleman, keep your motherfucken mouth shut."

20. TREACHEROUS BREAST

Victor, Wynne, 18 August 1965

   This toast probably derives from a literary source, but Victor insists he never saw it in print; he says he learned the poem from another inmate in the penitentiary. I asked him about the apparent incoherence in the sixth line ("was ever poled in the latter soup"), but he said, "that's the way I learned it." Either Victor or his source lost the original line and maintained the incoherence because of the rest of the couplet. The toast is another misogynistic homiletic: the good safecracker ("yegg") faces the chair not because he has been a criminal but because of "some two-faceted cocaine broad."

20   TREACHEROUS BREAST

Lend me your ears if you want to hear
the guiles of a treacherous breast,
how I found romance in a woman's glance
and urged my conscience to rest.
I was a yegg and one of the toughest of yeggs
was ever poled in the latter soup
till I met a moll with the face of a doll
that put my head in a loop.

I never will forget the night that we met,
it was at a dance out on the Lower East side.
I had just got back with a load of jack
from out where the big shot reside.
She lamped my roll [saw my money], fell heart and soul,
and wanted to dance with me.
Her body divine rested close to mine
and her moistured lips was free.
But that's all right, I cuss that night,
as I sit here to wait my doom,
'cause tomorrow I die and my fat must fry
in that chair in yonder's room.
But I want you to know before I go
it's not death that I avoid.
But it's hell to learn when you have to burn
for some two-faceted cocaine broad.
Now the safes that I've cracked and the jewelry I've sacked
I laid the swag at her feet,
and we should have been rich if that dirty bitch
don't have me fooled complete.
But there come a day when I had to lay
in my hideout way far from town.
And I sent word by another bird
to beware of the big shakedown.
'Cause you see I couldn't stew, for my love was new
and I would fret about her like that.
It was living hell when darkness fell
and I beat it back to the flat.
I pulled off my sneaks to avoid the squeaks
and mounted the darkened stairs.
I turned to stone when the pleadin' tones
of my loved one reached me there.
Sayin', "Don't let me croak for a shot of dope,
I'm ready to turn him in.
Give me a sniff or another little whiff,
I'll tell it all—you win."
Then with a lowered head the world turned red
and I flatted and slammed the door.
My six-gun spoke with a puff of smoke

and a fly-cop fell to the floor.
The other dick made an exit quick
leavin' me with only the girl,
with an urgent will and a mind to kill
and my brains was in a dizzy whirl.
'Course they found me there by her curly hair
pressed close to my lip half-crazed,
and her brilliant eyes [which] had told me lies
was open wide and glazed.
The purple mark showed up in the dark
was on her slender brown throat.
Tomorrow I die and here am I,
and my memories are long, long ago.

21. THREE WHORES SETTIN' DOWN IN BOSTON

Louis, Ramsey, 6 July 1964

Legman cites a similar song, "A Talk of 10 Wives on their
Husbands' Ware," originally published in 1871 from a 1460
manuscript. He also prints a two-stanza poem about "Three Old
Whores from Canada," which is similar to part of this toast (1964:
414-415). Vicarion (1959:67) publishes a song similar to this in the
comparisons of vagina size, but lacking the conversation about
whores and customers. There is a version in manuscript from an
inmate in an Ohio prison in the John A. Lomax Papers.

21   THREE WHORES SETTIN' DOWN IN BOSTON

There was three whores settin' down in Boston,
was talkin' 'bout my cunt is bigger 'n your'n, my cunt is bigger 'n your'n.
The first whore say, the first whore say, the first whore say,
"My pussy's big as the moon,
it goes up in January and don't come down till June."
The second one say, "My cunt is bigger 'n your'n,"
say, "it's bigger than the whole Brazos River," say, "ships sails in and ships sails
    out."
The third whore said, "My old cock [vagina] is bigger 'n the world."

Say, "I have three mens and don't worry my mind."
There was three whores that begin the same old talk.
They say, "What makes you hot?"
They say, "Make me hot when a sucker get up on top a me and don't make me
    bust my nut."
This third whore say, she was a Mexican whore, she say, "What makes you
    mad?"
She say, "That's when a sonofagun get up on top a me and play around and
    play around with my pussy."
Well, there's old Liza sittin' in the corner, say, "Girl, what make you hot?"
They say, "What make me hot? When a son of a bitch fuck me and ain't got no
    money."

22. PIMPING SAM

A. "Pimping Sam," Henry, Ramsey, 2 July 1964
B. "Wicked Nell," Phil, Wynne, 7 July 1964
C. "Wicked Nell," recorded by James Beyers from the perform-
   ance of Rudy Ray Moore, June 1970, Buffalo, New York
D. "The Pimp," Slim, Jefferson City, 23 June 1964

   This toast consists of a series of brags and insults, cast largely in
terms of status symbols well known on the street. I have based
discussion on the A-text, since it is the most interesting, but the
major points are applicable to the other two texts as well.
   Sam meets Nell while working a con game and brings her to the
city to see if she can hustle in the big time. Once there, she attacks
him on all the Pimp's status points. She claims he knows nothing
about women, that she is smarter than he, that he may look all
right in his fancy clothes but he lacks the hipness they proclaim.
She tells him how many times she fools pimps and takes off with
their money. But the folklore of the street has it the other way
around: the Pimp takes the woman's money, his clothes do reflect
his character, and he, in his infinite wisdom, is destined to
manipulate her as mere puppet.
   Sam responds with a statement about his reputation, about his
toughness—with women. He brags in a formulaic sextet about his
sexual prodigies; he sends her off after a trick and threatens to
"put this Stacey Adam [a brand of shoe popular with Southern
pimps] in your motherfucken ass." Then he insults her trade, the

very thing which presumably makes her valuable to him. Fellation, as I noted in the Introduction, is *not* generally acceptable among lower-class blacks, especially older ones (and this toast, according to the informant, is at least twenty-five years old), though whores are expected to perform it on request; in the toast world fellation is an indicator of submission. But even his insults to her tricking ability give way before something else, an anachronistic attack on her hair style: "Black, nappy-haired motherfucker . . . your hair was incorrect." The toast ends not with her capitulation and his triumph but with an extraordinary insult. That insult is formulaic and has a life of its own. It appears in this collection as #98, "And May Your Life Become Unlivable, Boy," and in a toast published by Abrahams, "The Big Man" (1970A:162) which is mostly like #26, "Sweet Lovin' Rose."

The splendid brag halfway into the poem has wide distribution. H. Rap Brown quotes a long poem he says he used to recite, part of which (in Dundes, 1973:354-355) goes:

Man, you must don't know who I am.
I'm sweet peeter jeeter the womb beater
The baby maker the cradleshaker
The deerslayer the buckbinder the woman finder
Known from the Gold Coast to the rocky shores of Maine
Rap is my name and love is my game.

In an autobiographical toast collected in Los Angeles by Anthony M. Reynolds (1974:6-8) another variant appears:

And I'm a cover shaker
And I'm a slat breaker,
And I'm a baby maker.
I'm a binder, the grinder,
The weak spot finder.

Sections of the toast float in tradition, but the whole poem seems to have moved about the country as well. Reynolds prints a toast he titles "Gambling Bess" (1974:25-26), which follows the general movement of the Texas version and has a similar ending.

There is a curious line in the Texas texts: "Now this bitch was three-quarter Kelsey, and she had mollyglass hair" (22A), and "She was three-quarter Kelsey with mardiglascar hair" (22B). Henry, who recited the A-text, used the term three-quarter Kelsey" again in his version of #40, "Dance of the Freaks." Neither

Henry nor Phil could define either "Kelsey" or "mollyglass/mardi-glascar," so I assumed the line was something misremembered and garbled that had stayed in the poem because the line was needed for the couplet. The best Henry could do, when asked for a definition, was, "I don't know, but it's some kind of mixture, she's some kind of mixture, her skin, you know." No slang dictionary I could find contained either term. Reynolds, in his version from Los Angeles, has a line: "Now this bitch was three-quarter Kelsey, and she had mollyglass hair." Neither of his informants could define the term either. It seemed unlikely that a line that existed for prosodic reasons only would survive a geographical transplant. In a recent letter Reynolds told me of a reference he had gotten from David Evans: "David L. Cohn in his book *Where I Was Born and Raised,* University of Notre Dame Press, 1967 (first published 1935), p. 21, quotes a conversation between a Negro woman and someone accusing her of stabbing another Negro:

'I'm no Nigger,' she said. 'My grandma told me not to let no-body call me no Nigger. I'm a Molly Glasser and an ink spetter.' Upon examination it developed that she was descended from the tribe of Malagasi. They were a strong and superior people who themselves had owned slaves.

Since the Malagasy people are a mixture of Indonesians and Africans, it would explain the difference in hair referred to in the various toasts."

Since the term "Molly Glasser" had some currency in the thirties, and since Reynolds' informant and Henry both were in their fifties at the time of recording and did not know its meaning, we are probably safe in assuming that the toast is at least forty years old. Such African references are extremely rare in black folklore now; this one brings up once again the difficulty in judging just how old the toast tradition really is.

The D-text, "The Pimp," begins with some lines similar to #26, "Sweet Lovin' Rose," but then it quickly goes into a whore/pimp insult and brag exchange.

More than anything else, the poem is about insult and reputation. Mimi Clar Melnick's comment about boasts in blues applies quite well to the pimp:

What, then, is the Negro blues boaster seeking? Largely, he is after status, and he gains it in a number of ways. First, he must exhibit tangible possessions which verify his personal importance and symbolize his own worth—possessions such as expensive ("sharp") clothes, fancy cars, women (pretty and in large quantity), and in some instances liquor and weapons. The most powerful of his possessions, however, is money, for without this most omnipotent charm, the above items are difficult to attain. To possess "plenty money" puts everything and everyone at the boaster's disposal; a loss of money, therefore, means a loss of power.

Status also comes from the individual's style of living: his appearance, which he enhances with clothes and other possessions; his personality, which he colors with individual quirks in speech, gesture, and mannerism. Values are placed on certain types of behavior: the big spender, the big drinker, the good lover (1973:268).

One could substitute "pimp" for "blues boaster" and change nothing except one sentence: to the pimp, a loss of power means a loss of money, and then everything else goes. It is enough to observe that the role of the showy male in emotionally charged transient relationships is one in which appearance and reputation are critical for status. Role alone will not suffice: a doctor in jeans is still a doctor, but a pimp without flashy clothes and a sharp car is nobody at all.

22A   PIMPING SAM

While sittin' here chattin' with you
it brings back memories of a bitch I once knew.
She was three-quarter Kelsey with mossy glossy hair,
she was a stompdown mudkicker and her mug was fair.
Now I met this broad while playin' short coin in the golden west,
I brought the whore to the city to see if she could stand the test.
And while we was sittin' down shootin' the bull and my ends was pretty low,
she say, "Shit, I know more now, daddy, than you'll ever know."
Say, "When I first met you, sweet papa, you tried to shoot me a line a bull,"
say, "but you can't look up a she-mule's ass and tell the load she'll pull."
Say, "Now, you handsome and everything and looks real nice in your clothes,
but you ought to cop yourself a job, fool, 'cause you can't play whores."
Say, "I'm known from the Golden Gates of Frisco to the Frisco Bay,
I'm known to beat you halfassed pimps at any game you try to play.

I'm know to beat you chickenshit pimps at any game you try to rule,
and buy clothes and furs with your money and play you for a goddamned
     fool."
Said, "So long, Pimping Sam, tell all your pimping friends
that you've met Wicked Nell from the banks of the Burnin' Hell,"
say, "This pussy's good and it's gotta sell."
Say, "Hold on, bitch, you travelin' too fast:
I'm supposed to be draggin' my foot out your motherfucken ass."
Say, "Bitch, I'm also known from the Golden Gates of Frisco to the Eagle's
     Pass,
I'm known to play bigtime landlords, kick chickenshit whores right in their
     motherfucken ass.
And if my luck continue to hold out in the future like it has in the past,
I'm gonna continue to kick you chickenshit whores right in your motherfucken
     ass."
Say, "Bitch, this is Pimping Sam, the world's wonder,
long-dick buck-bender, all-night grinder, womb-finder,
sheet-shaker, baby-maker, and money-taker."
Say, "Here come a trick, bitch," say, "catch him, catch him, and catch him
     quick,
catch him if you have to suck his motherfucken dick."
Say, "Catch him, whore, catch him and catch him fast,
catch him before I put this Stacey Adam in your motherfucken ass."
Say, "And lay that money on Pimping Sam,"
say, "for this is Pimping Sam from Alabam',
and for one jive bitch like you I don't give a damn."
Say, "And, anyhow, whore, shut up talkin' to me
'fore I tell the people your past pedigree.
Like rotten wood, you ass ain't no good, all beat and clappy,
get your kicks from suckin' dicks and fuckin' your bald-headed pappy."
Say, "Bitch, from the dicks you done sucked and the men you done fucked,"
say, "you oughta be held.
But look at you, all with a shitty smell.
Tellin' me about you can trick when you don't know how—"
say, "black, nappy-haired motherfucker, you oughta be in Georgia pullin' a
     motherfucken plow."
Say, "You know, I knew you when your drawers was funky and your hair was
     incorrect,"
say, "free-fuckin' bitch," say, "I oughta break your goddamned neck."
Say, "I hope the whole world turn against you and you fall down at my feet,

I hope crabs big as cockroaches crawl around your ass and eat,"
say, I hope the sun quit shinin' on you and your life be in a terrible wreck,
hope you fall through the loops a your own ass and break your motherfucken
neck."

22B   WICKED NELL

While sittin' down in deep meditation, little girl, lookin' at you,
you bring back my remembrance, once there was a little girl I knew.
Say now, she wasn't so good-lookin', but she could stand the test,
I made this little girl while I was playin' small towns in the West.
She was three-quarter Kelsey with mardiglascar hair,
she's a stompdown mudkicker and her mug was fair.
Now I jived this little broad and carried her to the East
and when my dough got low, boy, this was her beef.
She said, "Don't try to jive me, pretty papa," she said, "I'm the little girl they
call Wicked Nell,"
say, "I'm a coast guard cutter and I'm the burning hell."
Say, "I'm known from the Big Apple Block to the Frisco Bay,"
say, "I can show any pennyweight thief or grift any kind a game they try to
play."
She said, "Now, boy, when you first met me, how bad you would fool,
but you can't look up a mare mule's ass and tell what kind of a load she'll pull."
She said, "You're a long, tall papa," says, "you looks good in your clothes,"
say, "you may be a gambler, but you can't play whores."
She says, "I know all the niggers and whores that's famed,
such as Black Boot of Chicago and Chippy Maine."
I said, "Just a minute, old broad, now you knife your jib whilst I'll crack my
whip,
now you stand pat and I'm gonna show you some speed."
Say, "I'm known from Big Apple Block to the Eagle Pass,"
says, "I been playin' bigtime landladies and kickin' whores like you right
square in the ass."
Say, "I've had a dozen women standin' in their doors,
didn't let a day go by that I didn't stomp and kick some whore."
Say, "Now you come tellin' me 'bout you the little girl they call Wicked Nell,
come tell me 'bout you's a coast guard cutter and a burnin' hell,
now you come tell 'bout when I first met you, how bad I was fooled,

takin' you to be a little chippy just out a school.
Yes I set down and tried to charge your cunt with the bull,
but you can't look up a mare mule's ass and tell what kind a load she'll pull.
Now you come tellin' me 'bout I look handsome in my clothes —
it ain't a goddamn thing you can tell me about whores.
Now you come tellin' about you know all the niggers and whores that's fame,
such as Black Boot a Chicago and Chippy Maine.
Now you's all right, little girl, with them few nickels you knocked,
but when it come down to a mudkicker, little girl, your name didn't go down
     in the book."
Say, "Now you righteous in your togs, you righteous in looks,
now when it come down to big time hustlin' your name ain't even wrote on the
     book."

22C   WICKED NELL

While sittin' and thinking in deep meditation
shuckin' and jivin', dope-poppin', lollygaggin', eatin' chitlin' stew,
I'm reminded of a girl I once knew.
She was no bathing beauty, she didn't have long black hair,
but she was a stone good mudkicker and her mug was fair.
I pulled this little chick and moved out West and settled down out there.
When I first met her, baby, I thought she was a little girl just out of school,
but if you listen close, I'll tell you how bad I was fooled.
While playin' small towns back East, my bankroll got low.
She said, "Look here, pretty papa, you can't jive me,"
she said, "I forgot more than you'll ever know."
Said, "I'm Wicked Nell, the chorus girl hot from Burning Hell.
When you first met me you tried to fill me full of bull,
but you can't look up a mare mule's ass and tell how big a load she can pull.
But, baby, I'm gonna tell you what: I've beat chumps for their money and
     their clothes too,
I would a beat 'em for their tobacco, but all fools don't chew.
So I been from New York to the Frisco Bay,
I fucked all pimps like you with the game you tryin' to play."
Say, "But you good-lookin', kid, and look all right in your clothes,
but, baby, you oughta corner you a mule, 'cause you ain't shit tryin' to pimp
     whores."

This made Pimpin' Sam mad. He said, "Shut up!
Shut up, bitch, don't you say another motherfucken word,
if you do I'll put my foot in your ass about somethin' I heard.
Now you run around here with your nose all snotty,
if you don't know what the game is all about, you better ask somebody.
Now your tits is hangin' down like a shithouse bucket,
and your pussy is so funky that a dog wouldn't even suck it."
He said, "Bitch, there's a dick, and touch it, touch it, touch it quick,
you better touch it if you got to suck his motherfucken dick."
She said, "Look here, daddy, I ain't got any more clothes."
He said, "Tuck it out the window, bitch, you ain't goin' outdoors."
Then he looked at her and he said
"So you that little girl they call Wicked Nell,
the chorus girl hot from Burning Hell."
Said, "Bitch, I'll jump up in your pussy like it was stone
'cause I'm that notorious hustler called Pimping Sam."
Said, "I've been from the Golden Gates of California to the shores of Maine,
I know all the whores and the bulldaggers and cocksuckers by their natural
        name.
I been from New York City to Eagle Pass
playin' society whores and kickin' your kind of bitches in their no-good ass.
Now you were all right down home with the few nickels you knocked,
but, bitch, out here you're squarer than a block.
You did your bit girl, with all right looks,
but to a pimp like me, you ain't even in the book.
So you gonna try to play the game and have success,"
said, "you better ask me about it, goddam Bulldaggin' Bess."
Said, "To tell you the truth, bitch, you should be back on the farm singin' to
        your uncle Ned,
'cause the only way you can make a pimp like me a dime is to go out for your
        motherfucken head."
Said, "And furthermore I'll tell you somethin' whores do for me every day,
        that you could never do,
that's fuck, suck me, and give me that money too."
Said, "I got eight or ten whores standin' in line, and ain't a day pass
I don't kick four or five a them in their motherfucken ass."
Said, "And I'll throw a bitch like you out a bed at half-past four
and make her jump in Lake Michigan if it's ninety below."
Said, "And you better not shudder when you come to shore,
'cause if you do I'll make you jump over there and swim some cocksucken
        more."

Said, "Now the pistol's on the dresser and the razor's in the drawer,
and if you think about ere a one of them I'll break your motherfucken jaw.
And, bitch, don't you roll your eyes and give me no sass,
'cause I'll make these brand-new Stetsons sing a song in your ass.
Now if you ever think about going back home to Chitlin' Switch,
I want you to tell everybody that you met Pimpin' Sam, a bad, bad,
    sonofabitch."

22D   THE PIMP

Say, you want you a bitch that can burglarize, rob, and steal,
well you better do like my brother, get you a whore out a the field.
'Cause boy, when you all hooked up and locked up in jail,
it's that country bitch that come down and go your bail.
Now don't get the idea that you so motherfucken cool
that every whore you meet you can play her for a goddamned fool.
See, I thought I had me a whore that was young, dumb, and right out of
    school,
but listen to me and I'll tell you how I got fooled.
I bought my bitch a buggy and I wheeled her back East,
but when my money run out this was that poor whore's beef:
"Slim, I'll admit you look good in your tailorcut clothes,
but you's a lyin' motherfucker if you think you can play whores."
Say, "You layin' around here thinkin' you got sugar on your dick,
why the look on your face makes my pussy sick."
Say, "I only stuck with you fool because your line is funny,
but you'd get us both jailed if you ever got any big-time money."
Say, "I shouldn't pull your coat but I guess I might as well,
I'm that wicked bitch they call Kansas City Nell.
I'm known from the golden coasts of California to the rocky shores of Maine,
teachin' all you petty larceny motherfuckers this nickel-assed game."
But I leaned 'way back,
bit the butt off a sixty-cent Christian [cigar], and this is what I cracked:
"Shut up whore and let a man have the floor,
you talk too much to be a nickel-assed whore.
I should kneebone you, jump on you, pour gasoline over you and set your
    motherfucken ass on fire,

go to Chicago, cop me a bigtime whore, come back and watch your greasy ass
     fry.
You lay it around here and bitch that I can't play no two games at once and
     have no success:
I taught Diamond-tooth Floss and Bulldaggin' Bess.
Evidently whore you don't know who I am,
I'm that lousy motherfucker they call Pimpin' Sam.
I'm known from the Little Eagle Rock to the Big Eagle Pass
for rompin' and stompin' in a poor whore's ass.
Now here come a freight train, bitch, you catch it and catch it fast,
before I wear these Stacy Adams out in your goddamned ass.
Evidently, bitch, you don't know that I'm a playboy,
I played the big-time fancy women, even a Persian queen,
I'm a poor whore's paradise and a rich whore's sugar and cream."

23. HUSTLIN' DAN

Tom, Ellis, 24 March 1966

   This is another toast in which the central action consists of
brags, not performance. The whore is sitting at the bar in San
Francisco's best hotel, the St. Francis. The pimp first pretends he
is a trick, but she won't have anything to do with a pickup: she
works the telephone and gets two thousand dollars a trick; she
makes so much money she can throw Dan a hundred-dollar bill to
go buy a lollipop. He swings into a brag about his property and
status, whereupon she immediately decides to go home with him.
The coin for sexual success becomes reputation and assertion of
reputation, not money itself.

23   HUSTLIN' DAN

I'm gonna tell you a story about a hell of a bitch,
'course she's out of circulation now doing a seven-year hitch.
I met the broad when I was in San Francisco, I was out on the run
to score me a stable of bitches to work on my pappy's farm.
She was sittin' in St. Francis bar, she had sharp flaming red hair,
I could tell by the clothes she wore that she had that old sophisticated air.

Now the bartender told me that her name was MollyBelle,
so I decided to go over to her table and anchor a little old spell.
I says, "Say, pretty baby, why are you so all alone
when a stud like me is so far away from home?"
Bitch looked at me from toe to head
and, man, you know what that who' said?
She said, "Go on, trick, and leave me alone,
can't you see I'm waiting on a telephone?"
She said, "I just turned a two-grand trick and I'm waiting for more."
Say, "Take this hundred-dollar bill and run down to the store."
Say, "Now the store is run by a man named Mr. Rocker,
tell him MollyBelle sent you and to give you an all-day sucker.
And when you get that all-day sucker you take the change and split,
'cause I ain't got the time to listen to your bullshit."
I said, "Bitch, if you through,"
I say, "let me tell you a chickenshit thing or two."
I say, "I just left a stable of whores just like you.
They was all two-grand-a-day bitches but a pitiful few.
At the early age of fifteen
I was the hustlest motherfucker the world ever seen.
'Cause I made most of my money playing flim-flam,
and I'm the best in whorepickin' in the city of Alabam'."
I said, "I own property in Los Angeles and a part of Chi,
I got land in Oklahoma City that Henry Ford can't buy.
Never in this world have I felt all alone,
to me Nick the Greek wasn't shit and neither was Al Capone."
The bitch looked at me and said, "Daddy, if the things that you say are true,"
say, "Come on and take Molly home with you."
Say, "But just before you start out to play this old game,"
say, "tell me, baby, what's your name?"
"In Japan they called me Hookie-shookie Dan
because I shot more heroin than any living man.
Well in Mexico they called me Señor Glover
because I'm the world's greatest lover.
But in New Orleans where I saw the seven-year itch,
they called me Buggu the Gigilo because I beat every bitch.
Well now, throughout this world where a broad can catch a man,
I'm internationally known as Hustlin' Dan."

24. PING PONG JOE

Danny, Jefferson City, 13 August 1962

Although this toast voices a number of folk notions in familiar form, it doesn't hang together as a narrative. Some sections probably are omitted. Ping Pong Joe is described as rather scrofulous, down and out, and usually in withdrawal because he didn't have enough dope. A whore named Lila offers him money for dope if he'll perform cunnilingus, but Joe manages to get out some verbal insult, even though he can't manage any physical abuse. Impressed, Lila agreed to be his whore. He becomes a successful pimp, but the same whores who took him on because he was a junkie reject him because he is a junkie; the poem doesn't explain the change in attitude. He ends up back on the corner, ready for anything, even to "suck a pussy," as low as he might fall.

24   PING PONG JOE

Here's the story about a young guy named Ping Pong Joe,
a pretty motherfucker with a mudkickin' whore.
He had educated paws and charm,
but all his profit went dead in his arm.
Now let me tell you about Joe and how Joe got his start
and how Joe broke a many a young whore's heart.
Now Joe was just a junkie that looked like a tramp
with his eyes runnin' water and his belly full a cramps.
When he raised his arm it had him funky,
but he was just a chill fuck sicken junkie.
About this time came along this mudkickin' whore,
an international bitch that knowed the score.
She said, "Come here, junkie boy, with your mouth all full a spit,"
Say, "If you suck Lila's pussy, she'll buy you some shit."
He said, "You cold-blooded whore," said, "you know I'm sick,
and 'fore I'd suck your pussy, bitch, I'd just downright quit."
Say, "You jive bitch, high off of that grass,
if I wasn't so sick I'd get up and put my feet in your motherfucken ass."
She said, "You're young and fine and you want to score,
from now on, Jack, I'm gonna be your whore."

Now she named him Ping Pong Joe and put him on his feet,
and he was the sharpest junkie, Jack, to ever hit the streets.
And the coldest too.
He'd work his whores in snow and rain
to shoot heroin, morphine, cocaine in his burned-out veins.
Well naturally all the whores got tired of that stud
and went back on their own just a steady kickin' mud.
Now if you see Joe standing on the corner with one shirt and one pair a pants,
even a cold-blooded dope fiend need a second chance.
Turn him on and he'll talk some shit,
suck a pussy and give a ditch dick a fit.
That's a junkie.

25. DON'T LOOK SO DOWNHEARTED, BUDDY

A. "Don't Look So Downhearted, Buddy," Phil, Wynne, 7 July 1964
B. "Don't Feel So Downhearted, Buddy," Bobby, Jefferson City, 22 June 1964

26. SWEET LOVIN' ROSE

A. "Sweet Lovin' Rose," Frank, Ellis, 22 March 1966
B. "No Good Whore and Crime Don't Pay," Sam, Michigan City, 30 March 1962
C. "Whores Are No Good and Crime Don't Pay," manuscript given me by Winslow, Ramsey, 1964
D. "No Good Whore," Henry, Ramsey, 2 July 1964

Except for the eight lines of cynical advice at the end of the B-text, the two versions of "Don't Look So Downhearted, Buddy" are fairly similar. I include both to give some sense of how minor variation occurs in the toasts. A similar poem in the Lomax Papers, dated March 5, 1935, was sent Lomax from the U.S. Hospital for Defective Delinquents.

See Labov, et al. for a variant of "Sweet Lovin' Rose" (1973:336-337). The closing section of the A-text of "Rose" is similar to versions of #55, "Once I Lived the Life of a Millionaire."

It is a good example of how sections from the toasts can be moved about as complete units by competent performers. A few of the lines in "Rose" appear in "The Big Man," in Abrahams (1970A:161). Reynolds reports a Los Angeles version (1974:28).

Except for #39, "Winehead Girl," monogamy is hardly the style of the toast protagonists, so we can read the unambiguous double standard of these toasts as part of the general misogynistic pattern.

Two of the texts, 25-B and 26-B, were told by white informants.

25A DON'T LOOK SO DOWNHEARTED, BUDDY

Say, don't look so downhearted, buddy,
'cause you don't receive any mail,
the women soon forget you livin',
they can't use you when you get locked up in jail.
Now you're young and believe what they tell you
about stickin' through to the end,
but a bim that won't bolt while you doin' a little jolt
is just one out of a thousand, my friend.
Say, now I'm old in the racket now, buddy,
I've had pretty girls by the scores.
They once was all I thought of,
but they don't even get a tumble from me any more.
Now I did a hitch in San Quentin,
just to keep an old moll out a the stir,
but don't you think I was sick when I found out the dick
that pinched me was livin' with her?
Now there's old Sue in St. Louis,
she squalled when the judge give me ten.
She had all the swag and said she would keep it
till I was out free again.
Well, I sent her a kite [letter] by my cellmate,
the boy had just finished his hitch and was free,
but together they flown and left me all alone,
now I was just a sucker, you see.
So I married a old bimbo in St. Paul,
I bought preacher, rings, license, and all.

We lived happily together for six months,
and I took another fall.
She swore that she would stick.
Oh, so she did it,
for five long years she was waitin' at the prison gate.
But when I got home, boy, I had five kids to own.
Now do you blame me for pullin' my freight?

25B   DON'T FEEL SO DOWNHEARTED, BUDDY

Say, don't feel so downhearted, old buddy,
just because you don't get any mail.
These women they soon forget you
if they can't use a good daddy in jail.
You're just young and believe what they tell you,
when they say, "Daddy, I'll stick to the end."
But for the girl that don't bolt when you're doin' a jolt
is one in a million, my friend.
You see, I'm old in the rackets,
I've loved pretty girls by the score,
in fact they used to be all I could think of,
but I just don't take a tumble no more.
I once did a stretch in Jeff City
just to keep a pretty broad out of stir.
Maybe you think I wasn't sick when I heard that the dick
that pinched me was livin' with her.
Then there was a gal down in old Kansas City
who wept when they handed me ten.
She had the loot and promised to keep it
until I was free again.
So I sent her a kite by a cellmate
who had did his time and was free.
But together they flew, what the hell could I do,
I was just a poor convict, you see.
So I met and married a bingo [bimbo]
yes, marriage license, wedding rings, and all.
For six months we lived happily together,
till I landed a stretch in San Paul.

She promised to wait and she did
after six years she was there at the gate.
But when I got home I had six kids to own
—now do you blame me for pulling my frieght?
Now don't let this one love bother you, old buddy,
'cause there's still plenty of broads on the street.
And when you're free you can get one,
for the price of a flop and some eat.
I know you loved her, old buddy,
but you'll love plenty more of 'em too.
But don't believe 'em, just love 'em and leave 'em,
that's all an ex-convict can do.

26A   SWEET LOVIN' ROSE

I don't want no woman that's gonna rob and steal,
I'm gonna get a woman from some old Texas cotton field,
because those city women just aren't any good,
they're worse than a cow that chews on his cud.
They'll fuck you, they'll suck you, they'll make you take a prisoner's chance,
but, pal, there isn't any doubt,
one of those whores aren't going to make you any hustle when you get busted
     out.
Oh, she'll bring you chewing gum and cigarettes while you down in jail,
and swear by God she gonna get you out on bail,
but you know right then and there that that's a damned lie
because she's free to signify, jive, and stay high.
On the time of your trial she'll be there and that's no shit,
not to do you any good but to see how much time you gonna get.
When the judge pass sentence the bitch almost smile
because she knows she's free to signify, jive, stay high, for a good long while.
After you been on Ellis 'bout a month or two or more
here comes a letter from this no-good whore
and it reads like this:
"Say, dad, I went to see your lawyer today but he wasn't in,
I sure gotta be to see you, but I don't know when."
You go back to your cell with a uplifted heart,
thinkin' that skunky-assed whore out there tryin' to do her part.
After you haven't got much time, about six months to go,

here comes another letter from this skunky-assed whore,
and it reads like this:
"Say, dad, I heard about you just before your little old fall.
Say, that C-note I sent you, you didn't lose in a crap game at all.
[They] tell me you pitched a party with some punk named Bess,
tell me you bought that no-good whore a dress,
and God knows what you did with the rest."
Say, "I'm goin' back to Arkansas to see my maw and paw.
And by the way, I've been having cock trouble lately, I think I need a rest.
Don't you think that's best?"
And with these last few words the no-good whore will close:
"Please remember me as your sweet lovin' Rose."
Now after I had did my time and been on the streets about a month or two or
    more,
who should approach me but this no-good whore.
She said, "Hi, dad, may I have a dime, please,
for a cup of coffee or a piece of cheese?"
I said, "Rose, before I'd give you a dime you'd have to swim a shitty river
and don't get wet,
win money in a poker game and not even bet,
you'd have to fuck a she-lion till her eyelashes flutter,
look up a Jersey's ass and tell me the price of her milk and butter.
You'd have to fall off the Empire State building and down on your head,
get up and run around two or three times to show me that you ain't dead.
You'd have to swim Lake Erie at forty below
and I'll stomp corns on your ass if you even look toward shore.
You have to know a friend that who is a friend that could be a friend of mine,
before I reach in my pocket to give you a chickenshit dime."

26B   NO GOOD WHORE AND CRIME DON'T PAY

Say, boys, you can all have all these whores that rob and steal,
I'm gonna get me one from the cotton field.
For these city whores are no good,
they're lower than a cow that chews the cud.
And it'll be proven out beyond a doubt
that you'll soon find these city whores out.
They'll bring you cigarettes and candy to the jail

with a whole line of shit: "Daddy, I'm gonna get you out on bail."
Now that whore knows she's lyin',
all she's figurin' on doin' is gettin' on high.
Oh, she'll come to your trial, that ain't no shit,
not to do you any good, but just to see how much time you're gonna get.
And when that judge pass that sentence that whore damn near smile:
she knows she's free to fuck and signify for a long, long while.
Now after you're up the river for a couple of months or more,
you receive a twelve-page letter from this no-good whore.
First she's talkin' about things goin' on:
"Now, daddy, I will be to see you, but, honey, I don't know when.
You know, I was in to see your lawyer, but he wasn't in.
You know, I would send you somethin' but things is so tight,
I had to kick back a pocketbook from last Saturday night."
Now this whore would close,
"Now, daddy, don't you forget your sweet lovin' Rose."
Days would drift and linger for a couple of months or more
and I'd receive another scratch from this no-good whore.
First she's beggin' me to understand,
"Now, daddy, I ain't gonna quit you for no other man.
But I got a letter from maw and paw
and they want me back in Arkansas."
Now, you know, that whore's all packed, she thinks it's best,
but the doctor told me she had female trouble and she needed rest.
Now some men are weak more than they can bear,
they'd kill that whore and they'd die in the electric chair.
But I ain't goin' that way, I learned better a long time ago:
these whores ain't no good, boy, and that crime just don't pay.

26C   WHORES ARE NO GOOD AND CRIME DON'T PAY

When I do this sentence it'll be my last rap,
I'm through with night life and all of that crap.
Now most of you boys will get out and get you a gal and rob and steal,
not me, I'll get me a gal from the ole cotton field.

Now those city gals, they ain't no good,
they're lower than a cow that chews her cud.
They'll stick with you through thick and thin,
but when the going gets tough they'll call it the end.

When you get busted and throwed in the county jail,
they'll bring up a lawyer that can't even go your bail.
They'll come to see you and eye at the jailers and wink at the finks,
and tell you she loves you, when the whole damn story stinks.

Now she'll be at your trial and that ain't no shit,
not to do any good, just to see how much time you'll get.
When the judge says "Ten years," she'll only smile,
'cause she knows she can trifle for a long, long while.

She'll go home and call your friends and say, "Jack's in the clink,
so why not come over and bring me a drink."
And while you're down there shaking that ten,
that whore's out there drinking the best kind of gin.

After you've been up the river a year or more,
you'll get a letter from that no-good whore.
She'll say, "Daddy, I was up to see your lawyer the other day, but he wasn't in,
I'll be down to see you, but God knows when.

"I'd send you some cigarettes and stuff,
but you know the going out here is pretty damn tough.
I know this ain't much, but I'd better close,
this is from your darling, darling Rose."

Now while you're down there on those mile-long turn rows in that hot burning
    heat,
that no-good whore is out there cooling it between two white linen sheets.

In about a month or two more,
you'll get another letter from that no-good whore.
And you'll take it pretty hard,
'cause it'll be ten lines on a penny postcard.
She'll say, "Darling, I want you to understand,
that I wouldn't put you down for no other man.
But ma and pa done up and moved to Arkansas, and the doctor thought it
    best,
said I had female trouble and needed a long, long rest.
Well I guess I'd better close,
this is from your darling, darling Rose."

Now most of you boys would break out of that joint and go kill that bitch,
and sit in the chair while the man pulled the switch.
But believe me, man, I know what's best,
I'd leave her alone and forget the rest.

For I did my ten years, ten years to the day,
and all I learned is whores are no good — and crime don't pay.

26D   NO GOOD WHORE

Say, she'll be in the courtroom on the day a your trial,
she'll sit up like a innocent child.
Say, she'll watch the judge as he grip his pen,
and give you five, six, eight, or maybe ten.
And then she'll rare back and smile,
she say, "I'll be a free woman for a damn long while."
Say, and after you been down six months or more,
you'll get a letter from that chickenshit whore.
She'll say, "I went to see your lawyer, but he wasn't in."
Say, "I'll be to see you, God knows when."
She'll say, "'Cause you know, right now, daddy, things a little tight,"
say, "I ain't doin' nothin' but eatin' chicken and fucking every night."

(Another inmate listening nearby added: "Say you look around at your friend
and you say: 'A whore's no good and crime don't pay'.")

27. STRANGE, STRANGE THINGS

Phil, Wynne, 20 August 1965

28. YOU TOLD ME A LIE

Phil, Wynne, 7 July 1964

29. COCAINE NELL

Phil, Wynne, 18 August 1965

These toasts express a misogyny similar to that found in the preceding two. "You Told Me a Lie" tells of a women who hid her paycheck; most of the poem is an invective similar to the one at the end of #22, "Pimping Sam." In the other two Phil speaks of women who are there to be used sexually, but who see the man only as a source of money. I once pointed out to him that since men go to whorehouses to buy sexual partners it was a little odd to put down the women in those places for accepting the money. "Yeah," he said, "but whores are like that." The "buffet flats" and "gage pads" mentioned in "Strange, Strange Things" were Prohibition-era establishments, usually set up in a "landlady's" apartment. They weren't quite whorehouses — one might go there to drink or smoke marijuana (gage) — but hustling women frequently were in attendance. There is a fine description of such an establishment in Richard Wright's *Lawd Today* (1963: 198-214).

27   STRANGE, STRANGE THINGS

Said, it's strange, strange things, how we young fakes can be,
goin' in these old buffet flats spendin' our money free.
We don't ever think about the day we got to fall.
These old landladies in these old flats, they won't even pay us a call.
Though we'll get up every mornin' to go up on that stroll,
we'll stop in another one a them old flats, just to get a drink a that [alcohol].
We says that gives us workin' vim, boy, but it may just be our lucky day, and
    we take a healthy sting,
but before we think a home sweet home, we'll make another doorbell ring.
Now they'll open wide the welcome door and greet you with a smile,
they figure, "We done clipped some old chump," and ask us to stay awhile.
Now they'll set you down in their parlor and ask you, "Boy, what you say?"
Just studyin' trickeration, Jim, to make you throw your bucks away.
Now them old broads will come in, in them old friggish teddies, and start doin'
    the mess around —
that's the jive in the landladies con game to tear your bankroll down.
Now they'll start that old Victrola playin' some old low lonesome blues,
then your love will come down for some old no good broad, then you'll start to
    orderin' booze.
Boy, but the next day the roller may run down on ya, take you down to that
    lonesome old county jail.
You'll send for this same old landbroad to come and go your bail.

But, boy, you'll receive a nice little letter, sayin', "Boy, we doin' all that we can
    do for you."
But before you get out of that old jug you'll find your friends are few.
Now every word I say is logic, every word I say is true,
I'm cuttin' out from them old gage pads, boy, I don't know 'bout you.

28   YOU TOLD ME A LIE

Say, you told me a lie and it wasn't no need,
say, you cashed your check and said it was garnisheed.
Say, now that's your racket every time you come,
you ain't got nothin' but you will have some.
But I'm so glad, I'm about to shout,
that old bullshit's about played out.
I say, why who', before I'd touch your slimy thighs,
which a thousand crabs has bit,
I'd drink a gallon a drunkard's puke
and suck a clappy dick.
Say, now, I hope you sufferin' with the bleedin' piles
and corns grow on your feet,
and maggots as big as a horse turds
crawl up around your ass and eat.
Say, now, when you get old and your cards get cold,
when you stand on your life's last live deck,
I hope you slip through a loop a your ass
and break your motherfucken neck.

29   COCAINE NELL

Landlady, landlady, lock all your doors,
I'm gonna buy all your whiskey and then I'm gonna plow all your whores.
Says, then I'm gonna sniff a little coke and smoke some hop,
says, then I want to be loved till mornin', about five o'clock.
Then I'll put on my simp togs [sharp clothes] for I will have my gage,

to look your town over for some yellow babes.
'Cause I been down to the stir doin' a little time
for another guy's rap on the crosstown line.
But I'm back again, still holdin' my rep,
my body's hot and I'm full a pep.
I'm just from behind those gray prison walls,
so you can see why I'm got to get my ashes hauled.
So bring me some pajamas and jump in your gown,
let your butt get frisky and do the mess-around,
'cause, whore, I'm gonna sleigh-ride you and bulldag you too,
I'm gonna put you in the buck and airtight you just for luck,
then I'm gonna make you gaze in a lookin' glass
and throw some vaseline right in the crack a your ass,
then I'm gonna shove my rod in your open hole
and try to pacify your ornery soul.
'Cause whores are people I've never understood,
none ever mean a hustler any good.
They's all alike the whole world round,
they'll love a fake when he's up and hate him when he's down.
Boy, but I tried to be a gentleman and treat them all swell.
"But good treatment ruins a whore," says Cocaine Nell.

30. L.A. STREET

Joe, Ellis, 24 March 1966

It isn't the *vagina dentata,* but it's close: in return for giving up his manhood by performing cunnilingus, the woman gives the man the power of material possession. The great teenage male fantasy is to be selected from all the other horny teenagers by the most beautiful woman in the world. That is just what happens in this toast, and the moral is that there is a price to pay for such easy luxury. The word "cocksucker" is ambiguous in black slang, for "cock," usually means "vagina." The ambiguity is of course operative in the toast.

For another Texas version of this toast, see Abrahams (1970B:94-96). Part of Abrahams' "Just Looking for a Job" (1970A:166-170) is similar to "L.A. Street." For a California version, see Milner (1972:289-291).

L.A. STREET

As I was walkin' down L.A. Street
I was broke as hell but my clothes was neat.
Although I was broke I still felt fine,
I'd spent my last four bits for a jug of wine.
Now I was standing on the corner of Hollywood and Grand,
leaning up against the lamp-post in a three-point stand.
Boys, I was thinking every way in the world how I could make me some
     money,
when I heard a soft, tender voice behind me say, "Come here, honey."
Now I turned around and what did I see,
it was a chick in a Cadillac beckoned for me.
Now I went on out to the big Cadillac,
she said, "Hey, little daddy, when did you get back?"
Well you know I had to play like I was in the know,
so I tell her I just come in a couple of hours ago.
She said, "Well, little daddy, how about you and I havin' a good time,
smokin' some weed and drinkin' some wine?"
Now I'm gonna tell you fellas, that kind of puzzled me to a T,
out of all the available mens in L.A., why in the hell did she pick on me?
She said, "Well, little daddy, I saw you standin' on the corner so nice and neat,
I knew right then that you was hard to beat."
I said, "Okay, cutie, just one more thing before we go,
I been playing a fast game of Cotch and I lost all my dough."
She said, "Cool, daddy, pay that no mind,
since I invited you for this stroll,"
say, "you furnish the time, I'll furnish the gold."
So we made a few joints and then we drove up in Beverly Hills
where you couldn't smell nothing but old roses and daffodils.
She drove me to her pad, she said, "Welcome home.
This is your castle, daddy, and inside is your throne."
Now I looked all around and everything was groovy,
you know, just like one a them big motherfuckers you see in the movie.
She said, "Sit down, little daddy, and play your favorite song,
I'm goin' in to change clothes but I won't be long."

Now boys, she fell back out in a skin-tight gown,
that showed her shape from her shoulders on down.
Now I jumped up and grabbed her, hugged her real tight,
and asked her politely could I spend the night.
She said, "Yeah, cool daddy, if you know what to do,
you can spend this night and the rest of them too."
Now fellas, I have to admit I was a little green,
so I tell her to break it on down and tell me what she mean.
She said, "Well, you know, daddy, you know you can find a grinder any time
    that can grind a while,
but tonight I want it did on the Hollywood style."
She said, "I want you to fall down on your bended knees
and eat this pussy like a rat eat cheese.
I don't want you to slacken up one bit
until I pull your ears and make you quit."
Now boys, I got so mad I could jump and shout,
I said, "Bitch, what in hell is you talkin' about?"
Say, "I like cheese and I ain't no rat,
I'm crazy about pussy, but not like that."
I said, "Who', before I scale your rusty thighs and suck your bloodshot tits,
I'll drink a gallon a rattlesnake blood and swim in a ocean of shit."
She said, "Well, little daddy, I guess you and I are through,
'cause if you can't eat this pussy there's nothin' else you can do."
So I gets my hat and I started to go,
'course I don't get no farther than the front door.
She said, "Hey, little daddy, wait one minute,
you may still eat this pussy if you know what's in it.
Breakfast in bed, diamond ring,
Cadillac car, and everything."
I said, "Look here, woman, the reason I ain't married and ain't got no wife,
I was intending to be a playboy all a my life,
but if eatin' pussy is all I got to do,
shit, I guess I'll string along with you."
So I turned around with my head hung in sorrow:
I was a playboy today, but I'll be a cocksucker tomorrow.

31. THE LAME AND THE WHORE

Peter, Wynne, 18 March 1966

"The Lame and the Whore" begins as an attack on incompetent pimps who are easily sweet-talked by their own whores, but turns into a series of incredible abuses of the woman. The violence with which the hatred is expressed may be more excessive than in most of the other poems, but it is simply an extension of the same misogyny: if the woman is there to be sold, then she's an object; if the pimp is to maintain his status, he cannot treat an object as if it were human; if he is going to keep his object from becoming human, he must keep it from having anything resembling choice or free will. That may not be how things work on the streets, but on the exaggerated stage of the toasts such caricatures become the norm.

31   THE LAME AND THE WHORE

It's a lowdown shame how some of you cocksuckin' lames
you all claim to be so hip,
every time you open your mouth I know you dead from the South,
and you're just another poor hustler's tip.
You claim to be a bigtime gambler and you got a fast moneymakin' whore,
and you supposed to be that whore's first love.
You're good at pickin' people's pockets and robbin' supermarkets
and you're a foxy boy in a pair of boxin' gloves.
But you play workin' men's wives, you'll even burglarize,
in fact, you're good at all you attempt,
but your greatest mistake is when you decided your fate
and thought that a lame like you could pimp.
Because I've been pinnin' your style for quite a while
and I can see you ain't down with the game,
why the very bitch could make you both rich
if you wasn't such a motherfucken lame.
Because you got one a those whores that look good in her clothes,
and she got that pretty velvet-like skin,
and without a guess, when she lift her dress
she's at least worth a fin.

Say, but that bitch you got, her cock gets hot,
and she's wild as a bitch can be,
and it's a lowdown shame how the bitch'll pull her train
and give all her pussy away free.
Then the bitch come draggin' it home with her sickpad on,
she talkin' shit, "Daddy, you sure is sweet.
When you go down to the store bring me back a box a Kotex,
and don't forget to bring us back something to eat.
Say, but before you go I want you to know,
that today I lost my job,
and the money I drew, I lost that too,
I cross my heart to God."
So there the bitch will lay, she's the picture of death,
not one cryin' penny in her pocket,
the bitch feelin' fine, her breath smellin' like beer, whiskey, and wine,
and her ass is smellin' like a dyin' fish market.
Say, you got to wake up, lame, and prove to this whore
that you are not no goddam fool,
say, you got to prove to this bitch that you are three-quarter jackass
and that the other part a you is mule.
Say, you got to rule that bitch, you got to school that bitch,
you got to teach her the Golden Rule,
you got to stomp that bitch, you got to tromp that bitch,
and use her like you would a tool.
You got to drive that bitch and got to ride that bitch
like you would a motherfucken mule.
And after the end of the month rolls around and that bitch's flag jump back in
        port [when she menstruates]
then keep every inch a your natural prick right down her pricksucken throat.
And if the bitch starts to complainin' that she got pyorrhea a her gums,
put you some pillows up under that whore's belly and then charge her asshole
        some.
Charge that bitch's ass and charge it hard,
till the bitch no more can feel one slidin' fart.
Then take the bitch out on the highway and drag her until she's damn near
        dead,
then take your pistol and shoot her right through her motherfucken head.
Then send you a message to Tom Devil, for to hell she's bound to go,
tell Tom Devil to use that bitch and to abruse [sic] that bitch, because she's just
        another no-good whore.

Say, "Please, Mr. Devil, just before you call your roll,
if you have got just one more trick left in hell, please charge that poor whore's
    soul.
And when her soul-fucking days are over and her pussy they no longer buy,
throw you some more brimstone in the furnace and throw her dogass in the
    fire.
And when her soul is burned to ashes, put them in a jar and send them to me,
so I can take them and show them to all these other free-fucking bitches
    who are going around and giving their pussy away free."

32. TOLEDO SLIM

Victor, Wynne, 18 August 1965

33. PRETTY PILL

Phil, Wynne, 7 July 1964

Crooks aren't a notably trustworthy crowd, and many of the
toasts deal with the problem of betrayal. In both of these poems
we hear of women who did their good men wrong: Tommy runs
off with Jackie Brown, and Pauline shacks up with Pretty Pill, "a
Frenchman . . . with a evil leer." Tommy, like a character in a
sentimental opera, dies of TB in Denver; Jackie Brown, Pretty
Pill, and Pauline are killed by the men they've wronged.

There is a version of "Toledo Slim" in Milburn (1930:192-197)
which is very close to the text Victor told. Victor learned his
version from Phil some years earlier in another prison; Phil said he
learned it from someone in the free world. The similarity of the
texts suggests some widely distributed printed source. The
"fragment hot" in Victor's text appears in Milburn as "fragrant
hop" (194), which makes more sense.

32   TOLEDO SLIM

I was seated in a poolroom on one cold December day,
telling jokes and funny stories, just to while the time away.
As the door it softly opened and a form crept slowly in,

all the boys stopped their kidding as they recognized Toledo Slim.
As he crept into the room and took a look around the place,
you could see the look of hunger upon his dirty brown face.
"Hello, there, Slim," said Boston Red, "you look like you on the poke.
You used to be one of the swellest dressed guys that lived in old New York.
Come and tell us what got you on the bum."
And this is the sad story that Slim begun:

He says, "It's true that I'm on the bum, boys, and I'm on the hog for fair,
but in my past life I led 'em all, and my roll was always there.
I never turned an old pal down, I spent my money free,
and all the cats along the line, they liked to stick with me.
Why, I was a all 'round hustler, and I trimmed a sucker right,
I never fleed from any game [if] there was greenbacks in sight.
But one day I met my fate, boys, and fell like a many mo',
that's why I'm on the bum, all worn out and sore.
It happened about five years ago, if I remember right,
I clipped a sucker for quite a roll and fell almost out of sight.
I took a stroll down the line and set 'em up to all the boys,
just to pass the time away I stopped in Kid McCoy's.
I was sittin' at the table, gettin' on a mighty stew,
a dead swell dame come sit beside me too.
I asked her would she have a drink, she sweetly said she would,
and when I gazed into her eyes I thought I understood.
Now you might think me fickle, but it isn't a dream,
when it come to peachy looks this Tommy was a queen.
We chewed the rag for quite a while and shot the con for fair
and when it came to spreadin' jive, you could gamble that I was there.
I told her I'd put her in a nice, furnished flat,
and when that joint closed that night I had my girlie pat.
The next day I saw the parson and we paid a month's rent down.
I would lay up in my downy bed, so humble and so snug
while she'd go out through the town and hustled the grub.
After the day had proved gloomy, back to my [?] I would stop,
I would lay around in the dugout while she cooked the fragment hot.
When winter blew 'round,
we had the swellest flat of any couple in that town.
One night I had a job to pull in one of the swellest homes in town,
and I got my tools and started out with my pal, Jackie Brown.
Everything was still and not a soul in sight,

we never thought we'd bump a pipe.
We got the swag and put it into a sheet and started down the block,
but as luck would have it, we bumped into a cop.
But we didn't dread it 'cause we were fleetin' greyhounds,
We started on the run
with the cop behind us, shootin' off his gun.
The cop that wounded me stopped to handcuff me and my pal got away
and I never saw his face again in a many, many day.
Now I guess you know the rest, they made short works of me,
They sent me up the river to do a little "V" [five-year sentence].
But I didn't worry, I thought my broad would stick
and keep my flat a-runnin' while I done my little trick.
I never thought she'd turn on me in forty thousand years,
and when I come to think of it, it almost brings me tears.
As the years rolled around on one bright sunshiny day,
I gets a big discharge back to big New York, so happy and so gay.
When I reached my flat I found my girl had gone,
had run away with Jackie Brown and left me all alone.
Then I start to boozing, going from bad to worse,
tryin' to drown my sorrow and forget the bitter curse.
But the sceneries of her pretty face was always on my mind,
and I searched the country over, no trace of her could I find.
I roamed the streets of [?], seeking in vain for my prey,
tryin' to find the guy that wrecked my life and stole my broad away.
I swore that I would have his life for the deed that he had done.
I searched the country over, knowing full well my day would come.
One day I met a wiseguy said he knew my pal full well,
he was livin' in Frisco and doin' very swell.
But the girl had died in Denver with consumption, so they say,
where my pal had left her for to starve in want of one tiny piece of bread.
Now this happened at a time when I didn't have one cent.
I beat my way to Frisco and my mind was [?] and bent.
One foggy night on Market Street I met him to his face.
And he tried to get the drops on me, but he was one minute late.
I sent a bullet crashing right through that traitor's brain,
and made my getaway on that boomin' eastbound train.

Some a you boys is speakin' about women, but I can tell you a thing or two,
one a my experiences with women when I was a young man like you.
But I haven't had much use for them since, for a pimp's life is a joke,
he's the lowest man in the underworld and a pimp's always broke.
When I first come to New Orleans I was a 'bo hopped off a jolt,
it was a very cold winter and I had no place to go.
As I walked down the narrow streets all I got was a cold hard stare,
for I was broke, down and out, and I knew nobody there.
So I started hittin' up the free lunch shacks just to keep myself alive,
till at last I lucked up on a chance to sleep in a Rampart Street dive.
I was just about to give it up, I felt myself slippin' down,
boys, that's when Pauline come into my life, she's the sweetest little girl in
      town.
Now Pauline was a real small girl with coal-dark eyes and hair,
and when it come to peachest looks, the little girl was there.
Now when I first met Pauline I sure did love her right,
she'd go out and bring me in fifteen or twenty bucks a night.
So I was layin' there livin' like a king
with all a Pauline's love and what money she could bring.
Then I started runnin' around with a wise mob, that's when I played the sap,
for some of our boys was drifters and some of our boys was macks.
One a our boys was a Frenchman, a guy with a evil leer,
he was very popular with the women, they called him Pretty Pill.
Now Pretty Pill was a good con man, he shoulda have never been broke,
but the trouble with the Frenchman, he was up against the coke.
Now Hypo, he was a gentleman, and Cokie, he was a rat,
a smoker can respect himself, but a drunkard can't do that.
So I'll get back to my story. I was with my girl about a year,
that's when some talk got started, the kind that I couldn't help but hear.
I never took a tumble till I begin to feel blue and lost,
then my buddy told me, said, "That girl is giving you the double cross."
We was heading up the old pike.
When my buddy told me, we smoked around five bombs [marijuana
      cigarettes],
I immediately got up and started loadin' up my gun.

My buddy wanted to go with me, but I told him he had better not,
as soon as I finished my business, I'd come back and smoke some hop [opium].
I searched the whole city over, I walked on every beat,
I couldn't find her anyplace, yet she was supposed to be hustlin' the street.
So I goes down to our cabin, she never knew I had a key,
and there as I opened the front door, boy, a funny feelin' run over me.
In the bed with my gal lay a man. As I walked across the flo' he turned ashy
    gray.
He tried to get the drop on me, boy, but I killed him where he lay.
Now Pauline, she grabbed at my feet, she tried to play the woman's part,
but I remember laughin' when I sent a bullet through her heart.
Now that's about all a my story, except I got away,
I haven't had a woman, not since until this day.
But I have did lots a smokin', and never intend to stop,
for the only time I forget the li'l girl is when I'm full a hop.

34. DOGASS PIMP

Phil, Wynne, 7 July 1964

   This toast offers an anomalous version of the usual male/female
relationship. The woman neither abuses nor cons the man; rather
it is he who is the villain because he can't satisfy her properly. The
woman is not praised because she is good—the poem doesn't go
that far—but the man is condemned because he is incompetent.

34   DOGASS PIMP

Say, now boys, I got something to tell you, just to get it off my mind.
Now you dogass pimps ought to get off the line.
Say, you runnin' around here messin' these good gals up,
when you know you can't hustle 'em and you sure can't fuck.
Now you tellin' people you livin' a underworld life
when you know darn well you just livin' through struggle and strife.
Say, now you lay too heavy and you fuck too long,
your dick too short and you put it in wrong.
Now this old way you got a tippin' through these alleys and backyards,
and when you get home to your money-woman, boy, I bet you can't raise a
    hard.

And when she wants some lovin' you plays off sick,
but you can't get by long with that old bullshit.
But if you do get by it's just through luck
'cause these womens ain't gonna give you their money and go on half-fucked.
Say, now to keep a good money-woman, boy, you got to be ready right off the
    rail,
and let your dick fall out your britches as hard as pessified steel.
And when you fall down on your good gal and lower your bone,
you got to make that pussy call your dick "Bad Mr. Al Capone."
And when she throw that pussy back at you,
you don't have any excuse, just rair back and hit it like big Babe Ruth.
Now you better take heed, papa, to what I'm tellin' you,
before you fall back off your porckchops down to your plain beef stew.
When your woman see you comin' she don the bathrobe and both feet hit the
    floor,
she just want some baby talk out a you.
She said, "Daddy, where you been?"
You said, "Bitch, I been out gamblin' and tryin' to win."
She say, "you know you lyin', motherfucker, you haven't laid a bet,
you standin' there all funky and your dick still wet."
Then you said, "Well, good gal, if you don't want your feelin's hurt,"
say, "Just give me back my thirty-five dollars and my silk nightshirt."
Well, papa, right then, that's when you plannin' to go,
'cause she figurin' on puttin' your black ass dead out in the snow.
Now you been foolin' with your oats, you been messin' with your hay,
you say, "If you take me back, baby, I'll do it the other way."
She say, "No, no, daddy," said, "the love I had for you is a thing of the past,
and will you kindly let my doorknob hit you dead in your black ass."
Then when early next moring when down the road you go,
the first thing you call her is a no good who'.
Now you just say that because she throwed you down.
As long as she stood your shit, she's the best gal in town.
Well, papa, my home ain't here, I just stopped to catch my wind,
I'm green and lucky and I'll soon be gone again,
'cause I'm a stomp-down globetrotter and please don't get me wrong:
I got mule piss in my blood and I can't stay hitched up long.

35. AIN'T IT A BITCH?

Peter, Wynne, 26 March 1966

Not only is this stanzaic, but each verse has a burden, quite rare for the toasts. Peter said he had learned this in a county jail some years before.

35   AIN'T IT A BITCH?

When all your money's gone and you drain your last cup,
you sittin' and thinkin' of the times when you once was up,
when all your friends has gone and left you and you flat in a ditch—
now hi, my jivin' Mike, ain't it a bitch?

When the skies turn dark and gray, the rain begin to pour,
you out wanderin' from door to door,
you get throwed in jail by some dirty old snitch—
now hi, my jivin' Mike, ain't it a bitch?

They take you down to the old county jail,
maybe three or four of your old used-to-be broads tell you, "Daddy, I'll go
        your bail."
But you feel like killin' one a those bitches, but you don't know which—
now hi, my jivin' Mike, ain't it a bitch?

When they take you to court you nearly beat the rap.
The district attorney bring up some damned old crap,
then the judge he fine you just like you was rich—
I can't take it, Mike, ain't it a bitch?

There stand a old broad in the courtroom you maybe done forgot all about,
starts to beefin' to the judge, "I'll bail him out."
While all the other chickenshit offenders they got to stand in the hitch—
now how are ya, my jivin' Mike, ain't it a bitch?

She takes you home and a drink makes you feel sort of spry,
then you light up a stick of tea and you both get high,
then you both get friggish and then you pull off every stitch—
you starts to slow jivin', Mike . . . ain't it a bitch?

36. IF YOU SEE MY LITTLE GIRL IN DENVER

A. "If You See My Little Girl in Denver," Phil, Wynne, 7 July 1964
B. "Lady Liberty," Slim, Jefferson City, 23 June 1964

Phil's text seems to be a conflation of two poems, one about a woman, the other a homiletic about money. Note the advice to have "fall money"—money put aside in case of an arrest. The dollar described has on it a "Liberty," so the toast must date from the days when silver dollars were still in general circulation. Both poems express the notion that the only woman one can trust is the one on the coin, for only the coin is consistent.

36A   IF YOU SEE MY LITTLE GIRL IN DENVER

Say, if you see my little girl in Denver, I know she gonna feel blue,
to hear that I fell on a armoured rap and cannot pull it through.
She know I always been her true disciple and come at every call,
I lose my freedom trying to kick some dough to spring her from her fall.
Now boys, whilst you out there slippin' and slidin' be sure to take your time
and anchor some a your lays in some First State Dime.
'Cause there ain't but one woman in this world for me,
her picture's on the dollar and they call her Liberty.
She'll feed you when you're hungry, she'll buy your clothes,
so try to get that woman, Jim, you won't never have to be drove.

36B   LADY LIBERTY

Gather round me, fellas, I have a story to tell,
I want you to listen carefully so you can learn this lesson well.
You see I fell in love with a brown-skin girl
who carried my heart for a whirl
but the bitch was like a timberwolf all year 'round.
She was on my side when I was on my feet and on my ass when I got down.
So, you see, fellas, I've traveled this wide world over now,
and I know there's only one bitch for me,
she has her face on a silver dollar and her name is Liberty.
She feeds me when I'm hungry and keeps my clothes out a soak [pawn],
and as long as I got this fabulous old broad I *can't* be broke.

A. "Corner of 47th and South Park," Phil, Wynne, 18 August
   1965
B. "Little Old Wicked Nell," Louis, Ramsey, 4 July 1964

The intersection is a famous one in Chicago, but the image of a
white hooker approaching black streetcorner dudes there is not
very realistic. Once again we have the motif of the woman
demanding cunnilingus and the man rejecting the demand. First
he recites his pedigree, then delivers a superfuck, after which she
becomes "a bitch a mine." Reynolds reports a similar text from
California (1974:26-27), one which includes portions of #55B,
"Down and Out."

The B-text becomes rather incoherent, but it has the usual
theme of the man responding to the whore's request with talk
about his reputation.

37A   CORNER OF 47TH AND SOUTH PARK

Say, I was standin' on the corner of Forty-seventh and South Park
where the pimps and the whores and also sissies pitch a bitch in the dark.
Say, it was seven-thirty, eight-thirty, or probably nine,
when a little fay [white] broad tipped up aside a me, said, "Daddy, I haven't
      made a dime."
I says, "Baby, what do you want me to do about that?
It's the facts a the business, do you hold me responsible for that?"
She sort a snarled and she started to run,
I said, "Come back, babe, I got one."
She said, "Come on, let's go upstairs and have some fun."
On our way upstairs I looked her over: boy, she was a cute little trick.
And when I got up in her bedroom, boy, I pulled out my dick.
She looked at me and she shook her head.
Now, boy, these are the words that that whore said:
She said, "Daddy, that won't please, if you wants to be with me,"
say, "you got to bear down on your knees
and eat my pussy like a rat eat cheese."
I said, "That's fine and dandy, baby, for somebody else, but no, no, not me."
I say, "I love my cheese, but I ain't no rat,

I go for pussy, too, but not like that."
I said, "'Course, you nice and clean and your drawers are silk trimmed with
 lace,
but there's no way on earth that you could back your funky ass up into my
 face."
She said, "Well, who are you?"
I said, "I'm a whore-fucker and a gambler,
card-bender and a rambler."
She said, "Well, you got to prove that to me."
So I fucked this whore from the livin' room to the dinin' room stairs,
she fell down on her knees, I thought she was gonna say her prayers—
but she done kissed me on the dick.
She said, "Daddy, you done fucked me till I farted, you done fucked me till I
 pissed,"
said, "now, if there ever was a heaven, it must be this."
I said, "Now, if I catch you around here reading these bulldaggers' mail
I'm gonna cut your pulltongue out and throw your ass in jail."
Say, now, if you don't believe my jellyroll is fine,
ask Good-Cock Lulu, that's a bitch a mine.

37B LITTLE OLD WICKED NELL

It was way back in old Frisco, that was where I first saw the light,
on the corner of Corn and Pine, that's where all the whores and sissies lie.
It was 'bout half-past eight, or was it nine o'clock, when a little girl came
 tippin' up to me,
said, "Daddy, I ain't made a dime."
I said, "Li'l girl, you gonna hold me responsible for that?"
She start to run away and I said, "Come back, baby, I got a dime."
She taken me up to her room, we had some drinks a wine.
I went to her body with my pride in my hands.
She said, "Mmm, mmm, you gonna put all that in me?"
She said, "If you want this here you got to eat it like a rat do cheese."
I said, "I go for cheese, but not like that,
I like cheese, but I ain't no rat."
She said, "Who is you?"
I declared who I were: "The Big Boy from Boston."
She say, "Tell me somethin' about yourself."

I told her, "I played the game with the Florida Kid all down in Key West."
She said, she said, "Tell me about yourself.
If you want this cheese you got to eat it like a rat do cheese."
I say, "I go for that, but not like that." Shakespeare.

38. LITTLE GIRL IN THE GAMBLER'S NEST

A. "Little Girl in the Gambler's Nest," Phil, Wynne, 18 August 1965
B. "While Playing Short Coin," Henry, Ramsey, 3 July 1964

38A   LITTLE GIRL IN THE GAMBLER'S NEST

I was dealing short coin in the Golden West,
I met a little girl in a gambler's nest.
I'd scored off all a my money and give it away
by gettin' caught bluffin' with a small trey.
Then I turned to this girl that was standin' nearby,
I stood there shuck and looked her square in the eye.
She said, "Stick around, daddy, till I get back,"
says, "I feel kind a lucky and I think I'll hit the track."
She went out that night and she made a healthy sting,
she clipped twenty-two hundred and a diamond ring.
Thirty minutes later she were at my pad,
we'd talk to each other about the little luck she had.
She said, "Let's blow this burg and travel 'round,"
said, "I can do lots of hustling in a larger town."
I said, "Tell me 'bout yourself," I demand of this dame.
I had her dough in my pocket, boy, and I didn't even know her name.
She said, "I just cut out of a stable," said, "I had a rat for a man,
he had two more rat broads and they all were on my hands."
She walked the streets every night, no different if it shine or rain,
and she never come in off the blocks until she had bagged her man.
Jack, she knew the con racket, 'cause I played it by her side,
if once she ever stopped a lame, he'd never make it by.

So what happened on one circus day down close to Madison Square,
she clipped for a week the gate receipts and give the town the air.
But a plainclothesman he trailed us down from New York to Los Angeles,
Jack, at first I couldn't believe it, it was almost like a movie play.
A California nabber took me, white slavery was my charge,
convicted me and in twenty-four hours in the big house I did lodge.
Now New York give my girl a ten-spot and the matron led her by her hand,
just thinkin' of ten long years in prison just for breakin' the laws of man.
So I'm just up out of San Quentin on my way back in the East
to get my little girl out of prison, perhaps my mind can see some peace.
From New York I will take a steamer, Jack, I will pay a first-class fare,
we'll settle in some European country and live our lives together there.
Jack, a con man, a cannon [pickpocket] or a fake of any kind,
make a C or so, the day after tomorrow you serving time.
So if you ever cross this sea to London or any other foreign land,
you'll probably see my name in lights as a successful businessman.
Of course I know there's some good hustlers, to them I extend my hand,
but these long jolts in American joints have made me a different man.

38B   **WHILE PLAYING SHORT COIN**

While playing short coin in the Golden West
I met a dead swell dame in a gambler's nest.
Boys, I had lose all my money, in fact I gave it away,
I got caught bluffin' with a small legay.
Say, now I turned to this dame who was anchored nearby
and start shuckin' and jivin' and lookin' at her dead in the eye.
She say, "Wait right here, daddy," say, "I be right back,"
say, "I feel sort of lucky, I think I'll hit the track."
An while she was gone she took off a hell of a sting,
she beat for twenty-two thousand and a diamond ring.
Say, and thirty minutes later we was at her pad
shuckin' and jivin' about the luck she'd had.
Say, she told me she had a rat for a man
and he had two or three rat whores and they was all on her hands.
She told me she could play confidence and I knew the game by size,
and every time we'd meet a sucker we'd carry him for a hell of a ride.

Now I know you're not going to believe what I'm about to say,
'cause to you it's going to sound like a movie play.
But it was one night right next to Madison Square,
she beat a sucker for his whole life savings and we had to blow and give the
    town some air.
But the New York dicks followed me to San Francisco,
white slavery was my charge.
They put me in the big house,
and at San Quentin I did lodge.
New York State gave my girl a ten-spot, the matron had her by the hand.
Now just to think: ten long summers for breakin' the laws of man.
But as I sit here in the cells of San Quentin, way down in the deep,
every time I close my eyes I can see this little broad in my sleep.
Say and if I'm ever free, I'll travel back East,
say, I'll get my little girl out where my mind can have some peace.
And from there we'll catch a freighter and I'll pay first-rate fare,
we'll journey to some European country, spend our lives happily there.
And one day you might cross the seas to London, or some other foreign land,
and see my name in lights: "Mr. Henry, successful business man."
Say, for there are a lot of hustlers, cannons, con-mens, and fakes,
to them I extend my hand.
But these long trails of these American stupes
have made me a better man.

39. WINEHEAD GIRL

Phil, Wynne, 18 August 1965

Henry told me he'd "made this one up," but a year later Phil told me he'd taught it to Henry "Short Coin" when they had done time in the same prison several years before. Henry's version is similar to Phil's in the rhyme scheme; his variations come mostly' in the first half-line and adjectives. The rhymes are the mnemonic, the closest thing to a constant these poems have, but there is room for a great deal of variation before them. Henry's text sometimes loses coherence (as "legay" in line four, which should be "treys," a low pair). The rhymes keep the thread of narrative going, but they permit the individual performer a great deal of narrative flexibility and help him get by bits of memory failure.

I wondered if "Winehead Girl" had come from a book, but Phil shook his head and said, "That was made up. Got it a long time ago. You know, guys lived that kind of lives and just make them up. There used to be a old boy there in Houston, just about anything could happen and he could just make poetry about it. Anything. Didn't care what it was."

These are the only two hustler poems in which the woman is praised, in which her competence and consistency appear as virtues. In "Little Girl in the Gambler's Nest," the narrator says he will get his woman out of jail and leave the country with her; in "Winehead Girl" the woman gives the true-hearted man permission to go get himself another woman since she's going to be out of circulation for good.

39   WINEHEAD GIRL

Say, now, some a you boys is down on these women because they drink wine,
but I must confess, they're just my kind.
Now I don't care how they dress or how they look,
as long as they drink wine, they ace-high in my book.
Now I ain't goin' by what I heard or what I read,
the best broad ever I had, they called her "Winehead."
I bumped into her one Saturday night about half-past ten,
she told me her troubles and I took her in.
She said, "Daddy, I'm a stranger here, just hit this town,"
say, "I followed a dope addict this far, and he put me down."
She said, "Everything he had I got it out a soak [hock]
but there's one thing, I'm so glad, daddy, he didn't leave me broke."
Now the other part a her story I didn't care,
but when she said she wasn't broke, boy, that's just what I wanted to hear.
She give me one round cool hundred dollars, said, "Daddy, is that all right?"
I said, "Yeah, you know it is, Winehead, and you won't have to work tonight."
Said, "Now let's get dressed and walk up the streets,"
Boy, she had clothes to put on her back and shoes to put on her feet.
So we goes on up the streets and we stops in a cafe just to get ourselves a lunch,
all of a sudden old Winehead, she got a hunch.
She said, "Wait here, daddy, I'll be right back and then we'll be ready to go."
She's back in ten minutes with a hundred mo'.
She says, "Come on, daddy, and let's go lay down,"

say, "I don't want to go too stout, I just hit this town."
So we goes on down to her pad, I wants to hear her whereabouts.
She say, "I made a clip upstate, and I'm on the scout."
I say, "You don't have to worry about that now, Winehead, 'cause I'm's your
    man,
now just don't go too stout and overplay your hand."
She said, "Daddy, you know I've been to school,
and you know by that I ain't nobody's fool."
So away one night old Winehead went out to make another haul,
her luck run out and poor Winehead got a fall.
I was down to the courthouse and I felt like cryin'
when the jury's bounced out of the box and give her ninety-nine.
She looked at me and she begin to smile.
I said, "Winehead, you want me to appeal and try to get you another trial?"
She said, "No, no, daddy, now let's get this straight,"
say, "If I beat this rap I'm wanted in another state."
Say, "'Course I appreciate you doin' all you can,
but my best advice is you try to get you another real good true friend."
Now, boy, that's the day I made up my mind
that any woman I get gonna have to drink wine.
Now that's about all my story and I don't have to lie,
I expect to keep some winehead until the day I die.

Freaks and Supersex

40. DANCE OF THE FREAKS

A. Henry, Ramsey, 2 July 1964
B. Manuscript sent by Phyllis Wallace of the Delinquency Study Project at Southern Illinois University as given to her by an informant in Chicago

41. FREAKS' BALL

A. "Freaks' Ball," Mack, Jefferson City, 24 June 1964
B. "Twenty-Two Twenty," Mack, Jefferson City, 24 June 1964
C. "Bulldaggers' Hall," Manuscript sent by Judy Kolbas as she recorded it in Wilson, New York, 6 August 1970, from a teenage informant who learned it from a girl in Pensacola, Florida

For short verses similar to sections of both these toasts, see Abrahams (1970A:167-169). Reynolds reports a version of "Freaks' Ball" (1974:27-28).

These poems are meant to shock; the pleasure they offer is in observation of excess and absurdity, not eroticism. The term "freak," in the argot of the toast-teller, means both oldtime movie monsters, such as Frankenstein and Dracula, and sexual deviants—bulldaggers (lesbians), punks (catamites), and so on. The violent and Pimp toasts are caricatures of scenes from the real life; these are cartoons from a fantasy world in which all that is fearful is made fully absurd.

It was cold and mist and rain in old Spokane
off the red light district of the coast,
where the whores got high off a good cocaine
and stood on the corners and boast.
Now there was Light-Haired Nell, French Estelle,
they was both three-quarter Kelsey to the bone,
there was Little Lindy Flo, a red-headed who',
and Light-Fingered Peggy Malone.
Now Peggy Malone had a face of stone,
long fluffy lips and red scarlet cheeks.
The bitch told of the place where she reached her peaks,
none other than in the dance of the motherfucken freaks.
Say, on the wall was gay fancy trimmin
and on the floor was belly-rubbin' women
and punks who ate shit from a spoon.
Say, there was asshole shellackers and shitpackers
and freaks who drunk blood from a menstruatin' womb.
Say at the party was a little French maid who had never been laid.
She shot a speedball toddy and fell out at the party.
Woke up disgusted with her asshole busted,
full of slime and corrupted come.
Now the funk and shit woulda made Count Dracula sick,
but it's good the Count didn't show,
for the Wolf Man was in the kitchen, bitchin'
with a hundred zombie whores.
Say, he tickled and sucked them whores to death,
and turned around and survived them with his funky smellin' breath.
Say now, like Little Jack Horner, sittin' in the corner,
the mummy was beatin' his meat,
but he was so long and lanky, and so motherfucken stanky,
till they threw him in the streets.
Say, and it was just about time for the party to close
when the hinges went to flyin' off the motherfucken doors
and to everybody's surmise [sic]

there stood that big bad motherfucker they call Frankenstein.
He had a mismatched body with two left heels,
long dick hangin' out like a four-yard eel.
He said, "I'm raggedy 'n' rimey,"
said, "I wasn't invited but I'm down here,
and I'm so happy I could shout
that eleven dozen a you bad motherfuckers couldn't put me out."
Say Frank grabbed a whore
and threw her to the shit-smellin' floor.
With her feet to the ceilin' the bitch start squealin',
but Frank kept one steady bolt.
And when it looked like the whore's eyes was about to jump out the sockets,
that's when the come shot out like a white skyrocket.
And then Frank got up to make his self a toast
and found his self disgusted,
with his asshole busted,
and the Wolf Man was makin' for the door.
So the bitch say she been a lot of places
and heard a lot of men speak,
but the damnedest place she'd ever been
was the dance of the motherfucken freaks.

40B   DANCE OF THE FREAKS

It was a cool and mystic rain
In old Spokane
In the red light district of the coast
Where whores get high
Off of good cocaine
And stood on the corner to boast

There was a little French Flo
The red headed whore
And light finger Peggy Malone
They told experience they had
With suckers, pimps and chumps
They been told how they came from the back street dumps

Peggy Malone told where she made her stake
None other than the dance of the freaks
They had bachelors who die for a trick
Fags are the saddest of bull dagger named Gladys
Who's ambition was only a dick

A little French maid who never been laid
Her cock was tight as a drum
She fell asleep and woke up with her ass full of blood and slimy come
They had shit packers — ass hole shellackers — freaks who got thrilled by their
　　　sists.
Cheap cock suckers — grand mother fuckers — they went far as drinkin piss

They had shit sandwiches — menstruating blood for mustard
Wolf man walked in the door — he threw nine sons of bitches on the floor
He tickled them whores to death — the revival of his funky breath
But the damnest dance I ever seen was the dance of the motherfucker freaks.
　　　(*From Manuscript*)

41A　　FREAKS' BALL

You should a been with me in the year of twenty-three,
now, there was freaks in the Knee-high Valley far as the eyes could see.
Jim, you talk about freaks, man, they was there,
bulldaggers and punks from almost everywhere.
Now the hostess of the evenin' was Free-Turn Flo,
she brought fifteen bulldaggers to put on the show.
Shit-eatin' Shorty, he was there from the start,
while Fart-sniffin' Joe was lookin' for a fart.
Terytestin' Peter began to pout —
he wanted a shit sandwich on rye to straighten him out.
Now there was Nailhead, Railhead, Long-Drinkawater,
Shorty, the Barber's wife, fucked her till she hollered.
There was Little Miss Vi from the Windy City of Chi,
she had a dick [clitoris] so long she had to be circumcised.
And there was Mumblepeg with a dick like a table peg,
her and her partner, Anna Funk.
The two whores got together and grind the pump.
Now wasn't a thing that these bitches wouldn't do.
Lizzy Lou fucked her mother, too.

Said, "Let's have a party, have some fun,
for God sake, fellas, don't forget the gun [hypodermic syringe],
'cause, man, I want some two in one [cocaine and heroin].
We gonna sing and dance till daylight,
we'll cut and shoot till midnight,
and we're not gonna stop to eat a goddam bite,
but for breakfast we shall have two stiff dicks tied in knots,
two whore's cunts fried in snot
and a cup of come coffee."
Now if you can think of anything any filthier than this,
we'll all have a highball of tomcat piss.

41B   TWENTY-TWO-TWENTY

Twenty-Two-Twenty told Automatic Jim to tell his fast-fucking sister Fanny,
tell his bald-head, bulldagging, cocksucking mammy:
"We gonna have a cocksuckers' ball down at the Motherfuckers' Hall.
We gonna fuck and fight till broad daylight
and make damn sure we get our business right.
Now I don't know what we gonna have for lunch,
but I got a damn good hunch:
three pickled dicks all tied in knots,
three big fat funky syphilitic cocks all fried in snot.
Now all you whores get together and get me a toddy,
'cause when my dick get hard, I'm gonna fuck everybody."

41C   BULLDAGGERS' HALL

Tonight we gonna have a ball
down to the old Bulldaggers' Hall.
When you go down the street, you tell every motherfucker you meet,
you tell old Pistol Pete to tell old Forty-Four Joe
to quit raising hell everywhere he go.
You tell old Razor-Cuttin' Annie to tell her fast-fucken mammy
they all three can come in for a quarter.
What we gonna do we gonna romp and tromp til midnight,
fuck and fight til daylight,

we ain't goin' home to eat a bite.
What we gonna have: stewed pussy fried in snot,
six dicks in a knot
and a bucket of shit stinkin' like a sonofabitch.

42. 'FLICTED ARM PETE

A. "'Flicted Arm Pete," Victor, Wynne, 18 August 1965
B. "'Flicted Arm Pete," Peter, Wynne, 18 March 1966
C. "Pisspot Pete," Bob, Connelly Migrant Camp, Barker, New
   York, 17 August 1970

Victor said, "I learned that from a boy way back in '36 I believe
it was." The poem has to do with a damaged hero (his arm is
"afflicted") and he compensates by being a superfuck. See
"Schoolteacher Lulu and Crabeye Pete" in Abrahams
(1970A:164-165). The third text is only partial, but the first two
are full treatments of the narrative. Taped seven months apart,
they are by the same performer. There are as many differences as
one would find between performances by two different performers,
evidence that toast performance is an act of oral composition in
which elements may combine and appear in many variations, even
within the confines of a fixed plot and within the repertory of a
single performer.

42A   'FLICTED ARM PETE

Say, down in a little old town called Louisville
lived a fast-fucking whore and her name was Lil.
Say, Lil had nips on her titties about the size of your thumb,
she had somethin' between her legs would make a dead man come.
So Lil lived the night life and she like to fuck
and from what I could hear she was pretty rough.
But out of a mountain a long-dick creeped,
a sonofabitch they called 'Flicted Arm Pete.
Pete fell in the joint with both hands full of dick,
about twelve inches long and six inches thick.
Lil looked and spied Pete and cold chills run down her bone,

she turned on her shoes and started to go home,
'cause she knew at last she'd met her mate,
but if she turned and run now, it would be a little too late.
So they picked a spot over the hill,
down back of the shithouse and by the old mill.
And they fucked and fucked for hours and hours,
and pushed against burrs, trees, and flowers.
Well, on the third, with a groan and a cough,
Lil passed out and left Pete jacking off.
He was over on the mountain behind the stump,
he was picking crabs from his big rusty rump.
He was rolling his dick in red cross tape
when the officer walked up and charged Pete with rape.
He said, "Hold on, officer, you've heard of me, of course,
unless you're one of the new motherfuckers that just got on the force."
Say, "I've fucked everything from the Gulf of Colorado to the rocky shores
    of Maine,
mules, cows, horses, and every goddamned thing."
He says, "Now you go on back down on your beat
and tell all the whores you met 'Flicted Arm Pete."
So one day Pete mounted a goat
and his backbone popped and that was all she wrote.
The day of the funeral all the undertakers frowned
'cause they had to jack him off to let the coffin top down.
He shot up a load as the lady went to bare [bier?].
She say, "I know he's got a home in this world somewhere."
Now, generations may come and generations may go,
but after 'Flicted Arm Pete there won't be no mo'.
And if anybody should happen to ask you who composed this toast,
just tell 'em it was Butt-Cut flashin' from coast to coast.

42B   'FLICTED ARM PETE

It was way down in this little town that they call Louisville,
there once lived a fast-fucking whore by the name of Lil.
Now Lil had nipples on her titties just about as thick as your thumb,
Lil had jaws on her pussy that would make a dead man come.
But one day out of the mountains came a long-dicked creep,

that was a sonofabitch that we all call 'Flicted Arm Pete.
Pete fell in a beer joint and had both his hands full a prick,
it was just about fourteen inches long, just about four inches thick.
Old Lil spied Pete out of the corner of her eyes, with cold chills to her bones
Lil turned in her shoes and she started to run home.
For she knew at last she had met her mate,
but if she left right then and there it would still be too late.
So him and Lil picked a little spot, it was just over a hill,
it was down back of one of those old dry shithouses, down by an old mill.
Old Lil and Pete fucked and they fucked for hours and hours,
pushin' up against creek banks, hedges, and stumps, even mashin' the little
    wild flowers.
Finally wasn't nothin' heard but a grunt, groan, and a cough,
Lil keeled over and died and left Pete jackin' off.
Later on that evenin' Pete topped him a mountain goat,
but Pete's backbone cracked and that was all she wrote.
They took old Pete and buried Pete down in the graveyard,
Pete was stone dead and Pete's prick was still hard.
Say they put old Pete about six feet down,
about four inches of Pete's prick still stood up above the ground.
They had to put old Pete about ten feet down,
but when they finally got old Pete buried all the undertakers frowned
because they had to jack Pete off to let the coffin lid down.

42C   PISSPOT PETE

There once lived a whore around this town
she swore no man could fuck her down
from out of the woods come Pisspot Pete
with eighteen pounds of red-hot meat.
I hurried to the moutain to get me a seat
to see old Pisspot Pete when he sunk his meat.
For days and nights the fuck went on
now Pisspot Pete is dead and gone.
But his dick's still hard and his toes stickin' up,
and that's how they killed old Pisspot Pete.

43. CASEY JONES

Slim, Jefferson City, 24 June 1964

See Laws (1964) entry G-1 for information on the song "Casey Jones." The second part of the toast is a variant of "The Farmer's Curst Wife" (Child:278) and is sometimes found in songs about Stackolee; see, for example, #2, "Stackolee in Hell." See also Norman Cohen's article on the ballad (1973).

43   CASEY JONES

They tell me that Casey Jones was a railroad man
and he jumped out a his train with his dick in his hand.
Said, "All a you whores that want to be screwed—"
At the word he had a hundred and ninety-two.
So he lines 'em all up against the wall,
bet his fireman five dollars he could fuck 'em all.
He got a hundred and ninety and his balls turned blue,
he took a shot of corn and fucked the other two.

Then Casey died and he went to hell,
he fucked the Devil's wife and fucked her well.
Two little devils started runnin' through the halls,
said, "Papa, catch him 'fore he fuck us all."
Now there set old Satan high on the shelf:
"You better run, motherfucker, I'm tryin' to save myself."

But Casey said, just before he died,
"There's a couple more things I'd like to ride:
tricycle, bicycle, automobile,
a crapped-up cart, and a Ferris wheel.
Say, you know, man, it's a goddamned shame,
I'm forty years' old and haven't rode nothin' but a motherfucken train."

44. COCAINE SHORTY

Mack, Jefferson City, 24 June 1964

Bob, Connelly Migrant Camp, Barker, New York, 17 August 1970

These two similar toasts are superfuck stories. The same theme
—and some of the same lines—appear in many versions of #52,
"*Titanic.*"

44   COCAINE SHORTY

Cocaine Shorty is my name
and fuckin' is my claim.
I can line ninety-eight whores up against a wall
and I'll bet you a dollar I can fuck 'em all.
I'll fuck ninety-six and my dick get slick,
go across the street and get a oyster stew,
and come back and fuck the other two.
Now I wouldn't be tryin' to win myself no woman,
Slim, I just like to hear them poor whores moan.
I'll tell you what to do:
you get me fifteen cents worth a porkchops and dime's worth a rice
and I'll crucify good pussy like the Jews crucified Christ.

45   HERBERT HOOVER

When Herbert Hoover was born
he kicked off his napkin with a stiff hard on.
He said, "Line up a hundred womens against the wall,
I bet ten dollars I fuck 'em all."
He fucked ninety-eight and the skin of his prick began to rub hot,
he went down to the cafe and got him a cup a coffee and oyster stew
and come back and fucked the other two.
When Herbert Hoover died he fucked the Devil.
Said, "Catch that sonofabitch 'cause he gonna fuck us all."

46. THE VOODOO QUEEN

Big Ten, Ellis, 21 August 1965

    This toast is discussed at length in the Introduction. The "Sheriff of the wing" who takes "the Voodoo Queen to be his wife" is the inmate in charge of the wing, not a guard.

46   THE VOODOO QUEEN

If I may borrow your ear, I promise you'll hear
the life of a treacherous bitch,
who sent her friend to hell and made the Big D jail,
and now she's servin' a twenty-two-year hitch.
Now she was a sexy maid, a shake dancer by trade,
and men was her favorite delight.
She had big eyes that smiled and the face of a child,
but her heart was black as night.
Without further ado I'd better mention to you,
so that you'll surely understand,
that this little bundle of joy was a sissy boy,
you know, a female man.
Why you laughing so, sonny? It's not so funny.
Why this statement wise folks will endorse.
For in the glorious past, great kings liked their ass,
and sex is just a matter of choice.
But back to our little joy: her life was dreadfully sad,
'cause one day on Main she caught a convict chain
and rode Black Betty [prison transfer bus] to her new pad.
The sign on the gate said Huntsville State,
with bullring of brass that glossed like glass.
Now, she wondered, was it real, all that cement and steel,
the machine gun, the picket, the boss?
That night in her cell, she cried like hell
and swore she would kill herself,
for a filthy past and a greasy ass
was all that the whore had left.
In the first interview the nut doctors knew
she was as freakish as a three-dollar bill.

So he said, "Let's ice this tramp 'cause on the nigger camp
somebody would surely get killed."
So they sent Miss Flamsey to the Number One Ramsey,
a place of sorrow and shame.
There's lots of lost souls in this stinkin' hellhole
and anything else a man can name.
They got the righteous dads and the so-called bads
and plenty of the snitching kind,
it's a homosexual den full of crazy men,
where a good man is hard to find.
Now the Voodoo Queen created a hell of a scene,
she was a punk so worthy to see.
We were workin' in the woods where the fuckin' was good,
under every brushpile, stump and tree.
But, as I recall, it was in the mess hall,
when every eye gleamed like glass,
just to glimpse of the girl of the real free world
who could shake a wicked ass.
Now before very long she was coming on strong,
performing with pride and grace.
With her silly pride she pulled a group aside
and boasted how she lived in the street.
Claimed she dressed like a star, had a Cadillac car,
and the choicest of food to eat.
But I got the word from that Jackson bird
he lied every step of the way;
said she was a homemade punk, a real-live skunk
that shit ten times a day.
He was quick to insist that the bitch was rich
and praised her as high as he could,
but it wasn't long before the dog done him wrong
and that's when he found out the bitch was no good.
But there were some that thought well of this daughter from hell
and claimed that her lovin' was hard to beat.
She was young and strong and her wind was long
and a shyster didn't stand a chance.
Her ass was as tight as a bulldog's bite
and her fee was a dollar in advance.
Now I saw that Dallas Kid when he lost his wig,
he was just as wild as a goose,

and Wonder Boy White wrote notes all night,
until she cut his ass loose.
Then Smilin' Moe, he went for the who',
but Mother Carrie caught him fair,
then the deputy lawman tried to take a hand,
but he was too damned square.
Of course there was lots more,
but their effort was mighty dim.
There was Whorehouse Jimmy, Mr. Eataplenty,
and my good pal Fakin' Slim,
there was Professor Fenny, who made eyes aplenty,
and yet talked that gangster talk,
and his good pal Boss pulled like a hoss
to prove that he could walk that walk.
But it was the Sheriff of the wing that made his sting
and promised her a happy life,
with high-handed pride he pushed Pretty Miss Blue-eyes aside
and took the Voodoo Queen to be his wife.

47. MARIE

Joe, Ellis, 24 March 1966

48. ANNABELLE JONES

A. Al, Ellis, 21 August 1966
B. Bob, Connelly Migrant Camp, Barker, New York, 17 August
   1970

These toasts are about transvestites. Joe claimed he composed both "Marie" and #46, "The Voodoo Queen." Bob learned his version of "Annabelle Jones" in northern Florida. Al said about his Texas version:

Have you ever read about this woman, a convict, a man? He was a female impersonator in Shreveport, Louisiana. Now, he was an escaped convict from someplace or other, I don't know just where it was. But from some place or another he escaped and he come to this Louisiana town, Shreveport. And he was trickin' with a woman's husband and she shot him. And that's when they come to find out that he was a man and a escaped convict. Now this thing he had for a vagina, or whatever you call it, I think he had it all patched up with feathers and first one thing and another. He used a flashlight battery under his arm, that put the heat in that vagina down there. And after he was shot, he wouldn't let nobody undress him until he got so weak and he couldn't help himself. Then they undressed him and found out what he was, where he was from, and everything.

47   MARIE

Now it was just getting dark in the Eastwood Park
where I met this beautiful girl.
She was four-foot-nine and dressed real fine,
her teeth was as white as pearl.
She had long curly locks and big fine hocks,
a lovely leg to caress and hold,
with great big eyes that hypnotized
she captured my heart and soul.
Now like a gentleman should, I introduced myself,
and I asked her name in reply.
"Marie," she said, as she dropped her head
and I sweetly asked her why.
Now she seemed kind of shy as I gave her the eye,
and I asked, "Are you all alone?"
"Um hm," she cried, "let's go for a ride,"
and as quick as a flash we was gone.
First the Five Star, then the People's Bar,
after that I can't recall;
but I do remember a bed and a curly head
and her body so warm and so small.
Now for the rest of the night I was out like a light,
and, Jim, I was in one hell of a spot,
and for the trim, you can believe me, Jim,
I don't know whether I copped it or not.
But I woke up in bed with an achin' head
about one the next afternoon.
Marie had cooked, and oh how sweet she looked

as she tidied up the room.
Now she tried to get away as I started to play
and my headache was gone with the wind.
We fretted and I sweated and I actually petted,
tryin' to get my old rod in.
Now a quick move she made and let down the shade
and turned out all the lights,
then she grabbed a jar and greased my bar,
sayin', "Daddy, I'm a little bit tight."
Now she squirmed, she scooted, she farted, and she pooted,
she bit my wrist, we hugged and kissed,
sweat literally poppin' from my ass,
with her legs on my shoulders I could hardly hold her,
the girl she was fuckin' too fast.
But we finally got through about half-past two.
I took a quick shower and ate,
then I changed my stride as I went outside
to kiss Marie at the gate.
Now later I had a chat with a hood named Pat
concernin' my girl Marie,
and without thinkin' twice I took his advice
on how sharp a quick marriage would be.
Now for two long years I watched her shed lots of tears,
for each time we trimmed at night,
she grabbed that jar and greased my bar,
sayin', "Daddy, I'm still too tight."
Now one night I came home half high
and started to grind the old-fashioned way, I was takin' my time.
Now Marie fell asleep and my chance to peep
and I was horrified to find,
she had two rusty nuts that swung from her butt
and a fuck-pole longer than mine.
Now in a daze it seemed I let out a scream,
and staggered around as if I was drunk.
It's a well-known fact, but honest, Jack,
Marie was no woman, she was a punk.

48A   ANNABELLE JONES

Annabelle Jones from Shrevesport City,
the way she fucked these men it's a goddamned pity.
She's a he-she woman with a sheepskin pussy,
lined it with feathers and covered with fat.
She got springs on her ass to make it tight like that.
She fuck by electricity, and she come by gas,
she got a Cadillac pussy and Lincoln ass.

48B   ANNABELLE JONES

Annabelle Jones, a noble kid,
she had a big fat pass she did the yo-yo with.
It was lined with wool and it was covered with fat,
had a drawstring in it to make it tight like that.
When Annabelle Jones wanna make a poor man moan,
She cock up her leg and turn the hotshot on.
If anybody ask you who told this toast,
tell 'em ole Bullshittin' R. L. from coast to coast.
'Cause it's poontang.

Signifying and Poolshooting Monkey

49. SIGNIFYING MONKEY

A. Victor, Wynne, 20 August 1965
B. Tom, Ellis, 24 March 1966
C. Eugene, Connelly Migrant Camp, Barker, New York, 22 August 1970
D. Henry, Ramsey, 17 November 1965
E. Hank, Michigan City, Indiana, 30 March 1962
F. Bobby, Jefferson City, 22 June 1964

50. POOLSHOOTING MONKEY

A. Tom, Ellis, 24 March 1966
B. Homer, Michigan City, Indiana, 24 April 1962
C. Joe, Ellis, 25 March 1966
D. Ray, Connelly Migrant Camp, Barker, New York, 17 August 1970

51. PARTYTIME MONKEY

Frank, Ellis, 22 March 1966

Although these three toasts are about a jungle monkey, they are not necessarily about the same character. The style and hustle of Signifying Monkey is different from the other two, and it is "Signifying Monkey" that is the main poem in the tradition. Nevertheless, sometimes texts are combined: 49D includes a long section of "Partytime Monkey," but the character in that portion of the poem is described as Signifying Monkey's brother; Ray's "Poolshooting Monkey" turns into "Signifying Monkey" halfway through. But those are exceptions: usually the texts are kept separate.

I asked Tom about the second ending to his version of "Signifying Monkey," and he said he added it himself; this is the only text I've heard in which Monkey is killed. Note that the only time either combatant uses the term "brother" is when he is in serious trouble. Note also how the second ending uses parts of the first ending formulaically. Opie (1959:38) has a short rhyme about "Signifying Monkey." Abrahams discusses the poem at some length (1970A:66-70, 113-119, 142-156). See also Labov, et al. (1973:339-340), Mitchell-Kernan (1973:362-324), and Abrahams (1970B:88-90). D. K. Wilgus sent me several versions from his Western Kentucky Archive, one of which begins, "'Way down yonder in the Burma Jungle . . .'" He sent also several versions from New Jersey. This is one of the best-known toasts, so well-known it is sometimes told by whites, as are the E- and F-texts here.

49A   SIGNIFYING MONKEY

Say deep down in the jungle in the coconut grove
lay the Signifying Monkey in his one-button roll.
Now the hat he wore was on the Esquire fold,
his shoes was on a triple-A last.
You could tell that he was a pimping motherfucker by the way his hair was
    gassed.
Now the Signifying Monkey told the big bad Lion one day,
said, "Jack, there's a bad motherfucker lyin' down your way."
He said, "And the way he talked about you, I know it ain't right,
when y'all meet, gonna be a hell of a fight."
He said, "You know the other day down on the ditch
he called your mother a no-good bitch."
The Lion jumped back with a mighty roar,
his tail stuck out like a forty-four,
he breezed down through the jungle in a hell of a breeze,
knockin' giraffes to their knees.

He run up on Brother Elephant down under the trees, just about asleep,
he said, "You big bad motherfucker, it's goin' be you or me."
The Elephant looked at him out a the corner of his eyes,
said, "Why don't you go on and pick on somebody your size?"
But the Lion jumped back and made a pass
and the Elephant knocked him dead on his ass.
They fought all night and they fought all day,
and I don't see how in the hell that Lion got away.
Early next mornin', most dead than alive,
he crawled back to his tree and there lay Brother Monkey with his signifyin'.
He said, "Now look at you, talking about you the king of the jungle, ain't that
     a bitch?
Your face is fucked up like the seven-year itch."
He said, "I," say, "I didn't get beat."
The Monkey said, "You a lyin' motherfucker," said, "you [I] had a ringside seat."
He said, "Shut up, motherfucker, and don't you roar,
if you do I'll jump down and kick your ass some more."
The Monkey got frantic and went jumpin' up and down,
both feet missed the limb and his ass hit the ground.
Like a boom a lightnin' from a streak a heat,
the Lion was on him with all four feet.
The Monkey said, "I know you think you raisin' hell,
but everybody seen me when I slipped and fell.
But if you let me get my nuts up out of this sand
I'll fight you just like a natural man."
He said, "And if you even give me a bid,"
say, "I'll whip your ass worse than that Elephant did."
The Lion jumped back and said, "Well, be ready, motherfucker, when I count
     to three,"
but the Monkey tore his ass back up that same damned tree.
He said, "Well, Brother Lion, the day have come at last,
that I have found a limb to fit your ass."
He said, "You might as well stop, there ain't no use a tryin',
because no motherfucker is gonna stop me from signifyin'."

49B   SIGNIFYING MONKEY

There hadn't been no shift for quite a bit
so the Monkey thought he'd start some of his signifyin' shit.
It was one bright summer day
the Monkey told the Lion, "There's a big bad burly motherfucker livin' down
       your way."
He said, "You know your mother that you love so dear?
Said anybody can have her for a ten-cent glass a beer."
He say, "You know your sister that's old and gray?"
Say, "He's the turd that caused her to be that way."
And the Lion knew that he didn't play the Dozens
and he knew the Elephant wasn't none of his cousins,
so he went out through the jungle with a mighty roar,
poppin' his tail like a forty-four,
knockin' giraffes to their knees
and knockin' coconuts from the trees.
He ran up on the Elephant under the coconut tree,
said, "Come on you big bad burly motherfucker, it's just you and me."
Now the Elephant looked at him glassly out of the corner of his eye,
said, "Go on, you tramp, pick on somebody your size."
The Lion jumped back like a little jitterbug to make his pass,
the Elephant sidestepped and knocked him dead on his ass,
broke three ribs and fucked up his face,
he knocked his asshole out of place.
They fought all night and they fought all day,
by the Lord's help the Lion got away.
Now the Lion come back more dead than alive,
that's when the Monkey started some more of his old signifying.
He said, "King of the Jungles, ain't you a bitch,
you look like someone with the seven-year itch."
He said, "When you left the lightnin' flashed and the bells rung,
you look like something been damn near hung."
He said, "Whup! Motherfucker, don't you roar,
I'll jump down on the ground and beat your funky ass some more."
Say, "While I'm swinging around in my tree,"

say, "I ought to swing over your chickenshit head and pee."
Say, "Everytime me and my old lady be tryin' to get a little bit,
here you come down through the jungle with that old 'Hi ho' shit."
Now the little old Monkey was dancing all around,
his feet slipped and his ass must have hit the ground.
Like a streak of lightning and a bolt of white heat,
the Lion was on the Monkey with all four feet.
Monkey looks up with tears in his eyes,
he say, "I'm sorry, brother Lion," say, "I apologize."
The Lion says, "Apologize, shit," say, "I'm gonna stop you from your
    signifyin'."
Now the Monkey got to think and think fast
if he wanna save his little old hairy ass.
He said, "Look, Brother Lion, everybody saw me when I fell out a my tree,"
he said, "they know good and well that you takin' advantage of me."
Said, "But if you let me get my balls out this sand
I'll fight your funky ass all over this land."
The Lion jumped back and braced for a fight,
the Monkey swings damn near out of sight.
For days and days the Monkey was gone,
the Lion thought the Monkey was never coming home.
But the Monkey come back with two forty-fives,
he said, "Come on, big old motherfucker, now you my size."
He said, "'Member that day when I fell out of my tree?"
He said, "You put your big funky feet all over me."
Said, "Remember when I looked up with tears in my eyes?
You wanted to fuck me up 'cause I wasn't your chickenshit size."
Lion looks around with a chickenshit grin,
he said, "Come on, Brother Monkey, me and you can be friends."
He said, "No more ro-roar shit will I carry on
when I think that you and the missus is at home."
He said, "Around your tree I won't trespass
because I want our friendship to last."
The Monkey still wasn't satisfied,
he had the Lion beat: he had two forty-fives.
He said, "Stick your nose in the sand,"
say, "I wanna hear you hollerin' all over God's land."
Once again the Monkey gets tickled and begins jumpin' up and down,
his feet missed the limb and his ass hit the ground.
Like a streak of lightnin' and a bolt of white heat

he was right back on his ass with all four feet.
Now deep in the jungles in the still of the night,
when the Lion roar all the rest of the monkeys get the hell out of sight.

49C   SIGNIFYING MONKEY

Back down in the jungle up under the stick
things been quiet for a pretty little bit.
One morning bright and soon,
that motherfucker come out a his room.
He wearin' a Buroo watch and a zootsuit,
couldn't [any]body tell that bitch he wasn't cute.
He got Mr. Lion, said, "Woooo, Mr. Lion,"
Said, "Somethin' come down here,"
say, "way he talk about your aunt, niece,
your grandma he say he ask her for a piece."
The Lion got so mad he jump up trimmin' the trees,
chopped baby giraffes, monkeys down on their knees.
He went on down the jungle way a jumpin' and pawin',
poppin' his tail worse 'n' a forty-four.
He saw Mr. Elephant layin' side a the tree
say, "Get up big rusty motherfucker, [it's] you or me."
Elephant looked out a the corner of his eye,
say, go get somebody your size."
Like a streak of lightnin' and a bolt a heat,
that Lion was on that motherfucker with all four feet.
When that Lion backed and made a pass,
the Elephant slapped him, knocked him dead on his ass.
He drew back in the jungle, more dead than alive,
that motherfucken Monkey starts some of his signifyin'.
"Ooo, Mr. Lion, you talk about you were fast,
Look a there, you ain't got no hair to cover your ass."
He drew back in the jungle more dead than alive,
that's when that Monkey jumped up and started his signifyin'.
Said, "Look here," say, "every time me and my wife go to get a little bit,
you come with that 'owe you' shit."
Say, "Anyway, get out from under my tree before I take a notion to pee."
He jumped from limb to limb and all the way around,
his foot it slipped and his black ass hit the ground.

And that Lion covered him.
He said, "Look here, Mr. Lion, hold it!" say, "let's fight fair.
You stand over here and I stand over there."
That Lion backed up prepared to fight,
That motherfucker swung plumb out of sight.
Who ask you composed this toast —
Eugene Smith from coast to coast.

49D   SIGNIFYING MONKEY

It was early in the morning one bright summer day,
the Lion was comin' down the Monkey's way.
The Monkey laid up in a tree and he thought up a scheme,
and thought he'd try one a his fantastic dreams.
He say, "Hey, Brother Lion, a big sonofabitch just went down the way,
and he talked about your family in a hell of a way,
a whole lot of things I'm afraid to say.
The way he talked about you and your father was a damned sin,
said you and your grandmother wasn't even no kin."
Lion got mad, he bent back on his knees,
he went through the jungle knockin' down coconut trees.
That's when he spotted the big motherfucker up under the tree,
he say, "Hey! big bad sonofabitch, it's gonna be you and me!"
The Elephant looked out a the corner of his eyes,
said, "Why don't you find somebody to fuck with more your size?"
The Lion made a fancy pass,
the Elephant stepped aside and kicked him dead in his ass.
They fought all that night and they fought all the day,
I still don't see how in hell the Lion got away.
He come back through the jungle next day more dead than alive,
that's when the Monkey started his jive.
Say, "You left yesterday ringing like bells,
and you come back this evenin' all whipped up like hell."
Say, "Your nose is snotty,
and if you know how to fight I'm gonna fuck you in the ass somebody."
Say, "Everytime me and my wife go on the beach to get a little bit,"
say, "Here you come with that roarin' shit."
Say, "Get out from under my tree
before I swing out and pee."

The Monkey got happy and he jumped up and down,
his two foot slipped and his little ass hit the ground.
Like a bolt of lightnin' and a scribe [sic] a wheat,
the Lion was on him with all four feet.
Say, he say, "I'm not gonna whip your ass 'cause that Elephant whipped mine,
I'm gonna whip your ass for signifying'."
Monkey lay down there with his nuts in the sand,
he said, "Let me get up," he said, "And I'll fight you like a natural man."
The Lion jumped back, all squared off for a fight,
that's when the Monkey jumped damn near out of sight.

Now the Monkey had a brother who was two part kale,
and every time he turned around there's a lie he would tell.
Now this Monkey wore a tog a Mexican stitches
and every time you saw him he had a Cadillac full a monkey bitches.
He wore a hat and the color was brown,
and every time you saw him the Cadillac was draggin' the ground.
This Monkey went to the party and knocked on the door,
he said, "Yes, I'm rugged, I'm ragged, I'm 'round here,
I know goddam well I wasn't invited but I'm down here."
Say, "I measure forty-two inches across my chest
and I fear not a livin' sonofabitch between God and Death.
I was born in the Battle of Butcher Knives,
sprinkled in the eyes with a forty-five."
Say, "Lion is my prochates [protegees]
and tigers is my associates.
When the snake look me in the eye
he crawled over to the side and died.
'Cause I put chains on lightning and shackles on thunder
and I walk through the grave make the dead wonder."
He say, "I got a back pocket full a whiskey and a front pocket full a gin,"
he say, "if you all don't open the door I'm gonna kick the motherfucker in."
Say, "If you got any young whores in the house you better start 'em walking',
'cause you all done made me mad and I'm fixin' to do some bad goddam
        talkin'!"

Down in the jungle about treetop deep
a signifying Monkey was a wantin' some sleep.
Now, he'd been tryin' for a week or more,
and every time he'd go to sleep a damn Lion would roar.
One bright and sunny day
he told him about a bad bastard over the other way.
Said, "The way he talks, I know it ain't right,
if you two meet there'll be a hell of a fight."
Said, "That wasn't all I heared him say,
why, he done talked about your mama in a hell of a way.
He called her a bitch and a dirty whore,
if I hadn't left he'd a called her more.
Why, he [said he] screwed your mother, your sister, and your niece,
and the next time he sees your grandma, he's gonna ask her for a piece.
And I'd rather be deaf, dumb, and blind
than to have some bastard talk about a family of mine."
Say, old man Lion jumped up in a hell of a rage,
like a cowboy on a rampage.
Says, "Excuse me, Monkey, but I'm gonna go
get this motherfucker talks about my mama so."
Why, he left the jungle with such a breeze,
he knocked all the coconuts off a the trees
and slapped a big giraffe right down on his knees.
Then he saw Elephant layin' over and under the tree,
he said, "Get up, motherfucker, it's either you or me."
Now the Elephant kind of gazed from the corner of his eyes,
and said, "Lion, you better get on somebody more your size."
But the Lion made a pass,
and the Elephant slapped him on his ass.
Why, he kicked him in the head and stomped him in the face,
and broke three ribs and knocked his ass out a place.
Well, they fought that night and part of the next day,
I ain't never figured out how that Lion got away.
But he come out a that jungle more dead than alive,
and then that Monkey started to signifyin':

Said, "O ho, motherfucker," says, "why when you left this jungle it rung,
now you comin' back fit to be hung."
Said, "Your face fucked up like the seven-year itch—
King a the Jungles: ain't you a bitch?"
Said, "Don't say you wasn't beat,
why I was there with a ringside seat.
That sonofabitch kicked you in the nuts and stomped you in the head,
I laughed till I shit, 'cause I thought you was dead."
Said, "Done got to where me and my girl can't get a little bit
unless you come around with your roarin' shit."
Said, "Now, you better not roar.
If you do, I'll just walk down out a this tree and kick your ass some more."
Well, the Monkey got excited and jumped up and down,
his foot missed the limb and his ass hit the ground.
Like a streak of lightning and a wave a heat
that Lion had him with all four feet.
Mr. Monkey looked up with tears in his eyes,
"Mr. Lion, please, I want to apologize."
He said, "There ain't gonna be no apologizin' or cryin',
I'm putting an end to your signifyin'."
He said, "Why you big burly bastard, you're in for all sorts of hell,
this whole damn jungle saw how I slipped and fell.
Why, if you'd let me up like a right man should,
I'd kick your ass plumb out a the wood."
Said, "I'd snap at ya, I'd grab at ya, I'd even make a pass,
why, I'd jerk your big, burly head through your little red ass."
That the first time this Lion's ever been challenged by somebody under his size.
Why, he backed up and squared off to fight
and that damned Monkey took a hell of a flight.
Far in the nearest coconut tree
as high as the naked eye could see,
that sonofabitch he flew.
Scratched his head and scratched his chin,
says, "Piss on you , Lion, you're fucked again!"

Deep down in the jungle in the coconut grove
lived the most Signifying Monkey that the world ever knowed.
His eyes were red and his ass was sore,
and everytime he dozed that Lion'd roar.
The Monkey told the Lion one bright summer day,
"There's a bad motherfucker heading your way.
He talked about your brother, put your sister in the shelf,
the way he talked about your mother I wouldn't say to myself."
Now the Lion let out a ferocious rage
just like a young jitterbug blowin' his cage.
Went through the jungle at a terrible pace,
like a young sixteen-year-old with a cunt in his face.
Went through the jungle 'tween coconut trees,
knocking down giraffes to their motherfucken knees.
Then he spied the Elephant under a sycamore tree,
said, "Come on, bad motherfucker, it's just you and me."
The Elephant got up and was in the groove,
said, "You must be constipated and want your bowels removed."
The Lion let out a ferocious roar
and his tail shot out like a forty-four.
He made a pass at the Elephant's back,
the Elephant sidestepped and knocked him dead on his hairy ass.
He broke six ribs, fucked up his face,
jumped on his stomach, and knocked his ass out of place.
They fought all day, and they fought all night,
the Lion begin to wonder if he gonna win this fight.
They fought all night and they fought all day,
the Lion begin to wonder if he gonna get away.
They fought and they fought till the Lion said "Quits,"
'cause he swore he'd get the sonofabitch start this signifying shit.
So back through the jungle more dead than alive,
and that's when the Monkey start his signifying jive.
Said, "Oh, Mr. Lion, you don't look so well,
why it looks like you caught natural hell.
When you left, this old jungle rung,

now you come back damn near hung.
King of the Jungle, why ain't you a bitch?
You look more like a whore with the seven-year itch.
Said, "Now, you sonofabitch, don't you roar,
'cause I'll get down out of this tree and kick your hairy ass some more."
Said, "Every time me and my wife try to get a little bit,
you come around with this 'hi-ho' shit."
Now the Lion looked up to the Monkey, "You know I didn't get beat."
He said, "You're a lyin' motherfucker, I had a ringside seat."
The Lion looked up out of his one good eye,
said, "Lord, let that skinny little bastard fall out of that tree before I die."
The Monkey got frantic, jumped up and down,
his left foot missed, his skinny ass hit the ground.
Like a streak of bolt and a flash of heat,
the Lion was on him with all four feet.
He beat the Monkey till his nose bleed,
that's when the Monkey started his plead.
He said, "Oh, Mr. Lion, almighty friend,
don't you remember the other night we got drunk on gin?"
"Old Kangaroo Kate with the slick-lining jive
gave us some trim for your eighty-five."
Said, "Now, I got a wife with thirteen kids.
What the hell would they do if they found me dead?"
Said, "Monkey, I'm not kicking your ass for lyin',
I'm kicking your hairy ass for signifyin'."
Little by little and bit by bit,
I'm gonna put a stop to all this signifyin' shit."
The Monkey looked up with tears in his eyes,
said, "Mr. Lion, I apologize."
Lion said, "I've heard that shit before,
Monkey, I'm not letting your ass go no more."
The Monkey said, "Let me get my teeth out of the grit and balls out of the
    sand,
and I'll fight your ass like a *real* he-man."
So the Lion stepped back to the end of the curve,
'cause that was the boldest challenge he'd ever heard.
But faster than the hand or the human eye could see,
the Monkey was back in the coconut tree.
Said, "Now, you better be on your way, you hairy slut,
before I split your fucken hair with a coconut."

50A   POOLSHOOTING MONKEY

I don't know but I was told,
the Monkey went out on his morning stroll.
He had on a double-breasted suit and long black robe,
he had his hat crushed down in a Esquire fold.
He had on a long black pair of shoes on a triple-A last,
he had a walkin' stick on his arm and his hair was gassed,
and everybody could tell by the clothes he wore
that he was a poolshooting Monkey from Coconut Grove.
Now the old Baboon was settin' inside on a stool
waitin' on just any old fool.
The Monkey walks in and says, "You know,
I just love and enjoy to see the eight-ball roll."
The Baboon says, "Look, Brother Monkey," say, "down here we shoot the
    eight-ball for fun,
but now if you got any old gold in your clothes, I'll shoot you a little sixty-one."
The Monkey said, "Get you cue stick from the wall,"
said, "now y'all watch this ugly motherfucker when he bust them balls."
The Baboon bust the balls and his tar-ball scratched,
the Monkey set back and relaxed.
The Monkey got up and made the one, two, and three.
He said, "Watch 'em, houseman, while I go pee."
He come from the shitter and he chalked his stick,
he made the four, five, and six.
He made the seven and eight and he banked the nine,
he played the ten, eleven, and twelve in the side.
He played a double combination on the thirteen and fourteen
and raised his cue stick and give the fifteen a chance to ride.
Now the Baboon looks around with a chickenshit grin at all his friends,
he said, "Boys, pool ain't my game but cooncan I'm bound to win."
The Monkey said, "Find a stump that'll fit your rump,
I'll skin you some coon if you don't jump."
Now as the cards was dealt the Baboon spread the one, two, and three and cut
    short fives,
hot boilin' water jumped from his eyes.

That old Bullfrog was settin' on the side,
he dug the switch was made and fell over and died.
Now the Monkey played the one, two, and three and ditched the queen,
he made a switch with the deck that the world never seen.
He said, "I'm pat to aces and I'm pat to queens,"
he said, "I'm pat to your big funky ass if you start any motherfucken thing."
The Baboon jumped up and he grabbed his hat and he grabbed his coat,
he said, "That's all, Brother Monkey," said, "that's all she wrote."
The Monkey said, "Wait a minute, man, just before you go,"
say, "if anybody ask you who win your gold,
you tell 'em that poolshootin' motherfucker out a Coconut Grove."
So now I don't know, but I was told,
the Monkey continued on his morning stroll.

50B   POOLSHOOTING MONKEY

It was in Speero's poolroom in the year eighteen-ten,
the Baboon ran the joint, but it really Mr. Gorilla's den.
Now one day Mr. Bear comes slowly walkin' in,
walked over to the rack, grabbed his cue, and stepped back.
He said, "How about now?
What ugly motherfucker wanna shoot me one?"
Now 'way over in the corner all snuggled by the stove
sit the little old Monkey from the Coconut Grove.
From his ass pocket he drew his cue,
he say, "Hit 'em, big motherfucker," say, "I believe I do."
Two little monkeys had 'em a seat just as high as they could sit,
said, "It ain't gonna be no fun if you folks don't bet."
The Monkey said, "Well, Brother Bear, I been playin' for five but I'm gonna
    play you for ten."
Say, "You flip the coin and see who wins."
Now the Bear flipped the coin and the Monkey win,
picked up his cue and run from the one to the ten,
shot the rest of them straight in.
Bear said, "Houseman, rack 'em and rack 'em quick,"
say, "this little ugly motherfucker think he's slick."
Now the Bear bust the balls and made a few strikes,
but over in the third his tarball scratched.
Said, "Rack 'em."

Little Monkey run the balls, run the one, two, and three,
he stopped and winked his eye at the houseman and said, "I got to go take a
     pee."
He come back and run the four, five, six, seven,
crossbanked the eight, nine, ten, had a dead position of the eleven.
Bear said, "Houseman," say, "don't stand there and stutter,"
say, "I want you to ask that little ugly motherfucker if he goin' any further."
Say, "Now I know you boys think I'm a goddamned fool,
but this little Monkey motherfucker just hustles natural rotation pool."
Said, "Say, ugly Monkey, think you want to have some fun,"
say, "why don't you get you a deck of cards where I can coon you some?"
He said, "Well you get you a stump to fit your rump,
if I don't make you shit, I'll make you jump."
Now they cooned all night and just about the break a day,
the Monkey had the Bear throwin' his high cards away.
Every time the Bear lay a spread the Monkey picked up his discard.
He say, "Hack it, Mr. Buttercup, switch it Mr. Bear,
it look right shitty, but it's eleven cards there."
Now the Bear played the four, five, and six,
he left the little Monkey in a hell of a fix.
The Monkey sevened, mapped the mountain, played the jack, king, and
     queen,
and played a switch on the Bear he ain't never seen.
He said, "Hack it, Mr. Buttercup, switch it, Mr. Bear,
it looks right shitty, but it's eleven cards there."
The Bear said, "Look here, Brother Monkey, I didn't mind you winnin' my
     money as long as you was winnin' it fair,
but I'm gonna break your goddamned neck about that 'switch it, Mr. Bear.'"

50 C   POOLSHOOTING MONKEY

It was in Speero's poolroom back in nineteen-ten,
the gorillas had it, but it was the monkeys' den.
Now the Baboon come strollin' past,
said, "I'm a bad motherfucker and I don't bar none,
is there anybody here would like to try me one?"
Well, Mr. Monkey jumped up and grabbed him a cue,
said, "Yes, motherfucker, I believe I do."

Now the two little Baboons jumped up and said,
"We gonna get us a seat just as high as we can sit,
but it ain't no fun if you motherfuckers don't bet."
So they bets a ten.
Little Monkey leans over and he makes the one, two, and three,
he lays his cuestick on the table and he went to take a pee.
He come back in and then he looked down the line,
he made the four, five, six, seven, and the eight and the nine.
Now it was hid behind the eleven-ball, he couldn't see the ten,
he shot a six-inch curve and kicked that one in.
He ran the eleven and he made the twelve,
and they both went down to the corner like a bat out of hell.
Now the thirteen-ball was a spot shot and, not to fail,
he kicked it on down to the corner rail.
He banked the fourteen-ball across the side,
he shot the fifteen-ball in like a shot out a forty-five.
Then he looked over there at the Baboon and said, "Ain't no need a standin'
    over there with your eyes all green,
because I'm the pool-shootenest motherfucker you ever seen."
Said, "Lookahere, rackman, don't stand there studyin',"
say, "ask this motherfucker do he wanna play another one."
Now the Baboon reached for the rack and the two little Baboons jumped down
    and said,
"Go ahead on and play, you can beat that fool."
He said, "No, Jack, that's his game, hustlin' rotation pool."
Said, "But I don't drink whiskey and I don't drink rum,
just as steady as my nerves is now, I'll coon the motherfucker some."
Now the Monkey said, "Jack, where I come from they call me Cooncan Bill,"
says, "I take a deck a forty and give a chump the chills.
Now if you find a stump that'll fit your rump
I got to beat you if you just don't jump."
Well now they cooned all night and they cooned all day,
the little Monkey had the Baboon throwin' his out cards away.
And every time little Monkey would fold he'd say,
"Fuck it, Mr. Buttercup, fuck it, Mr. Bear,
it looks mighty shitty, but it's eleven cards there."
And he'd flip the last card in the Baboon's face.
The Baboon said, "Looka here, Mr. Monkey, it's all right when you fall from
    your wrist,"
say, "but you makes me mad like a motherfucker when you do like this."

Monkey say, "I knowed you wasn't gonna play this game right,
you done lost your little hand, now you wanna fight.
But you bad motherfucker if you fuck with me," says, "I'll tell you what I'm
    gonna do,
I'm killin' you."
The Baboon said, "Look, Mr. Monkey, don't feel that way,"
says, "I'm gonna play you again when I get my check—off the W.P.A."

50D   POOLSHOOTING MONKEY

Deep down in the stick
the animals had a game, but the Baboon thought he was the motherfucken
    slick.
Up popped a Monkey from the coconut grove,
he's a pool-shooting motherfucker, now Richard knows.
He came up to Richard one bright sunny day,
said, "I'll shoot you a game a pool when I'm down your way."
He wore a double-breast suit and a two-button roll.
So the Monkey went to the poolroom and he tossed for the break.
He won.
He set the one, two, and three,
he said, "Hold my stick, motherfucker, while I go outdoors and pee."
He come back in, he shot the four and the five,
that's when hot boilin' water come out the Baboon's eyes.
He hit the six, seven, kicked the eight corner pocket in the left corner side.
The Baboon walked like a three-legged stool,
said, "He's a ugly motherfucker but he sure can pool."
Down in the jungle by the coconut grove,
was a Signifyin' Monkey and everbody knew him.
One bright sunny day the Monkey told the Lion,
"Say, I went to a party last night and it was a cryin' shame,
if was you, I'd change my name,
the way the Elephant talked about you.
He called your mama a cocksucker, your dad a cotton-picker,
your sister a bulldagger."
Then that Lion was up like a bolt a heat,
knockin' giraffes to their motherfucken feet.
He said, "Come out, motherfucker, up, it's you or me."

Elephant looked out with a tear in his eye.
Said, "Look, mother, pick on somebody your goddam size."
The Lion made a hell of a roar,
his tail straight out like a forty-four.
He then made a hell of a pass,
the Elephant sideswiped him, put two toes down the crack of his ass.
They fought all night and they fought all day,
I don't see how in the hell that poor Lion got away.
He went back through that jungle more dead than alive,
that's when that Monkey started his motherfucken signifyin'.
He said, "Yeah, motherfucker, you told me you was the jungle king,
and now I see you ain't a goddamned thing."
He said, "And don't you roar,
'cause I'm gonna beat your goddamned ass some more."
The Monkey jumped from limb to limb,
his right foot slipped and his ass hit the ground.
The Lion was on him with a bolt of heat.
Monkey said, "Mr. Lion, Mr. Lion, I apologize."
Said, "If you let me get my nuts up off this sand,"
say, "I fight you like a natural man."
The Lion stepped back for a hellofa fight,
the Monkey jumped damn near out of sight.
He went to beating his wife, beating the shit out of his wife.
He said, "Cook me some biscuits."
"Hey, baby," she said, "Hey, babe, what you beatin' me?"
He said, "For thirty long years I been climbing a tree,
damn if I don't believe you pushing me."

51   PARTYTIME MONKEY

Back on the nineteenth of June
all the animals gave a party back down at Brother Coon's.
When the Monkey heard the news he got all excited,
but he was real hot when he found out he wasn't invited.
He say, "I know, when the time come I'll just go."
The next mornin' at the crack of dawn,
he was up tryin' a brand new rig on.
He had a red vest with a bow in the back,

he had a shirt and shoes to match,
he had a yellow tie with a purple suit,
he was clean and he knew it, too.
He went on down to the barber shop to get him a shave and a shine,
he looked at his watch and said, "It's partying time."
He went on to the party and they called him a disgrace
and slammed the door in his motherfucken face.
He said, "I know." He went home and reached over a silver door
and brought down a long forty-four.
He said, "Honey, give me a ten, I'm gonna buy some gin."
He went and bought a fifth a whiskey and a fifth a gin,
he put the whiskey in his pocket and he drank the gin.
He says, "Now I'm gonna kick this partytime door in."
He went to the party, he jumped and shout,
he said, "Who's the bad suckers thought to leave me out?
On some sonofabitch I'm not gonna have no pity,
I'm gonna kick ass until the shoelaces get shitty."
He said, "Listen, you sissies, I don't play,"
he said, "I quit school 'cause they had recess one day.
If there's any schoolgirls in the house will they kindly take a walk,
'cause I'm a drunk sonofabitch and I'm full a bad talk."
He said, "I'm the baddest sonofabitch that ever walked the earth,"
he said, "the doctor ain't spanked me durin' the time of my birth."
'Bout that time he spied the Lion.
He jumped on the table, pissed in the Lion's cup,
said, "Now bad sonofabitch, drink it up.
Get on your knees and say a little prayer
before I put the butt of this forty-four down your motherfucken hair."
The Lion said, "I know you all hot and excited,
you mad 'cause you didn't get invited,"
he say, "but it was the Coon that told us yesterday about a quarter past noon.
He said, "Next time y'all have a party and I get all excited,
there gonna be some badassed happenings if I don't get invited."
He say, "I do what I please,
talk shit, stay drunk seven days a week."

The *Titanic* Toasts

52. *TITANIC*

A. Tom, Ellis, 24 March 1966
B. Joe, Ellis, 25 March 1966
C. Mack, Jefferson City, 24 June 1964
D. Slim, Jefferson City, 24 June 1964
E. Slim, Jefferson City, 14 August 1962
F. Richard, Connelly Migrant Camp, Barker, New York, 17 August 1970
G. Roswell, Wilson, New York, recorded by Judy Kolbas, August 1970
H. Rudy Ray Moore, recorded by James Beyers in the Governor's Inn, Buffalo, New York, June 1970
I. Victor, Wynne, 20 August 1965
J. John, Ramsey, 17 August 1965

Shortly before midnight, April 14, 1912, the White Star liner *Titanic,* on its maiden voyage from Southampton to New York, sheared its side on an iceberg 1300 miles from its destination. The next day, with over 1500 of its passengers and crew, the *Titanic* sank in the icy waters of the North Atlantic. It was the major disaster of the era, and it struck the imaginations of the rich, who lost friends and relatives on the ship, and the poor, to whom the ship represented the great shining and glistening world forever denied them and anyone they would ever know. The newspapers were full of it, people talked about it. The event went into the folk tradition in three ways: a little-known Negro spiritual, a well-known camp and college song, and the widely-known toast. Although Leadbelly wrote a song about the sinking of the *Titanic* (Lomax, 1936:182), it never entered tradition. The folk chose to support one built upon an older spiritual, one that had also served to document the Galveston Flood (see Lomax, 1941:26-27).

The toast seems to exist in black communities throughout the country. Though one of the three most frequently told toasts, it is the only one of the three I have never heard told by whites. The reasons should be obvious.

The A-text, like most versions, has a beginning which sacrifices chronology for euphony ("Fourth a May" is much easier to rhyme and say than "Fourteenth of April"). The narrator situates himself far from the action; we hear no more of his first person in the poem after the introductory lines. The action proper begins with those in command—the captain and the sergeant in this version—"havin' some words" (squabbling like fools when they should be tending to the ship). Shine tells them what is going on, but they reject his information. He in turn rejects them; "but there's one time you white folks ain't gonna shit on Shine," and leaves the ship with "a thousand millionaires lookin' at him." But money is not his first temptation; rather it is the rich man's daughter, standing clumsily "with her drawers around her knees and underskirt around her neck," who offers him sex, which he rejects, then marriage, which he also rejects. Another black, Jim, leaving the ship sees another woman on the deck who makes Shine the same offer. "Jim climbed his black ass back up on that ship," and we hear no more of him. He is the kind of fool Shine is not; he can't delay gratification, and so presumably drowns along with the rich whites. Shine meets the shark, which he outswims, and there is a sulking line I've heard in no other version: "Swim, black motherfucker, 'cause I don't like black meat." While the *Titanic* is going down, Shine is in Los Angeles; by the time it has gone under, he is across the country "damn near drunk." The poem concludes with a quatrain that is really a separate piece, one that not only has an independent existence as a drinking toast, but is on occasion appended to other poems.

Each version of the toast, except the short B-text, ends with a detachable group of lines, lines from another poem. It is almost as if when Shine reaches dry land he is no longer the same man he was at sea, and must therefore be given another, more familiar, identity, one appropriate to a cool stud on dry land.

Except for Jim and the Shark's line, neither of which appears in any other version, the A-text follows the general pattern of the toast. In many versions Shine is propositioned by two women or by one woman twice; the first offer has to do with sex, the second with marriage, and he rejects both.

The F-text is interesting because of its use of uncoupled lines ("So John jumped and began to swim," and "So John said, 'I want me some cock'"), which demonstrates that the poem is perceived in structural blocks. More important is the narrator's confusion of Shine the swimmer with John the trickster. John is the clever slave in antebellum Negro folktales, the man who usually outwits his brutal or clumsy or naive master; after Emancipation, John becomes the hero of the John/boss stories, many of which are the same as the John/master stories altered to fit the new situation. He is the hero who by his wit and acuteness time and again outwits the boss, and sometimes other blacks, and manages to get favors or privileges he would not otherwise get or manages to get off scot-free for deeds that should have gotten him in trouble (See Dorson, 1967, *passim*). But there are no toasts in which John is the protagonist, none at all; he belongs to another world entirely. Shine is no trickster. He has verbal ability and obvious pleasure in saying things, but he tricks no one; his mode is common sense. He is practical in the extreme. It is not until the very end of the narrative in all versions, when he is safe on dry land, that he ceases to be busy and becomes silly or foolish or exhibitionistic. Why should this narrator—and others not printed here—confuse him with John? The link might be that John saves himself by outsmarting the white man; Shine saves himself by refusing the white man's bribes. It is important to remember that Shine does not reject the values of sex and money—only the *place*. He says those things are fine—but not on a sinking ship.

Rudy Ray Moore's nightclub version is similar to the others, but it has four mentions of the word "black" and only one of the word "white." It seems at first curious that in a version for popular consumption there should be little racism if that were really what made the poem work. His ending sequence beginning with "But if I die . . ." is a drinking toast, and his last three lines, beginning with the prose line "Shine died and went to hell," is most commonly found in one of the poems about the badman Stackolee. The uncoupled prose line signals formulaic material from other sources.

B, the shortest text, is a good example of how a mediocre performer can recite the basic structure of the poem. The B-text is bare, lacking the modular units, the extra exchanges in couplets with people on the ship, and the extensions at the end. In the C-text, for example, "The captain and the major was havin' a few words / and the old *Titanic* hit the first iceberg," then a little later, "Captain and the major had a few more words, / and the old *Titanic* hit the second iceberg." Such incremental repetition is the mark of a better folk poet, one who understands the genre and knows how to manipulate his audience and has a stanzaic repertory large enough to effect such manipulation. The temptation sequence in the C-text begins with the captain's offer of money (while four thousand millionaires watch), next a thousand whores offer Shine sex, then the captain's daughter offers him marriage. The C-text has a line similar to the end of the B-text, "I just left the big motherfucker fifteen minutes ago," but it adds a different quatrain.

The C- and H-texts present the captain's daughter as being pregnant. I'm not sure about the meaning of this, unless it is a way of suggesting that she is not the nice virgin a captain's daughter is supposed to be, that trading sex for favors is nothing new to her, that the only thing new is the big step of offering the trade to a black man. But Shine knows any fool can get pregnant and will have no part of her.

The same performer recited the D- and E-texts (one was 1964, the other in 1962), but the earlier text has a character not found anywhere else: the big man from Wall Street. Shine says to him, "You don't like my color and you down on my race / get your ass overboard and give these sharks a chase." The character disappears from the action for ten lines, but then he is reintroduced in a line so long it adds to the comic effect: "Big motherfucker from Wall Street told the sharks, 'I'm a big motherfucker from Wall Street, you got to let me be.'" The shark's reply is short and simple: "Here in this water, your ass belongs to me."

Richie, who recited the F-text, is one of a group of migrant workers who make their permanent homes in northern Florida; this accounts for the reference to Jacksonville near the end of the poem in a slot usually filled by New York or Harlem. All the Florida versions I collected end with Shine's master sexual feat, but this version also has tacked on a slightly garbled version of another toast about a sexual hero who loses his genitals because of venereal disease.

The twelve-year-old boy who recited the G-texts recited much of the narrative in prose; only the indented lines were recited with a verse stress. The term "jelly" in that text is a euphemism for sexual intercourse. John's J-text is almost completely sanitary; for some reason he didn't want to use the regular words that day. I include it to give some idea of the kind of manipulation a performer can do with a well-known text.

For more on *Titanic* see Abrahams (1970A:101-103, 120-129, and 1970B:44-45), Jackson (1972B), and Labov et al. (1973:334-336). A rather bizarre text is described by Eddington (1973:648).

52A   *TITANIC*

All the old folks say the fourth a May was a hell of a day.
I was in a little seaport town and the great *Titanic* was goin' down.
Now the sergeant and captain was havin' some words
when they hit that big iceberg.
Up come Shine from down below,
he said, "Captain, captain," say, "you don't know,"
say, "we got nine feet of water over the boiler-room floor."
And the captain said, "Go on back and start stackin' sacks,
we got nine water pumps to keep the water back."
Up come Shine from down below,
he said, "Captain, captain," says, "You don't know,
we got forty feet of water over the boiler-room floor."
He said, "Go on back and start stackin' sacks,
we got nine water pumps to keep the water back."
Shine said, "Your shittin' is good and your shittin' is fine,"
say, "but there's one time you white folks ain't gonna shit on Shine."
Now a thousand millionaires was lookin' at him
when he jumped in the ocean and he begin to swim.
Rich man's daughter came up on deck
with her drawers around her knees and underskirt around her neck.
Like a noonday clock Shine stopped
and his eyes fell dead on that cock.
She says, "Shine, oh, Shine," says, "save me please,"
say, "I give you all the pussy that your eyes may see."
He said, "I know you got your pussy and that's true,
but there's some girls on land got good a pussy as you."
She said, "Shine, oh, Shine," say, "please save my life,"
say, "I'll make you a lawfully wedded wife."
He said, "Your shittin' is good and your shittin' is fine,
but first I got to save this black ass of mine."
Now was another fella by the name of Jim,

he jumped in the ocean and he begin to swim.
Another girl ran up on deck
with her drawers around her knees and underskirt around *her* neck.
Like a noonday clock Jim stopped
and his eyes fell dead on that cock.
Now she had long black hair that hang from the crown of her head to the nape
of her belly,
she had a twenty-pound pussy that shook like jelly.
Say, "Shine, oh, Shine," says, "save me please,
I'll give you everything that your eyes may see."
And before the last word could fall from her lip,
Jim climbed his black ass back up on that ship.
Up come a shark from the bottom of the sea,
said, "Look what godalmighty done sent to me."
Shine bowed his neck and showed his ass,
"Get out the way, let a *big* shark pass."
And after old shark seen that Shine had him beat,
he said, "Swim, black motherfucker, 'cause I don't like black meat."
About four-thirty when the *Titanic* was sinkin',
Shine done swimmed on over in Los Angeles and started drinkin'.
But now when he heard the *Titanic* had sunk
he was in New York damn near drunk.
He said, "Ladies and gentlemen," say, "when I die don't ya'll bury me at all,
soak my balls in alcohol and lay my old rod up across my breast,
and tell all the peoples old Shine has gone to rest."

52B   *TITANIC*

It was sad indeed, it was sad in mind,
April the fourteenth of nineteen-twelve was a hell of a time,
when the news reached a seaport town
that the great *Titanic* was a sinking down.
Up popped Shine from the deck below,
says, "Captain, captain," says, "you don't know."
Says, "There's about forty feet of water on the boiler-room floor."
He said, "Never mind, Shine, you go on back, and keep stackin' them sacks,
I got forty-eight pumps to keep the water back."
Shine said, "Well, that seems damned funny, it may be damned fine,

but I'm gonna try to save this black ass of mine."
So Shine jumped overboard and begin to swim,
and all the people standin' on deck watchin' him.
Captain's daughter ran on the deck with her dress above her head and her
    teddies below her knees,
and said, "Shine, Shine, won't you save poor me?"
Say, "I'll make you as rich as any shine can be."
Shine said, "Miss, I know you is pretty and that is true,
but there's women on the shore can make a ass out a you."
Captain said, "Shine, Shine, you save poor me,
I make you as rich as a shine can be."
Shine say, "There's fish in the ocean, whales in the sea,
captain, get your ass in the water and swim like me."
So Shine turned over and began to swim,
people on the deck were still watchin' him.
A whale jumped up in the middle of the sea,
said, "Put a 'special delivery' on his black ass for me."
Shine said, "Your eyes may roll and your teeth may grit,
but if you're figurin' on eatin' me you can can that shit."
Shine continued to swim, he looked back, he ducked his head, he showed his
    ass,
"Look out sharks and fishes and let me pass."
He swimmed on till he came to a New York town,
and people asked had the *Titanic* gone down.
Shine said, "Hell, yeah." They said, "How do you know?"
He said, "I left the big motherfucker sinkin' about thirty minutes ago."

52C   *TITANIC*

In the year of eighteen-twelve
so many lives were lost it's hard to tell.
Now the story's true in every way,
but the third of May was a hell of a day.
The captain and the major was havin' a few words
and the old *Titanic* hit the first iceberg.
Shine come from the decks below,
he said, "Captain, captain, don't you know:
there's forty foot a water on the boiler-room floor."

Captain say, "Shine, Shine, that can't be a fact,
I got too many pumps to keep that water back.
Go back and get another blow."
Captain and the major had a few more words,
and the old *Titanic* hit the second iceberg.
Shine come from below the deck
with a lifesaver around his neck.
He say, "Captain, captain, I can't work no more.
Don't you know there's forty foot a water on the boiler-room floor."
Captain say, "Shine, Shine, that can't be a fact,
I got four hundred pumps to keep that water back.
Go back and hit another blow."
Shine said, "Captain, captain, can't you see,
this ain't no time to bullshit me!"
I'd rather be out on that big ocean going 'round and 'round
than be on this big motherfucker slowly sinkin' down."
Shine jumped in the water and commenced to swim,
four thousand millionaires watchin' him.
Captain say, "Shine, Shine, save poor me,
I'll make you richer than old John D."
Shine turned around and took another notion,
say, "Captain, your money's counterfeit in this big-assed ocean."
Then from below the deck came a thousand whores
with their drawers in their hands and their tits around their neck.
They say, "Shine, Shine, save poor me,
I got the best white pussy you ever did see."
He says, "I'm sorry, ladies, but I [gotta] go,
but there's better pussy on yonder shore."
Then from below the deck came the Captain's daughter
with her drawers in her hand and her tits around her neck.
She said, "Shine, Shine, save poor me,
I'll make you the best white wife you ever did see."
He say, "I'm sorry, lady, but you 'bout to have a kid,
so jump and split the water like old Shine did."
Shine took a overhand stroke
that carried him five miles from that sinkin' boat.
Up popped a whale with a slimy ass,
say, "You a long time coming, but you here at last."
Shine said, "You swallowed old Jonah and spit him on dry land,
but you'll never swallow me 'cause I'm a hell of a man."

Folks on the land were singin' "Nearer my God to Thee,"
The sharks in the ocean were singin', "Bring your ass to me."
Shine split the water like the battleship *Maine,*
the way he hit that New York harbor was a goddamned shame.
He spread it around town
that the *Titanic* was slowly sinking down.
They say, "Shine, how you know?"
He say, "I just left that big motherfucker fifteen minutes ago."
When the news reached Harlem that the *Titanic* had sunk,
Shine was in a whorehouse damn near drunk.
He said, "Now, whore, don't sit there with your mouth poked out,
'cause I'm a swimmin' motherfucker and a water trout."

52D   *TITANIC*

I don't know, but my folks say,
eighth a May was a hell of a day.
News reached the little seaport town
that the old *Titanic* was about to go down.
They tell me on board was a fella called Shine,
he was so dark he changed the world's mind.
Shine came up from the bottom deck below,
he said, "Captain, there's water runnin' all in the firebox door,
and I believe this big motherfucker's gonna overflow."
Captain said, "Shine," say, "You go back down,
I got forty horsepower to keep the water pumped down."
Shine went down and came up with a teacup in his hand,
He said, "Look here, captain," says, "I'm a scared man.
I'd rather be out there on that iceberg goin' around and 'round
than to be on this big raggedy motherfucker when it's goin' down."
Shine hit the water and he began to swim,
with ninety-nine millionaires lookin' at him.
Captain came out on the second deck, he said, "Shine, Shine, if you save poor
        me,"
say, "I'll make you as rich as any black man can be."
Shine said, "There's fish in the ocean, there's whales in the sea,
Captain, get your ass overboard and swim like me."
Now the captain's daughter came out on the second deck,

brassiere in her hand and drawers around her neck.
She say, "Shine, Shine, if you save poor me,"
say, "I'll give you all this white ass your eyes can see."
Shine say, "One thing about you white folks I couldn't understand:
you all wouldn't offer me that pussy when we was all on land."
Now Shine was swimin', he was screamin' and yellin',
his ass was kicking water like a motorboat propeller.
Swimmed on down by the Elbow Bend,
there he met the devil and all a his friends.
Shark told Shine, say, "A bite a your ass would be a wonderful taste,"
Shine said, "Man, it sure be a motherfucken race."
Then a stewardess came out on the second deck,
in his hand he held a book a check.
"Shine, Shine, you save poor me,"
say, "I'll make you as rich as any black man can be."
Shine says, "Your money's good, it's good as gold,
but there's other shit on the other shore."
Say, when the news finally got around
that the old *Titanic* had finally gone down,
there was Shine on Main Street, damn near drunk,
tellin' every motherfucker how the *Titanic* sunk.
Now a whore said, "Shine," say, "darlin'," say, "why didn't you drown?"
Said, "I had a cork in my ass, baby, and I couldn't go down."

52E   *TITANIC*

The eighth a May was a hell of a day.
I don't know, but my folks say.
The news reached the little seaport town
that the old *Titanic* was finally goin' down.
Say now there was a fella on board they called Shine,
he was jet black and he change anybody's mind.
Shine came up from the bottom deck below,
said, "Captain, water's runnin' all in the firebox doors,
and I believe to my soul
this big motherfucker's fixin' to overflow."
Captain says, "Shine," says, "you go back down,
I got forty horsepower to keep the water pumped down."

Shine went down and came up with a teacup in his hand,
he said, "Look here, captain, say, I'm a scared man.
I'd rather be out there on that iceberg goin' around and 'round
than to be on this big motherfucker when it's goin' down."
Shine jumped overboard and he begin to swim,
with ninety-nine millionaires lookin' at him.
Shine swimmed on down by the Elbow Bend,
there he met the devil and all a his friends.
Big man from Wall Street came on the second deck.
In his hand he held a book a checks.
He said, "Shine, Shine, if you save poor me,"
say, "I'll make you as rich as any black man can be."
Shine said, "You don't like my color and you down on my race,
get your ass overboard and give these sharks a chase."
Say, the captain's daughter came out on the second deck
with her drawers in her hand and brassiere around her neck.
She said, "Shine, Shine, if you save poor me,"
say, "I'll give you all this ass your eyes can see."
Shine said, "There's fish in the ocean, there's whales in the sea,
get your ass overboard and swim like me."
Now Shine was swimmin' and screamin' and yellin',
his ass was kickin' water like a motorboat propeller.
Shine was doin' ninety, he begin to choke,
fell on his back and he begin to float.
Big motherfucker from Wall Street told the sharks, "I'm a big motherfucker
      from Wall Street, you got to let me be."
Sharks say, "Here in this water, your ass belongs to me."
Shark told Shine, say, "A bite of your ass be a wonderful taste."
Shine say, "Man, it sure be a motherfucken race."
Now when the news finally got around
that the old *Titanic* had finally gone down,
there was Shine on Main Street damn near drunk
telling everybody how the *Titanic* sunk.
A bitch said, "Shine," say, "daddy," say, "why didn't you drown?"
He said, "I had a cork in my ass, baby, and I couldn't go down!"

The tenth of May was a hell of a day
when the great *Titanic* was sinkin' away.
Hit the iceberg, that's what Richard [the performer] heard.
Shine on the fifth floor, captain on the sixth floor.
Shine come up from the deck below,
big old black dick all over the floor.
Saying, "Captain, this here gonna sink."
He say, "John, oh, John, fear no doubt,
I got forty-nine pumps to keep the water out.
So go and pump a little more."
Shit! Shine come up from deck below,
draggin big old black dick all over the floor.
"Captain," he say, "we gonna sink."
He say, "John, oh, John, fear no doubt,
I got forty-nine pumps to keep the water out."
John say, "Yeah, captain, your word might be true,
but here's one goddamned day your word won't do."
So John jumped and begin to swim
with all those millionaires looking after him.
A millionaire's daughter came up on deck,
had her drawers around her neck.
She had nips on her titties sweet as plums,
she had hair on her cock [that would] make a dead man come.
[On another occasion Richard said: "She had nips on her titty that make a
dead man come, / She had hairs on her cock that make a dead man run."]
She said, "Shine, oh, Shine, please save me,
I give you more pussy than a motherfucker see."
Shine say, "A nickel is a nickel, a dime is a dime,
get your motherfucken ass over the side and swim like mine."
Shine made two strokes
and water shot out a his ass like a two-ton motorboat.
So Shine begin to swim, runnin' with a shark.
Shark say, "Shine, oh, Shine, you better swim fast,
I got thirty-two teeth in the crack of your ass."
Shine say, "I outswim the white man, I outswim the Jew,

I know motherfucken well I can outswim you."
The little baby shark say, "Mama, mama, fear no doubt,
he swim like a fish and he taste like a trout."
Say when the great *Titanic* had sunk,
John was in Jacksonville damn near drunk.
So John said, "I want me some cock.
Now I'm gonna line a hundred whores up against the wall,"
say, "I'm gonna fuck 'em all in a hour's time."
So John fucked ninety-eight and he thought he was through.
He said, "Beat it, whore, I'm gonna get me a oyster stew."
He come back and fucked the other two.
He went to the doc, said, "I'm stupid like a goddamned fool."
Doctor cut his nuts off up to his dick.
He said, "Doctor, doctor, are you through?"
He said, "Hell, no, motherfucker, your dick's goin' too!"

52G   *TITANIC*

This is about Shine O Shine. The captain was on his boat and he was
white. Shine runnin' around, he say, "Captain, water on the first floor!"
   "I don't give a damn if it's on the second floor."
   He say, "Captain, water on the second floor!"
   "I don't give a damn if it's on the third floor."
   "Captain, captain, water on the third floor!"
   "I don't care if it's on the fourth floor."
   "Captain, captain, water on the fourth floor."
So the ship sunk. Everybody started strokin' out. Shine O Shine, he
strokin' on. So Shine met up with the captain. He say,
   "Shine O Shine, please save me,
   I give you more money than your eyes can see."
Shine O Shine say,
   "Money on land, money on sea,
   Money on land is just for me."
Shine kept on a strokin'. He
met up with the captain's wife. She say,
   "Shine O Shine, please save me,
   I give you more jelly than your eyes can see."
   He say, "Jelly on land, jelly on the sea,
   Jelly on the land is just for me."

And here go the captain's daughter, same age Shine is, and,
    "Shine O Shine, please save me,
    I give you more than your eyes can see."
[Miss Kolbas says, "More what?" and the narrator and two friends, also twelve,
        burst out laughing.]
He met up with a shark. He say,
    "Shine O Shine, you're strokin' fine,
    miss one stroke, your ass is mine."
That's what the shark say. Shark took after Shine O Shine who was strokin'
out. So Shine got on land, So Shine say,
    "I lay a hundred womens against the wall,
    I fucked ninety-eight, my balls turned blue,
    I bet you a hundred dollars I fuck the other two."

52H   *TITANIC*

The twelfth of May was one hell of a day
when the news got around to all the seaport towns
that the great *Titanic* was sinkin' down.
Up stepped a black man from the deck below that they called Shine,
hollerin', "Captain, captain, don't you know,
there's forty feet of water on the boiler-room floor."
The captain said, "Go back, you dirty black,
we got a thousand pumps to keep this water back."
Shine bent back below and begin to think,
said, "Hm, this big bad motherfucker is bound to sink."
Shine said, "There's fish in the ocean, crabs in the sea,
but it's one time you good cool white people ain't gonna bullshit me."
Shine went on the deck, jumped overboard,
waved his ass, begin to swim,
with a thousand millionaires lookin' at him.
The captain's wife stepped on the deck,
sayin', "Shine, Shine, please save poor me,
I'll give you all the good pussy you can see."
Shine said, "Oh, pussy's good, and that is true,
but there's some whores down on Fifth Street'll make a ass out a you.
There's pussy on land and pussy on sea,
I got twenty-five whores in New York just waitin' for me."

Captain's daughter stepped on the deck,
said, "Shine, Shine, please save poor me."
Said, "I'll name this little kid after thee."
Shine said, "Bitch, you're knocked up and goin' [to] have a kid,
but your ass got to hit this water just like old Shine's did."
Here come the captain.
Say, "Shine, Shine, please save me,
I make you rich as any shine can be."
Shine said, "Captain, to save you would be very fine,
but I got to first save this black ass of mine."
Said, "There's money on land and money on sea,
I got a thousand dollars in New York just waitin' on me."
Shine said, "Shark, look out!"
Said, "I know some of this black ass you'd like to taste,
but from here to New York is gonna be one hell of a race."
When the news got around the world that the great *Titanic* had sunk,
Shine was in Harlem on 125th Street damn near drunk.
Shine spent all of his money, fucked his twenty-five women, dick got sore,
went to the doctor, doctor said, "Shine, I'm gonna have to cut your dick off."
Shine said, "Doctor, you'd better cut it off down to the motherfucken bone,
'cause if you leave any meat, I'm gonna fuck right on.
But if I should die have my balls soaked in alcohol, lay my ticker on my chest,
and tell all these goodtime bitches old Shine has gone to rest."
Shine died and went to hell.
The devil said, "All you bitches you better climb the walls,
'cause old Shine's come down here to fuck us all."

521   *TITANIC*

It was sad indeed, it was sad in mind,
that eighteen hundred was a hell of a time.
In nineteen-twelve was too sad to tell
when the news reached all the towns
that the big *Titanic* was sinkin' down.
The captain and the major was having a few words
when the *Titanic* hit the big iceberg.
Say, Shine jumped up from the boiler-room floor,
he said, "Captain, captain, don't you know,
we have forty feet of water below."

He says, "Go on back down, there is no doubt,
we got four, five pumps to keep the water out."
He said, "But captain, captain, don't you know
that this big motherfucker's gonna overflow."
So he jumped overboard and begin to swim
and there's quite a few wealthy peoples lookin' at him.
The rich man's daughter jumped up on the top deck
with her drawers on the floor and dress around her neck.
She said, "Come back, Shine, and save poor me,
I'll make you rich as a shine can be."
Shine say, "White girl, you must think I'm blind,
but I first got to save my black behind."
She said, "Well come back, Shine, and save poor me,
and I'll give you anything in sight you see."
Shine looked back and waved his hand,
said, "You wouldn't give me that pussy when we was on land."
He said, "Now you may be pretty and that is true,
but there's bitches in Brooklyn will make a ass out a you."
So old whale turned over in the bottom of the sea,
said, "Lawd," said, "look what I've done found."
Shine says, "You's a lyin' motherfucker, 'cause I'm New York bound."
He said, "You swallowed Jonah four hundred years ago,
but I'm gonna wear your big ass out from here to shore."
But late over in the evenin' when the water got cool,
Shine said, "If I can just pull to New York harbor I'll be a swimmin' fool.
And if these old sharks will give me any kind of break,
I'm gonna quit this cold-assed ocean and the five great lakes."
Now Shine didn't know he was raisin' no hell,
till he quit the cold-assed ocean and hit the Panama Canal.
He passed the cruisers, destroyers, the sea-goin' plane,
he passed the battleship *Luxion,* the *Washington,* and *Maine.*
He said, "Now I oughta go 'round through Russia, that's the Bering Strait,
but it's best to hold this chickenshit Pacific till the Golden Gate."
When Shine reached New York people was on the panic,
they talkin' about the great *Titanic.*
Shine staggled [sic] through the crowd just about drunk.
He said, "There ain't no use a talkin'," say, "'cause that big motherfucker done
   sunk."
They said, "Shine, oh, Shine, how do you know?"
He said, "I just left the big swimming motherfucker forty years ago."

52J   *TITANIC*

Boys, you remember way back on the day of the eighth of May
the year of nineteen and twelve, was a hell of a day.
Up popped little Shine from the deck below,
sayin', "Captain, captain, you don't know,
'bout forty feet of water on this boiler-room floor."
He said, "Never mind, Shine," say, "You go on back and keep stackin' them
    sacks,
I got forty-eight pumps to keep the water back."
Shine says, "That seems mighty funny 'cause maybe you doin' fine,
I'm tryin' to save this old black body of mine."
So Shine jumped overboard and begin to swim,
all the people were standin' on deck watchin' him.
The captain's daughter jumped on the deck
with her dress above her head and her teddies below her knees.
Sayin', "Shine, Shine," say, "save poor me,"
say, "I'll make you as rich as any shine can be."
He say, "Miss, I know you's pretty and that is true,"
said, "there's women on the shore will make a ass out a you."
Well, Shine turned over and begin to swim
and the people were still watchin' him.
Say, a whale popped up in the middle of the sea
and said, "Put a special delivery on Shine's black ass for me."
Shine say, "Your eyes may roll and your teeth may grit,
but none of this black ass you gonna git."
He swimmed and swimmed till he came to a seaport town.
The people asked had the *Titanic* gone down.
Shine said, "Hell, yeah," they said, "How do you know?"
"I left the big sonofagun sinkin' thirty minutes ago."

Miscellaneous Narratives

53. UPS ON THE FARM

Peter, Wynne, 18 March 1966

"This here is free world," Peter said, "a colored guy made this up." Other than *"Titanic,"* this is the only toast I've heard that expressly deals with white/black problems. Here it is a matter of the white man's trying to screw the black out of his wages. Notice the black's refusal to have the white call him "boy ," and his use of the jargon terms, "Mr. Whitey," and "paddy," and also that the puzzled white is given the cliche gesture of the dumb black in American films before 1955: "He pulls off his hat and begin to scratchin' his hair." A similar prose tale, "Its and Ifs," is found in Dorson (1967:307).

53   UPS ON THE FARM

An old farmer stopped me on the street one day,
I stopped to listen to his conversation and these is the words that he had to say:
"Say, boy, I don't mean you no harm,
but would there be any chance of me gettin' you to go out on my farm?"
I said, "Look here, Mr. Whitey, I want you to understand,
I'm not no boy, I'm a full grown man.
Now talk to me just like I'd talk to you —
what in the hell is out on your farm that you want me to do?"

He said, "Well, I want you to chop and I want you to plow,
I want you to feed my mules, want you to milk my cow."
I told him to stop right there 'fore he said any more,
I told him in front I wasn't goin' to go.
I told him I wasn't going to chop his cotton and wasn't goin' to plow his corn,
if I saw a mule runnin' off at the world, I'd tell him to go ahead on.
I told this paddy and solemnly did swear,
no more farm for me — too damn many ups out there.
He pulls off his hat and begin to scratchin' his hair,
say, "What you mean by the farm, you say it's 'too many ups out there?'"
I say, "Well, on the farm, early in the mornin' when you wake up,
the next thing you do you got to get up,
there it is, it's a rush up.
You got to get in the lot before sunup,
when you get to the lot you got to catch up,
when you get to the field you got to hook up.
Say the next thing you hollering is to 'Come up.'
All day long you plowing God's ground up,
when you get in at night you all stiffed and stoved up.
Say, on Saturday there's the man you got to look up,
you tryin' to get him to settle up.
He tell you you ain't paid for the groceries you got last week and you done
    already eat up.
That may make you mad and you may frown up,
maybe start to giving him some of that big head up,
and right there them farmers is liable to bunch up,
and right there is where you liable to get fucked up."

54. I GOT A JOB IN FLORIDA FOR CROFT

Eugene, Connelly Migrant Camp, Barker, New York, 22 August
    1970

   This poem also deals with the problems of the farm worker
trying to get his pay, but there is no certainty that Croft, presum-
ably white, has anything to do with the action after the first line.
The violence is connected with the foreman, who may be black.
Notice the curious use of the word "bitch" for a male — either an
inversion or elliptical for "son of a bitch."

54 I GOT A JOB DOWN IN FLORIDA FOR CROFT

I got a job down in Florida for Croft.
The foreman got drunk and cut the payroll off.
I said, "Look here, man, when you fuck with my money you fuckin' with me."
He said, "Aw, boy, go on, I'll pay you next week."
I said, "Uh uh, me and *my* family got to eat."
I grabbed that bitch and knocked him on the floor,
he scuffled down there like somebody having a stroke.
I grabbed him again and slapped him other side of the jaw
a babe jumped up and said, "Don't hit him or do I call the law?"
I said, "Look here, do anybody know this bitch before I take his life?"
Another babe jumped, "Yeah, I'm his wife."
I said, "Looka here: All 'round my house is painted in red,
up over my door is skeleton head,
I buy my groceries and I pay my rent,
I don't ask no motherfucker for a damned cent."
But you think I say this shit to be funny:
that bitch went on and got my money.

55. ONCE I LIVED THE LIFE OF A MILLIONAIRE

A. "Once I Lived the Life of a Millionaire," John, Ramsey, 17
   November 1965
B. "Down and Out," Homer, Jefferson City, 24 April 1962

This toast is partially parallel to Jimmy Cox's Depression song, "Down and Out" (in Shirley, 1963:87-89), but there is no way to tell which was in circulation first. Labov et al. (1973:337) include part of this text. Abrahams (1970B:124-125) prints a text from Austin.

55A ONCE I LIVED THE LIFE OF A MILLIONAIRE

Once I lived the life of a millionaire,
I spent my money and I didn't seem to care.
I'd take my friends out for a good time,
bought 'em whiskey, beer, and wine.
Finally I got broke and got in soak,
I asked one for a dime, he wanted to cut my throat.
Boys, you must learn what it's all about,
'cause nobody knows you when you're down and out.
But if ever I get my hand on a dollar again,
I'm holdin' it till the eagle turn to a sittin' hen,
and 'fore a joker can get a dime,
he got to be born bald-headed, crippled, and blind.
He got to have both his legs cut off above his knees,
suffering with the tuberculosis and the heart disease,
and from his blind eyes he got to be sheddin' briny tears
and got to be wearin' his crutches up under his ears,
even got to have that old German flu,
and every rib in his body cryin', "What shall I do?"
He got to show me a letter written in red
that his grandma is sick and his grandpa dead,
and I got to see the hearse standin' before the door
with the motor runnin' just rarin' to go.
But he got to come over with another letter at the very same time
that his mama is sick and his papa is dyin'.
Now if he come to me with that kind a line,
maybe I'll make up my mind to loan him a dime.

55B DOWN AND OUT

Boys, I used to live the life of a millionaire,
spendin' my money without a care,
and takin' my friends out for a good time,
buyin' good whiskey and the best of wine.

Now that I has fell so low
I has no friends and no place to go.
But I've made up in my mind that I was gonna take a dollar to be my friend
and I'm gonna hold that motherfucker until the eagle grin.
Say, now, Jack, that I'm back on my feet
many of my old friends I can meet.
Now one day while walkin' down the street
I met a pal a mine called Piccolo Pete.
He said, "How are ya there, pal a mine?"
Said, "How's chances a me borrowin' a dime?"
I said, "Lookit here, Jack, I'm not flyin' no more kites
and I'm not sayin' this to bring on no fights,
but you gotta be born blind, crippled, and cannot see,
and both your legs cut off up above the knee,
you gotta have the T.B. and the German flu,
you gotta have crabs crawlin' up and down your back singin' 'Yankee Doodle
    Do,'
you gotta walk a barb-wire fence twenty miles or more,
just to wrassle with a she-lion and dare the he-lion to roar,
you got to wrassle with the he-lion and throw him down in a gutter,
you got to look up a cow's asshole and tell me the price a butter,
you got to bring me the Wriggly Building in a paper sack,
and kiss a camel in his ass and draw the hump out a his back.
You got to show me the place where Eve and Adam hid,
and walk the water like the good Lord did,
and when elephants start roostin' in trees
and poor people stop eatin' black-eyed peas,
you bring me the news that your grandma's dyin'
and you mammy's pussy is runnin' your pappy blind,
and your sister got the pox all around her belly,
and your whole damn family's got a stroke from cryin',
you come go with me and I *might* introduce you to a friend of mine
and maybe he'll loan you a thin, thin dime,
because Jack, I've made up in my mind that I was gonna take a dollar to be my
    friend,
and I'm gonna hold that motherfucker just as tight as I can,
because, Jack, that's the only friend."

56. LIFE'S A FUNNY OLD PROPOSITION

Slim, Jefferson City, 13 August 1962

Slim said, "You go through life, you stumble along, you pick up bits here and there and, I don't know, you get it all together . . . . Here's one my father told me." A similar poem, "The Great Jest," was sent to John A. Lomax from the Federal penitentiary at Leavenworth sometime in the 1930s (John A. Lomax Papers), so, although I have not been able to find the printed source, I assume a version of this must have been published somewhere.

56   LIFE'S A FUNNY OLD PROPOSITION

Life's a funny old proposition, from the cradle to the grave,
and it matters not your calling, be you rich man, beggar, or slave.
A man comes to birth on this funny old earth with not a chance in a million to
　　win,
to find that he's through and his funeral is due before he can even begin.
He gets one fleeting look at life's mystery book and the curtain rings down the
　　show,
before he gets set, he finds he's all wet, washed up and ready to go.
He'll stumble and strive with this thing called life, but a man at his best is a
　　slave,
stumblin' at a grind like the rest of his kind till at last he pulls up in the grave.
The thing never stands, the tightly drawn strands seem to fall apart like
　　sand-woven rope,
and all you get is a record of debts you fail to cash in if you're broke.
Nine-tenths of the time you're not worth a dime, and the whole damned thing
　　was a joke.

57. HOBOES' CONVENTION

Victor, Wynne, 18 August 1965

Victor claims he wrote this after years of hoboing, but the poem is well known in hobo tradition. Milburn (1930:28-30) prints a similar text; most of the differences have to do with the order of events and some nicknames. Milburn says: "The gathering described took place in the summer of 1921, and came off successfully without any assistance from the Portland, Oregon, Chamber of Commerce. A delegate named George Liebst has been credited with the present song, but it follows closely earlier convention anthems, and its purpose, that of introducing monikas [hobo nicknames] is the same" (28). John A. Lomax received a variant of this poem from the United States Reformatory at Chilocothe, Ohio, taken down from the recitation of the "Kansas Kid" in July 1935.

57   HOBOES' CONVENTION

Say, you talk about your big convention, here's one you won't forget,
now get me straight there is none so great, [as] when all the hoboes met.
From Portland, Oregon, last year, they came from near and far,
on tops and blind where the cinders whine, they rode on every car.
It was on the third of June one Sunday afternoon, they gathered in a mass.
Some was from the Lone Star states, and some was from the Eagle Pass.
There was Texas Slim, he was from the Lone Star State, there was Jack the
     Katydid,
there was Lonesome Lou from Kalamazoo blew in with the San Diego Kid.
There was Denver Bob and Boston Red, blew in with Hell Fire Jack,
Andy Lang from the Lakeshore Gang and Big Mac from the Mackinac.
There's a few more 'bos I do not know, but if I can remember I will tell you so.
There was a hobo called New York Spike,
Candy Sweet from the Battle Creek, and Mississippi Ike.
Old Bill Boss peeled out a song, along with Desperate Sam,
while Paul the Shark from the Tourist Park clog-danced with Alabam'.
Shapeless Slim and Bashful Tim fixed up our jungle stew,
while Paul the Shark from the Tourist Park chopped meal for our menu.
Now old New York Bill dressed like a bull, he shook hands with Frisco Fred,
while little Halfbreed Joe from Mexico shot craps with Eastport Ed.
We gathered 'round the jungle fire, the night was passing fast.
We all had did time for other crimes and talk was of the past.
We set around the railroad yard until the morning sun;
from the town the cops come down, we had to beat it on the run.
We scattered through the railroad yards, we left the bulls far behind,
a thousand caught freights for other states, and me, I rode the blinds.

I got bluffed off in Denver, Colorado, a tired, hungry 'bo,
But when the train come through I'm goin' catch it, and I got to blow.
Now I hear the whistlin' down the block, I got to catch it on the fly,
Because it's that old number nine on the D and R G W line, I'm off again —
      bye, bye.

58. JUNKIES' BALL

Slim, Jefferson City, 13 August 1962

59. JUNKIES' HEAVEN

Nate, Ramsey, 17 November 1965

60. HOPHEAD WILLIE

Joe, Ellis, 24 March 1966

61. WILLIE THE WEEPER

Phil, Wynne, 7 July 1964

The list of names in the first part of "Junkies' Ball," as in #46, "Voodoo Queen," and #57, "Hoboes' Convention," follows the form and metric pattern of the hobo monika poems discussed by Milburn (1930:*passim*). Nate, himself a dope addict for many years, said he'd heard #59, "Junkies Heaven," a parody of "'Twas the Night before Christmas" recited by many other addicts. A different version, from New York, is reported by Labov et al. (1973: 342).

"Hophead Willie" and "Willie the Weeper" are both grand fantasies. "Hophead Willie" is perhaps the ultimate dream of the man who is down and out: coming back with a boxful of money to say a fine "fuck you" to those who weren't available when times were hard. "Willie the Weeper" has been around for a very long time. The Galveston (Texas) *News,* on 9 April 1911, in an article about smoking hop (opium), included a version of this poem. There is also a text in Kennedy (1962:82-83).

It was late one day and I was on my way
to dig my partner Dan.
See, Dan was goin' to court the next day
and we all knew he wasn't comin' back.
So we gave this thing and the junkies sing
while Dan talked shit to his partner Mike.
Now there was Hooshoo Bess and Teardrop Tess,
and, with the hair of his ass close to the curb,
Deacon Herb and Bakin' Soda Bo.
Standin' in the corner was Air Bubble Ann,
lookin' oh my God so foxy,
and over her head with her hair dyed red
was Jasper Ass Huntin' Roxy.
"Break out the dope, man, let's have some fun.
For God's sake, boys, don't forget the gun [hypodermic syringe]."
"Willie, my man, I missed my vein,"
cried Mike with a spike [hypodermic needle] in his arm.
"Don't give up hope when you blow off your dope,"
this was the thing I said.
"I'll give you some of mine any time
in turn for some of your motherfucken head [fellatio]."
"Is this a drunk or is this a skunk?"
asked Small Crack Nadine with a spike in her thigh.
"It's your stinkin' assed cunt, bitch," said Chi Chi the Snitch,
"you got your motherfucken dress too goddamned high."
Although little Herb never said a word,
we knew he loved Nadine like a square man did his wife,
and we also knew before the end of the day,
that joke was gonna cost T.J. his motherfucken life.
Now the whores was a sighin' and the funk was flyin',
Nadine broke the silence with a fart,
T.J. the Snitch made one last twitch
and died with a shank in his motherfucken heart.
"Throw him outside, let the cats lick his bones,
we don't want his death to spoil our fun."

And hurled right back the same voice cracked,
"'Cause, Jack, I want a shot of two-in-one [cocaine and morphine]."
"Hold it, now, you fellas know I'm the deacon of a church,
and it's my duty to say a word over the dead.
Oh, Lord up there, here comes this square,
broke, beat, and busted, and without a doubt
he has no friends. My God: Kick him out.
If you let this motherfucker through your pearly gates,
— my God, if you have ears please hear this prayer —
he'll give your angels a shot of cocaine
and the lousy motherfucker in Heaven'll nod till I get there."

59   JUNKIES' HEAVEN

It was the night before Christmas and all through the pad
cocaine and heroin was all the cats had.
Stuffed in the icebox, stacked real high,
they had cocaine cookies and morphine pie.
Now me and my pal Hookamonie and my pal Doc
had all settled down for a heroin shot,
while the rest of the cats was knocked out and snuggled in bed,
visions of opium just danced in their head.
The stockings was hung by the foot of the bunk,
hoping that St. Nick would soon fill 'em with junk.
While out on my lawn there rung such a platter,
I rose from my bed like prayers up and at 'em.
But what to my wonderin' eyes would appear?
A '59 Cad in second gear.
I knew in a minute the man was here.
He banged on my door and he kicked it rough,
he called me a dukie-head and demanded my stuff.
He lay the tracks of a new electric train,
he sprinkled my tree with flakes of cocaine.
The room was filled with reefer smoke,
one agent got high and soon told a joke.
Another agent sold his pussy for forty-four sticks,
he smoked like a madman and soon got his kick.
The cats put on a platter by Miles and Bird,

the terriblest jam I ever heard.
If any ask you who told this toast,
just tell 'em old Bullshitting Nate off the West Coast.

60   HOPHEAD WILLIE

So you say you're glad to see me, old pal.
Well, how in the hell did things ever get thataway?
After all this time I spent up the river not one word did you have to say.
All my friends put me down and not one letter did I get,
and my head hung low in deep regret.
For six long years I stood the task and took my bitters in-between,
just to find a friend in need is a friend indeed
and lost treasure is cash unseen.
But just today I got lucky, old man, I made me thirty million grand.
I bought eight Packards, six trucks, and a brand new movin' van,
I bought the east side of New York City and the west of dear old Chi,
I bought airports in California that Henry Ford had tried to buy,
I bought a boatload of silk just imported from Japan,
I bought me several fronts, old boy, and each one of them motherfuckers cost
        me a grand.
Now I got me a yacht on every ocean and just a flock of seaside grills,
I bought me fourteen furniture companies and twenty-eight lumber mills.
I bought me six brilliant nightclubs, all built on platoon ties,
I bought a independent railroad, Jim, just to ride for miles and miles.
I bought me six ruby duckeyes and a half a dozen sapphire vines,
I bought oil wells in Oklahoma and just a host of diamond mines.
I bought me nine bossalimas [Borsalinos], half a hundred Stetson hats,
I bought a 1965 Cadillac, Jim, and a high powerful smokin' flat.
Now I got a Chinaman doin' my cookin', I got a Frenchman mending my
        clothes,
I got a Irishman for a chauffeur, and they call my butler "Mose."
For breakfast I have tea, toast, and quail,
and a half a dozen Hollywood secretaries come read my morning mail.
And if I ever feel lonesome or feel just a little bit blue,
there's always five or six bitches come to spend an hour or two.
So you see, old pal, I no longer need your friendship as I did in the dear old
        days gone by,

I knew my day was sure to come, for I had the guts to try.
So bring on the drinks, let's drink them all,
I'm gonna buy you some motherfucken more.
Play "Flatfoot Floogie," Mr. Piano-player, I come from where the greenbacks
    grow.
Say, whose old dog is that running around?
Give him a stick, let the bedbugs bite, don't let the rats go wrong.
Call the stool pigeon over and play him a song.
And just one more thing before I go, to you, boy, this may sound silly,
but you can straighten 'em out in a jiff, old pal, just tell 'em they met
    Hophead Willie.

61   WILLIE THE WEEPER

Say, now, there's little Willie the Weeper,
he's a chimney sweeper.
He had a hop habit and he had it bad.
Now don't think this is real:
this is only a dream that a dope fiend had.

He dreamed he went down in Chinatown one Saturday night,
he know he'd find the lights always shining bright.
He called for the Chink to bring him some hop,
the poor boy started smokin' like he was never gonna stop.

He smoked and he smoked till he fell asleep,
he dreamed he was way out on the ocean deep,
he dreamed he was playin' stud poker when the ship first left the land,
he dreamed he won a cool million dollars on the very first hand.

He dreamed he won a million dollars all in nickels and dimes,
they counted them all over five thousand times.
He even sailed to the island of Siam,
he rubbed his eyes, said, "Now I wonder where in the hell I am."

He even shot dice with the king, he won a million mo',
but he had to leave the island 'cause the king got so'.
Now the queen said, "King, oh, King," said, "now can't you see,"
said, "Little Willie done busted every rich Jew in Galilee."

The king said, "Yeah, he busted me too, baby, and I don't give a damn
if he bust every motherfucker in Bethlehem.
But if you see the little lucky motherfucker before he go,
tell him I wants to sell Egypt and Jericho."

Now that's when the queen called him her little darlin', angel, pet,
she bought him a automobile with a silver disc wrench and a diamond steering
    wheel,
she gave him a rosebush and a diamond tree,
and she gave him forty-four whores just to keep his company.

Then the queen said, "Oh, yes, Willie," said, "the king told me to tell you
    before you go,
that he wanted to sell Egypt and Jericho."
He said, "No, babe, I can't use them 'cause I'm travelin' too fast,
and he's just like I want to see him, on his motherfucken ass.

And by you hangin' round here with him ain't profiting you a damn thing."
He said, "Motherfuck the sonofabitch that caused to call him king."
Said, "Now if you get your bags all packed and quit that big soft chair,"
says, "we'll catch the World-Trans airline and leave his broke ass here."

Now that's when Little Willie sailed to Monte Carlo where they played roll-y-
    ette,
he won another million dollars and he never lost a bet.
He even went to the race track and laid his famous bet,
now the horse he bet on, he ain't stopped runnin' yet.

Little Willie gambled and he gambled all the banks went broke,
Little Willie turned right over and taken him another smoke.
Now little Willie thought he'd charter him a ship to go sailin' back home.

When the ship struck the iceberg Little Willie fell on the flo'.
Now he's the same little raggedy motherfucker that he was before.
Says, now don't you get to drinkin' and smokin' and havin' your fun,
and go off in a dream like Little Willie done.

That's Willie the Weeper.

62. T.B. BEES

Jason, Ellis, 21 August 1965

The "bees" are the gobs of phlegm the tubercular patient coughs up. The toast seems well known in Texas. The main variations occur in the ending line. Others I have heard are "Won't you fill up my little bottle just to help me on my way?" and "Won't you give me one a those old Chesterfields to help me on my way?" One informant said, "A guy composed that and fell dead in 1935. His name was Stanley. That was his last name. And anything could happen, he'd make up some poetry about it. I knew him in thirty-five; that's when he fell dead."

62   **T.B. BEES**

Now, Alex, you know the T.B. Bee have been my complaint,
man, for me to live is a narrow chance.
I once was fat, but now I'm po',
it ain't a chance for me to get fat no mo'.
My people all told me and the doctor told me too,
"Jason, high climate would be the best for you."
I have a hackin' cough, sometimes I spits up blood,
I wanna say goodbye to my friends I love.
Man, I have light fevers and I sweats at night,
I have a poorly, poorly appetite,
I have a hurtin' in my knees,
I got a shortenin' in the breath and it's kinda hard to breathe.
I got a hurtin' in the back and a pain in my chest,
which you know a pain ain't nothin' but a letter from death.
Out of all these rules that we got to obey
we know that some kind of pain has got to carry us away.
Now boy, bein' as I'm goin' and you goin' to stay,
I'll take a good drink of this Thunderbird to help me on my way.
—Shakespeare.

63. THE CHINTZ

64. THE FLY

65. THE ALPHABET

66. THE SEVEN WISE MEN

67. GET IN OUT OF THE RAIN

Peter, Wynne, 26 March 1966

Peter said he made up "The Chintz" while "in jail when the chintzes [bedbugs] was in the mattress." About "The Alphabet": "This is the way I learned my alphabets when I was a little boy going to school. I never could get 'em in rotation until I learned 'em in this manner." He composed "Get in out of the Rain" about a friend in Dallas: "It was raining one day and he called me to come in out of the rain. And when I come in his house I stepped right in a pile of baby shit. He had a bunch of little babies, nasty babies running all around his house. When I got back home I made a poem about it."

63 THE CHINTZ

One night as I awoke a little wee chintz spoke to me as I raised my head.
He said, "Don't you get rough and don't you get tough, for you and I both
    must share this bed."
Now it was a cinch no wee brown chintz was gonna tell me what to do,
so I laughed out aloud and I tried to be proud when away from my bunk he
    flew.
But it is a fact, he did come back, but this time he was ten thousand strong,
and from the looks in their eyes I soon realized that all my pride it was gone.
They said, "So you're the lad and you tried to be bad but with us you can't
    compete,
we'll nibble all over your big red ass until you shit all over this sheet."
I said, "Why is it every night when I go to light you all come right straight to
    me?
There's other guys here in this same old place and they just as fat and juicy as
    me."
But they said, "Don't you get rough and don't you get tough, you lowdown
    dirty pup,
we'll nibble all over your big red ass and we'll eat your red ass up."
Now it won't be long before I'll be gone and then you think that won't be swell:
then some other lad who try to be bad will catch this same old nibblin' hell.

64   THE FLY

Say, a little fly flew past my door,
he flew into a grocery store.
He shit on the cheese, pissed on the ham,
then he wiped his ass on this grocery man.
When the grocery man seen what this little fly had done,
he went and got a flyspray gun.
And he chased this little fly up and down,
and tried to shoot him up his brown.
But this little fly was much too quick,
he showed this grocery man a trick.
He flew around the store again,
then went over and shit on the ham again.
And when he'd did his dirty work,
he flew over to the lady clerk,
and up her leg he took a stroll,
and he took a bath in that lady's hole.
The lady laughed and said, "Oh, my,
you are a very naughty fly."
What made her laugh, you all should know,
that funny sensation, it tickled her so.
She felt so good she rolled on the floor,
she said, "I never felt quite so good before."
But she closed her legs and she held her breath,
and this poor little fly, he was smothered to death.

65   THE ALPHABET

A is for ass, upon it we sit,
    it tunnels in and it's a passage for shit.
B is for balls, each man has a pair,
    with a wrinkled ole sac all covered with hair.
C is for cunt, juicy and slick,
    it's home-sweet-home for a little seven-inch prick.

D is for diddle, it never grows stale,
  there's nothing so good as a nice piece a tail.
E is for egg, it's laid in the grass,
  that's a object that falls from an old hen's ass.
F is for fart, a odor in the breeze,
  smells three times worse than limburger cheese.
G is for guts, they a tangled up mass,
  they separated your belly from the hole in your ass.
H is for hair, they surround the cunt,
  but to find that hole is a man's night hunt.
I is for Ireland, that's the home of the Mick,
  they fight their battle with a crowbar and pricks.
J is for jism, sticky like cream,
  spots up the sheets when dreamin' sweet dreams.
K is for king, wears a crown on his beam,
  but his favorite pastime is fuckin' the queen.
L is for love, it never sticks,
  starts at a man's head, but ends at his prick.
M is for marriage, that's when you get you a wife,
  then you got hell for the rest of your life.
N is for nature, supplies your balls with the sap,
  sometimes you end up a bad dose of clap.
O is for odor, it sures does smell,
  lower your arms, it's raisin' hell.
P is for prick, a pastified [petrified] prong,
  they ranks from seven to twelve inches long.
Q is for quiver, that's a sensational thump,
  when a man blow off his lungs in a woman's hump.
R is for rag to catch the flow from the womb,
  it substitutes for Kotex when menstruation is full bloom.
S is for soap, rub and rub fast,
  Lifeboy soap is good to bathe your ass.
T is for a woman's titties, they supposed to be sucked,
  but they never give milk until she's been fucked.
U is for urinate or a pot of piss,
  but excuse me for speaking such language as this.
V is for vine upon which it holds fast,
  I'll show you how it goes if you'll give me some ass.
W is for woman, she a blade a sin,
  she laughs or whines as you shove it in.

X is for X-ray, that's a magnifying glass,
    you should always use that when you want a enlarged ass.
Y is for yes, when a young girl gets hot,
    she needs a prick to cool her spot.
But Z is for zero, a temperature that's very, very cold,
    that's the temperature of a man's balls when he's around ninety years old.

66   THE SEVEN WISE MEN

There was once seven wise men, they had knowledge fine,
but to build a cunt was their one design.
The first one was a carpenter, he was tall and fit,
with his hatchet he made the slit.
The second one he was a blacksmith, he was black with coal,
he taken his sledgehammer and he made the hole.
The third one was a tailor, he was tall and thin,
with a piece of red flannel, he lined it within.
The fourth one was a furrier, he was old and stout,
with a old bearhide he lined it without.
The fifth was a fisherman, he was tall and bent,
with an old herring he gave it its scent.
The sixth was a preacher, that was old Reverend DeeDee,
he felt it, smelt it, and said it could pee.
But the seventh, he was a rabbi, that darned little runt,
he fucked it and blessed it and called it a cunt.

67   GET IN OUT OF THE RAIN

One day I stopped by this friend of mine's house,
but that's one day that I will never forget.
Man, you couldn't walk around this man's house
without steppin' in a pile of shit.
His windows they were all dirty and most of them were broken out,
and he had little pissy babies and they were running all about.
Snot was dripping from their little nostrils, looked just like the yella from the
    egg,
shit was oozing out their diapers down their filthy little legs.

Now next to this little youngest one was a little two-year-old,
and they all called him little Buster, damn his little soul.
Little Buster he came up to me and he crawled up on my knee,
gas from little Buster's ass burned blisters upon my thighs,
and the piss from little Buster's diapers drawed water to my eyes.
Now the head of that family, which I am gonna call no name,
but that was little Buster's daddy, and damned if he didn't smell the same.
The mama she was a little different, in her middle-age sag,
she was sportin' a pair of her husband's workshoes and wearin' a skirt made out
    of a burlap bag.
There were fourteen babies sleepin' in one bed,
they had seven at the foot, and they had seven at the head.
All the rest of 'em slept on a pallet on the floor
with the mama and the daddy and the baby boy called Joe.
Now you know I don't like to talk about people, because it's all in vain,
it's a sad situation and it's too hard to explain.
But I've said it once before and I'll say it once again:
if I ever stop by this house again, it'll be for the same thing—to get in out of
    the rain.

68   DRINKIN'

Mack, Ellis, 25 March 1966

When your heels fit together and your head feel queer,
your breath start to smellin' like the foam off a beer:
say, man, you been drinkin'.

You get up off the stool and you wobblin' in your knees,
when you staggle out the door you wobble in your knees,
and you wanna knock hell out a everybody you sees:
boy, you high.

Say, now, you staggle up to your house about a quarter to four,
and you knock on the door and your wife meets you at the door
and hits you 'cross the head with a two-by-four:
say, man, you drunk.

Say, she puts you to bed, you wake up in the mornin' about a quarter to ten,
and you count your money again,
then you say to yourself, say, "I have been a drunk motherfucker
but I'm sober again."

69   CONVICT'S PRAYER

Jason, Ellis, 21 August 1965

The warden is my shepherd, I shall always want.
He maketh me to lie down behind the green door,
he leadeth me beside the wagon of salty water,
he kills my soul.
He leadeth me away from the righteousness for his own sake.
Yea, though I walk down the alley of shadow and death
I fear all evil, for he is with me.
His pistol and solitary discomfort me.
He preparest a table for me with all of my enemies,
he balds my head with double-ought clippers, my cup stays empty.
Surely goodness and mercy shall find me one of these days in life
and I will drill away from this house for ever and ever. Hey man.

70. PEARL HARBOR

Neal, Wilson, New York, 6 August 1970; given to me by Judy Kol-
    bas as recorded by Eugene Williams, one of her students

71. HITLER, YOU LIED TO ME

Gene, Connelly Migrant Camp, Barker, New York, 22 August
    1970

   Both these toasts date from the 1940s. Neal said, "The soldier
that wrote this, he was from Beaton, Alabama; his name was Joe
Smith of the 146 Quartermasters. This was in 1943. I learned it
from him in Germany." These two toasts and #18, "Joe the
Grinder and G.I. Joe," are the only toasts I've heard about World
War II.

70   PEARL HARBOR

They say in nineteen hundred and forty-one,
that's when the European war begun.
Old Tojo came to the United States
and him and Mister Roosevelt oh communicate.
Roosevelt say, "Tojo, remember Pearl Harbor,
but you say, 'Damn Pearl Harbor and remember it yourself.'"
Our soldiers and our sailors they was a lying in the sun,
they was eating and fucking and having they fun.
They say, "Lo and behold, look up at the rising sun."
There was a thousand Japs dropping bombs by the ton.
They run out on the deck with their dick in their hand,
they was waiting for the captain to give the command.
But before the whole thing was through,
they found out the captain was fucking, too.
General MacArthur went up the mast,
and the Japs took a crack at his naked ass.
General MacMajor went up to take his place,
and a airplane pilot slung shit in his face.
Out of all the things I saw in my life,
wasn't a man on the island was fucking his wife.
But although they say, "Remember Pearl Harbor if any of us left,"
I say, "Damn Pearl Harbor and remember it yourself."

71   HITLER, YOU LIED TO ME

One morning there was a cloud couldn't be found,
that's when Tojo rose from [his] bed in his white evening gown.
He steps over to the phone, says, "Give me 2609,
I want to talk to a damn friend of mine."
Says, "Hitler, you lied to me."

Say, "You told me go in Pearl Harbor and drop the biggest bomb I had.
That didn't do a damn thing but make Uncle Sam mad."
Say, "But Hitler, you lied to me."

Say, "You know I got some Jap Zeros do very well,
but Uncle Sam got some P-38s burn up old hell."
Say, "But Hitler, you lied to me."

Say, "I'm short of ammunition,
my men on the firin' line short of ammunition
but don't mind dying."
Say, "But Hitler, you lied to me."

"Got me my wife, quiet as a mice,
pissin' and shittin' in the corner a my house.
But Hitler, you lied to me."

72   I USED TO BE A COWBOY

Skip, Cambridge, Massachusetts, 24 November 1964

I used to be a cowboy and I decided I'd quit,
I didn't have a damned thing and I didn't give a shit.
I went to my boss man and I asked him for my roll,
he say, "What you gonna do with it all?"
I said, "I'm goin' downtown and get a little tail."
And I was travelin' and I met a little schoolgirl and I offered her a quarter.
She said, "You must be a damned fool, man, I'm the cowboy's daughter."
And I grabbed her and I kissed her and I laid her on the grass,
I rammed this little golden rod straight up her ass.
And a few days after that I taken sick,
I take a dribblin' at the head and a leakin' at the dick.
I went to the doctor and he set me on the stool,
he said, "What you doin' sittin' up there lookin' like a damned fool?"
Say, "Ain't no use a you sittin' up there lookin' so damn glad,
'Cause I'm gonna cut your fucken dick off up to your damn ass."

73. I WOKE UP THIS MORNING WITH A HARD ON

Neal, Wilson, New York, 6 August 1970; given to me by Judy
    Kolbas as recorded by Eugene Williams

    Neal said he learned this from a girl in a work camp in Virginia.

I woke up this morning with a hard on,
I didn't have a damn thing to start on.

I met a little girl, like a mighty she would,
and I asked her for some just as hard as I could.

She walked down the street, like a mighty she would,
and I walked down behind her just as hard as I could.

She walked in the house, like a mighty she would,
and I went in behind her just as hard as I could.

She pulled off her clothes, like a mighty she would,
and I jumped out of mine just as hard as I could.

She got in the bed, like a mighty she would,
and I jumped over behind her, just as hard as I could.

She opened her legs, like a mighty she would,
and I jumped down between them just as hard as I could.

She booted upcuttin', like a mighty she would,
and I laid it back down just as hard as I could.

She got up and asked me for a dollar, like a mighty she could,
and I kicked her in the ass just as hard as I could.

74. RINGO

Neal, Wilson, New York, 6 August 1970; given to me by Judy Kol-
    bas as recorded by Eugene Williams

I recorded several versions of this poem in Texas in the early
1960s. Neal said he learned it in France while in the army from "a
boy who called himself Guitar Slim, from Humbolt, Tennessee.
He just loved to talk; he'd sit around and tell 'em all day, and I got
him to write me out a few of 'em so I could read 'em at times and
learn 'em." Vicarion (1959:25) has a similar poem, "A Clean

Story," in which the rhyme structure sets up expectations not fulfilled by the text.

74   RINGO

There was a poor man living in the country,
he was diggin in the rich man's ditch,
the rich man call the poor man
a lying son of a ---

Didn't I tell you to whip that boy
and whip him with a stick?
So when he get up big enough
he can skin back the head of his ---

Didn't I tell you about that little dog?
He was a pretty little dog was he.
I lent him to my friend last night
to keep her company.
And all around her bed that night,
the little dog begin to hunt,
all up under her petticoat,
smelling for her ---
Come from under there little dog,
you'll make my passion arise.

I had a can of beer last night,
I choose that for my part.
And I eat a can of pork and beans
and it's about to make me ---

Forty dollars, I shoot,
six bits, I pass.
And my gal took my last pair dice
and ran 'em up her ---

Ask me no question before I tell you a lie,
my gal 'cross town
she got the best ole ---
cock my pistol before I shoot.

75. THROUGH THE KEYHOLE IN THE DOOR

Peter, Wynne, 18 March 1966

There is a version of this in an untitled anonymous collection of bawdy songs from Air Force men in Guam, 1956-1959, in the files of the Institute for Sex Research in Bloomington, Indiana, which is similar to the version in Vicarion (1959:94). In both these versions—unlike the one here—the voyeur has sexual intercourse with the women at the end of the poem.

75   THROUGH THE KEYHOLE IN THE DOOR

This little girl left her parlor quite early, it was scarcely half-past nine,
and just like luck would have it, her room was right next to mine.
But I'm like old wise Columbus, I had me an idea to explore,
I taken me a snap position by the keyhole in her door.

There upon my knees I waited, I was as quiet as I could be,
I waited very patiently, at the things that I might see.
First she began unrobing and she pulls off her pretty dress,
gee, her undergarments, there were fifty more or less.

But to tell you the truth sincerely, it must have been a score,
but I could not tell exactly, through the keyhole in this door.
Upon her slender legs, sky-blue garters she wore,
they made a glimmerin' picture through this keyhole in the door.

Then up before this mirror the pretty maiden she stood,
she was admiring her pretty figure and it almost froze my blood.
My hair it stood up like bristles upon the wild and angry bowl,
I felt just like jumpin' through the keyhole in this door.

Then up before the fireplace her pretty feet to warm,
she had nothing but her teddies on to hide her pretty form.
I cried, "Pull off those teddies and I will ask you nothing more!"
Gee, I could see her do it, through this keyhole in the door.

Then up before the mirror, this pretty maiden she stood,
she was admiring her pretty figure, it almost froze my blood.
My hair it stood like bristles upon the wild and angry bowl,
I felt just like jumpin' again through this keyhole in this door.

If I had a been strong like Samson, I'd a broke this damned door down,
I'd of fucked that lovely maiden and beat it out of town.
But therefore I was not Samson, so I fucked my fist once more,
but I taken good aim and shot it — through this keyhole in this door.

Short Verses and Drinking Toasts

76   **MY UNCLE SAM**

Richard Connelly Migrant Camp, Barker, New York, 17 August
   1970

My Uncle Sam was a good old man,
he jumped out the window with his dick in his hand.
He said, "Excuse me, lady, I'm a nasty old man,
but I had my dick in the frying pan."

77   **MY UNCLE HAD A OLD GRAY HORSE**

John, Ramsey, 17 November 1965

My uncle had a old gray horse,
his left eye was out and his right eye was glass.
He had three stocking feet and a star on his ass,
Every time he pace his ass sucked wind,
A pretty good old pony for the shape he was in.

78   **MARY HAD A LITTLE LAMB**

Homer, Michigan City, Indiana, 24 April 1962

Mary had a little lamb for which she cared no particle,
it stuck its nose under Mary's clothes and smelled of Mary's article.
Now Mary was a brazen cuss and she didn't give a damn,
she let it have another whiff and it killed the poor little lamb.

Now Mary had a lamb, its fleece was white as snow,
and everywhere that Mary went this little lamb would go.
Now Mary went to shit one day and this little lamb went too.
He said, "Lookit here, Mary, I'd like to smell your ass when you get through."
Now Mary was a brazen cuss and she didn't give a damn,
and she let it have a couple of whiffs and it killed the poor little lamb.

79   MISS LOOKINGOOD

Al, Ellis, 22 March 1966

"Good morning, Miss Lookingood,
kiss my ass, I wish you would.
Here I stand with my dick on the hard
trying to get a piece of pussy with the help of God."

"Hey, Mr. Motherfucker, you'll have to see my sister Kate,
she got her bloomer legs all trimmed in red,
she'll fuck a young man till he fall dead."

Me and my buddy, we made a plot,
we was going to fuck every whore that had a cock.
Ain't but one thing my buddy done wrong,
he topped a whore with her sickness on.

80   BEND YOUR BACK

Al, Ellis, 21 August 1965

Bend your back when I say "Go,"
cut that tree and cut it low.
Use that ax till it blisters your hand,
when you leave here you'll be a better man.

81 THE ROOSTER CROWED

Bob, Connelly Migrant Camp, Barker, New York, 17 August 1970

The rooster crowed, the hen looked down,
says, "You want my jelly, have to run me down."
The Alabama rooster told the Georgia hen,
"I ain't had no lovin' since eighteen-ten.
Lift up your thing and throw up your tail,
I got to have this load, I got to go to jail."

82 THE HE-FROG

Bob, Connelly Migrant Camp, Barker, New York, 17 August 1970

The he-frog told the she-frog,
"Back up against that log.
I'm gonna show you
how to fuck a frog."

83 RUNNING THROUGH THE JUNGLE

Richard, Connelly Migrant Camp, Barker, New York, 17 August
1970

Running through the jungle with my dick in my hand,
I see a young girl and tell her I want some.
I looked up a tree, guess what I could see?
Pissed on me!
I picked up a rock, I hit him in the cock,
made the motherfucker run eighteen blocks.

84 SWINGING THROUGH THE TREES

Howard Nelson of Buffalo, New York, gave me this text as
reported to him by tenth-grade students in Middleport, New
York, sometime in the spring of 1973. After the opening couplet,

the rest of the verse is a floating stanza, one of those short brags
that can stand alone or appear as a section of another poem, as,
for example, the F-text of *Titanic*.

Swinging through the trees with my dick in my hand,
I'm a mean motherfucker, I'm a Tarzan man!
Line a hundred pussies up against the wall,
Bet a hundred dollars I could fuck'em all!
Fucked ninety-eight till my balls turned blue,
Then I wacked off—jacked off!—and fucked the other two!
  (*From Manuscript*)

85   PUSSY

Tom, Ellis, 22 March 1966

Pussy ain't nothin' but a hairy split,
the more you get it, the better it get.
You can wash your dick and you can wash it well,
but you can't get rid of that funky smell.

86   A GIRL TOLD ME

Joe, Ellis, 21 March 1966

A girl told me:
"Joe, a pussy ain't nothin' but slip and slide,
it keeps a man's dick hard all the time.
It got a mouth like a hog and jaws like a frog,
and eats more dick than a goddamned dog.
So, beware."

87   COCK IS

Bob, Connelly Migrant Camp, Barker, New York, 17 August 1970

Cock is a crickly creature,
all covered with wool.

It look like a monkey and smell like a bear,
but I wish my peter was there.

88   THE FORD

Richard, Connelly Migrant Camp, Barker, New York, 17 August
       1970

I got me a Ford since you seen me last,
it's a good old Ford, it won't run so fast.
All you got to do is get right in, set right down,
mash in on your clutch and let your lever down.
It's got a Hudson hood and a Chevrolet cab,
all four wheels, Jack, but still the bitch won't crank.
If you give me a little shove you could do me some good.
I'm goin' home and get three-quarter drunk,
I'm gonna sell that no-good sonofabitch right back to the junk.

89   FORTY-NINE FORD

Gene, Wynne, 18 March 1966

Forty-nine Ford and a tank full of gas,
a mouth full of titty and a hand full of ass.
Mother in a whorehouse, father in jail,
sister on the corner holler "Pussy for sale."
Way down in the woods where nobody goes,
there sit a girl without any clothes.
Along come Gene swingin' on a chain,
pulled down his zipper and out it came.
Three months later it began to swell,
six months later and all was well.
Nine months later and out it came:
a hairy little bastard swingin' on a chain.

Richard, Connelly Migrant Camp, Barker, New York, 17 August
    1970

Now I don't know whether it's true or not,
but I'm gonna say it like I know it:
they tell me when a man get old
his cods get cold,
they say the head a his peter stick up and turn blue,
and that's what's the matter with you.

91   I USED TO COULD DIDDLE ALL NIGHT LONG

Theo, Wynne, 7 July 1964

I used to could diddle all night long,
but since I got the age I am,
it takes me all night to diddle.
I used to could take the gals,
and she says, "Drive me quickly out of town
and give me pecker by the pound.
And don't stop at six or seven,
but cart me up to number eleven."

92-103. DRINKING TOASTS

   All the preceding toasts belong to the streetcorner/party/jail-
house tradition. The toasts that follow belong not only to that tra-
dition, but to the wider toasting tradition—that connected with
lifted glasses—as well. I did not focus on these in my field
collecting and I suspect there are a great many more of them in
the working repertory. Some, such as #98, "And May Your Life
Become Unlivable, Boy," sometimes figure as sections in the
narrative toasts.

92   WELL HERE'S TO THE FOOL THAT WRITES UPON THE SHITHOUSE WALLS

Mack, Jefferson City, 24 June 1964

Well here's to the fool that writes upon the shithouse walls,
may he roll his shit in little balls.
And he that reads those words of wit,
should eat those little balls of shit.

93   HERE'S TO THE LADY WITH THE LITTLE RED SHOES

Slim, Jefferson City, 24 June 1964

Here's to the lady with the little red shoes
who will smoke your cigarettes and drink your booze.
Says she knows every town on the map,
and three days after you fuck her you get the motherfucken clap.
She has no cherry, but she thinks it's no sin,
for she still has the box that the cherry came in.

94   WELL IF I HAD A DOG THAT COULD PISS THIS STUFF

Mack, Jefferson City, 24 June 1964

Well if I had a dog that could piss this stuff,
and I was sure he could piss enough,
I'd tie that son of a bitch to the head of my bed
and suck his dick till we both fell dead.

95   AND HERE'S TO THE DUCK THAT SWIM THE POND

Slim, Jefferson City, 24 June 1964

And here's to the duck that swim the pond
and never got a feather wet,

and here's to the lady who sells her ass
and ain't caught the syphilis yet.

96   WELL HERE'S TO THE CRANE THAT FLEW DOWN THE LANE

Mack, Jefferson City, 24 June 1964

Well here's to the crane that flew down the lane
and lit upon the mast pole.
Stretched his neck and shit a peck
and sparks flew from his asshole.

97A   HERE'S TO YOU, MAG, YOU DIRTY HAG

Slim, Jefferson City, 24 June 1964

Here's to you, Mag, you dirty hag,
your cunt's a drippin' shit,
scabby scabs is hanging from your tits.
Before I'd climb them slimy thighs
and suck your palsied tits,
I'd rather die of drippin' shit
and be bathed in drunken shit.

97B   MOTHERFUCK A WOMAN LAY FLAT ON HER BACK

Gene, Connelly Migrant Camp, Barker, New York, 22 August
     1970

Motherfuck a woman lay flat on her back
and give you some pussy for nothin'.
Before I'd get between those slimy thighs
and suck those skizzy tits,
I'd rather drink a barrel of buzzard puke
and swim in a river of shit.

98   AND MAY YOUR LIFE BECOME UNLIVABLE, BOY

Slim, Jefferson City, 24 June 1964

And may your life become unlivable, boy,
and bunions grow on your feet,
may crabs as big as a young man's fist
hang from your ass and eat.
And the whole world turn against you
and your life become a wreck,
may you slip down your own connivin' asshole
and break your motherfucken neck.

99   KNOCKIN' DOWN CHAIRS AND SLAMMIN' DOORS

Jim, Cambridge, Massachusetts, 26 November 1964

Knockin' down chairs and slammin' doors,
cussin' decent women for bitches and whores.
Says, "Wake up, gal, and make me a toddy,
when I get drunk, I'll screw anybody."

100   HICKORY WOOD IS THE BEST OF WOOD

Jim, Cambridge, Massachusetts, 26 November 1964

Hickory wood is the best of wood,
crackin' does the women good,
make them open their eyes and stretch their thighs,
give their ass exercise.

101   WHEN I BEGIN TO THINK WHEN I WAS A YOUNG MAN AND IN MY PRIME

Nate, Ramsey, 17 November 1965

When I begin to think when I was a young man and in my prime,
I used to didn't drink nothin' but that old dark port wine.
But now that I got old and I can plainly see,
Thunderbird's the only thing gonna save poor me.

102   THIS IS TO THE WOMEN OF TEXAS

John, Ramsey, 17 November 1965

This is to the women of Texas,
they is tall, handsome, and savage.
When you get a kiss from their lips all you smell
is snuff, tobacco, and cabbage.

103   TALK SOME SHIT, RICHARD

Ray, Connelly Migrant Camp, Barker, New York, 22 August 1970

Talk some shit, Richard,
talk some shit.
Well, goddammit, talk.
He don't wear no drawers.
This here's Richard,
you know what I mean?
This is my friend,
this is my kin,
I don't give a motherfuck
if he don't come in.
'Cause this is Richard,
Richard is my boy,
and talkin' shit
is my pride and motherfucken joy.
So if he talk shit he talk it fast.
I don't give a motherfuck if y'all kiss my motherfucken ass.
Talk some shit, Richard,
talk some shit.

Books and Articles Cited

Index of Names

Index of First Lines

Books and Articles Cited

Abrahams, Roger D. *Deep Down in the Jungle . . . : Negro Narrative from the Streets of Philadelphia,* rev. ed. Chicago, Aldine. (1970A)

———— *Positively Black.* Englewood Cliffs, N.J., Prentice-Hall. (1970B)

Agar, Michael H. "Folklore of the Heroin Addict: Two Examples," *Journal of American Folklore* 84:332 (1971), 175-185.

Anderson, Nels. *The Hobo: The Sociology of the Homeless Man.* Chicago, University of Chicago Press, 1961.

Auerbach, Eric. *Mimesis.* Garden City, Anchor, 1957.

Berryman, John. *77 Dream Songs.* New York, Farrar, Straus, 1964.

Brown, H. Rap. "Street Smarts," in Dundes, 1973:353-356. (An extract from Brown's *Die Nigger Die!*).

Cohen, Norman. "'Casey Jones': At the Crossroads of Two Ballad Traditions," *Western Folklore* 32 (1973), 77-103.

Coser, Lewis A. "The Functions of Social Conflict," in Coser and Rosenberg, 205-209.

———— and Bernard Rosenberg, eds. *Sociological Theory.* New York, Macmillan, 1964.

Dollard, John. "The Dozens: Dialectic of Insult," in Dundes, 1973:277-294. (Originally in *American Imago* I (1939), 3-25.)

Dorson, Richard M. *American Negro Folktales.* New York, Fawcett, 1967.

Dundes, Alan, ed. *Mother Wit from the Laughing Barrel: Readings in the Interpretation of Afro-American Folklore.* Englewood Cliffs, N.J., Prentice-Hall, 1973.

Durkheim, Emile. *The Rules of the Sociological Method,* trans. Sarah A. Solovay and John H. Mueller; ed. George E. G. Catlin. New York, The Free Press, 1964.

Eddington, Neil A. "Genital Superiority in Oakland Negro Folklore: A Theme," in Dundes, 1973:642-648.

Freud, Sigmund. "Contribution to the Psychology of Love: the Most Prevalent Form of Degradation in Erotic Life," trans. Joan Riviere, in *Collected Papers,* IV. New York, Basic Books, 1959: 203-216. (1959A)

———— "Medusa's Head," trans. James Strachey, in *Collected Papers,* V. New York, Basic Books, 1959:105-106. (1959B)

Friedland, William H., and Dorothy Nelkin. *Migrant: Agricultural Workers in America's Northeast.* New York, Holt, Rinehart and Winston, 1971.

Gebhard, Paul, John Gagnon, Wardell Pomeroy, and Cornelia Christenson. *Sex Offenders.* New York, Harper and Row, 1965.

Grier, William H., and Price M. Cobbs. *Black Rage.* New York, Basic Books, 1968.

Grotjahn, Martin. *Beyond Laughter*. New York, McGraw-Hill, 1966.

Guthrie, Woody. *Born to Win,* ed. Robert Shelton. New York, Anchor, 1966.

Hannerz, Ulf. "The Rhetoric of Soul: Identification in Negro Society," *Race* 9:4 (London), (1969), 453:465.

———— *Soulside.* New York, Columbia University Press, 1969.

Huizinga, Johann. *Homo Ludens: A Study of the Play Element in Culture.* Boston, Beacon Press, 1955.

Jackson, Bruce. "Circus and Street: Psychosocial Aspects of the Black Toast," *Journal of American Folklore* 85:336 (1972), 123-139. (1972A)

———— *In the Life: Versions of the Criminal Experience.* New York, Holt, Rinehart and Winston, 1972.

———— *The Negro and his Folklore in 19th Century Periodicals.* Austin, University of Texas Press and the American Folklore Society, 1967. (1967B)

———— "Stagolee Stories: A Badman Goes Gentle," *Southern Folklore Quarterly* 29:3 (1965), 188-194.

———— "The *'Titanic'* Toast." In Harry Levin, ed., *Veins of Humor,* Harvard English Studies 3, Cambridge, Mass., Harvard University Press, 1972. (1972B)

———— *Wake Up Dead Man: Afro-American Worksongs from Texas Prisons.* Cambridge, Mass., Harvard University Press, 1972. (1972C)

———— "What Happened to Jody," *Journal of American Folklore* 80:318 (1967), 388-396. (1967A)

Kennedy, Charles O'Brien, comp., *American Ballads.* New York, Crest, 1962.

Kinsey, Alfred C., Wardell B. Pomeroy, and Clyde E. Martin. "Social Level and Sexual Outlet," in Reinhart Bendix and Seymour M. Lipset, eds., *Class, Status and Power.* Glencoe, Ill., The Free Press, 1953:300-308.

Kochman, Thomas, ed. *Rappin' and Stylin' Out: Communications in Urban Black America.* Urbana, University of Illinois Press, 1972.

Labov, William, Paul Cohen, Clarence Robins, and John Lewis, "Toasts," in Dundes, 1973:329-347. (Originally in their *A Study of the Non-Standard English of Negro and Puerto Rican Speakers in New York,* II, "The Use of Language in the Speech Community." Cooperative Research Project No. 3288. New York, Columbia University, 1968. 55-75.)

Laws, G. Malcolm. *Native American Balladry,* rev. ed. Publications of the American Folklore Society. *Bibliographical and Special Series,* 1. Philadelphia, 1962.

Leach, Maria, ed. *Standard Dictionary of Folklore, Mythology and Legend.* New York, Funk and Wagnalls, 1950.

Legman, G. *The Horn Book.* New Hyde Park, N.Y., University Press, 1964.

Liebow, Elliot. *Tally's Corner: A Study of Negro Streetcorner Men.* Boston, Little, Brown, 1967.

Lomax, Alan. *The Folk Songs of North America.* Garden City, Doubleday, 1960.

Lomax, John A. and Alan. *Negro Folk Songs as Sung by Lead-Belly*. New York, Macmillan, 1936.

_____ *Our Singing Country*. New York, Macmillan, 1941.

Lorenz, Konrad. *On Aggression,* tr. Marjorie K. Wilson. New York, Harcourt Brace Jovanovich, 1971.

Lord, Albert B. *The Singer of Tales*. Cambridge, Mass., Harvard University Press, 1960.

Mead, George Herbert. "Psychology of Punitive Justice," in Coser and Rosenberg, 1964:591-597.

Melnick, Mimi Clar. "'I Can Peep Through Muddy Water and Spy Dry Land': Boasts in the Blues," in Dundes, 1973:267-276.

Milburn, George. *The Hobo's Hornbook*. New York, Ives Washburn, 1930.

Milner, Christina and Richard. *Black Players: The Secret World of Black Pimps*. Boston, Little, Brown, 1972.

Mitchell-Kernan, Claudia. "Signifying," in Dundes, 1973:310-328.

Opie, Iona and Peter. *The Lore and Language of Schoolchildren*. London, Oxford University Press, 1959.

Rainwater, Lee. "Crucible of Identity: The Negro Lower-Class Family," *Daedalus* 95:1 (1966), 172-216.

Reynolds, Anthony M. "Urban Negro Toasts: A Hustler's View from L. A." Xerox manuscript copy, 1974; forthcoming in *Western Folklore*.

Scott, Sir Harold, ed. *The Concise Encyclopedia of Crime and Criminals*. New York, Hawthorn Books, 1961.

Shirley, Kay, ed. *The Book of the Blues*. New York, Crown, 1963.

Vicarion, Count Palmiro. *Book of Bawdy Ballads*. Paris, Olympia, 1959.

Whitten, Norman E., Jr., and John F. Szwed, eds. *Afro-American Anthropology: Contemporary Perspectives*. New York, Free Press, 1970.

Wright, Richard. *Lawd Today*. New York, Avon, 1963.

Index of Names

(Names in capitals are informant pseudonyms)

Index of First Lines

About the Companion CD

The CD enclosed with this book contains the following toasts:

1. Life's a Funny Old Proposition
2. Signifying Monkey (50A)
3. Poolshooting Monkey (50C)
4. Titanic (52D)
5. Cocaine Nell
6. Life of a Junkie
7. Pingpong Joe
8. Dogass Pimp
9. Pimp's Toast
10. The Pimp (22D)
11. Corner of 47th and South Park (55D)
12. Down and Out (55B)
13. Feeble Old Man
14. Hoboes' Convention
15. Jesse James
16. 22-20, Freaks' Ball (41A), Cocaine Shorty, Casey Jones
17. Freaks' Ball (variant of 41A)
18. Voodoo Queen
19. Strange, Strange Things
20. The Teacher
21. Toledo Slim
22. Treacherous Breast
23. Winehead Girl
24. They Can't Do That